D1540095

Merchants and Capitalists

MERCHANTS AND CAPITALISTS

•

Industrialization and

Provincial Politics in

Mid-Nineteenth-Century France

•

DAVID M. GORDON

The University of Alabama Press

Copyright © 1985 by
The University of Alabama Press
University, Alabama 35486
All rights reserved
Manufactured in the United States of America

Library of Congress Cataloging in Publication Data

Gordon, David M., 1949–
  Merchants and capitalists.

  Bibliography: p.
  Includes index.
  1. Reims (France)—Politics and government.
2. Saint Etienne (Loire, France)—Politics and government. 3. Business and
politics—France—Reims—History—19th century. 4. Business and
politics—France—Saint Etienne (Loire)—History—19th century. I. Title
JS5205.R42G67 1985   320.8'0944'32   83-18266
ISBN 0-8173-0210-7

For my mother
MARY P. GORDON
and the memory of my father
MORRIS A. GORDON

Contents

Acknowledgments

This book would not be complete without an expression of thanks to all those who helped in its writing. I am very grateful for the assistance of the staffs of the Departmental Archives of the Loire and the Marne and of the personnel at the municipal libraries of St. Etienne and Reims. The inevitable financial burdens associated with a project of this kind were lightened by grants from the Alliance Française and Brown University. Adeline Daumard's suggestions about the use of the *Mutation après décès* were very helpful. Much good advice about the early versions of this manuscript was received from William Hudson, Joan Scott, Abbott Gleason, Norman Rich, and especially R. Burr Litchfield, whose enthusiasm for this project from its inception was most heartening. Portions of this work also received the benefit of the suggestions and criticisms of Kathryn Amdur, Paul Gallis, Jim Lehning, John Merriman, and Ann-Louise Shapiro. Trudie Calvert helped in the editing, and Charles Wetherell contributed to the technical preparation of the manuscript. I owe the greatest debt to my parents, who taught me to love learning and scholarship. All that is good in this work is as much theirs as mine.

Publication of this book has been assisted, in part, by financial assistance from the Andrew W. Mellon Foundation and the American Council of Learned Societies.

Merchants and Capitalists

Introduction

In the spring of 1869 the government of the Second Empire faced its greatest crisis since its establishment. Nowhere was this threat more evident than at St. Etienne, the nation's most important center of heavy industry, where the May elections promised to return diehard republicans to the Corps législatif. Popular hostility to the imperial government had been growing in this city, as in many others, for years, so that the prefect was unable to persuade any of the local notables to risk a humiliating defeat by standing as the government's candidate. Both the prefect and the *procureur général* sadly predicted the victory of "red republican demagogues," and the conservative press warned of a revolutionary threat unknown since the June days of 1848. Yet when the election was over, Frédéric Dorian, a millionaire steel manufacturer, emerged as the easy winner and unrivaled arbiter of local political fortunes, and the middle-class coalition he headed enjoyed more genuine popular support than any group of notables since the days of the July Monarchy. Dorian subsequently became one of the most popular figures in the capital, and middle-class republicans easily weathered the challenge of a short-lived commune at St. Etienne. The 1869 election thus did indeed bring about a major shift of local political power, but to the profit of members of the industrial bourgeoisie and their allies. More important the elections demonstrated the spread of republican sentiments among industrialists both here and elsewhere in France and their ability to win popular support on the basis of a moderate republican program. Accepting some of the reforms associated with the Second Republic, they were frequently able by the last years of the Second Empire to become the most popular political figures in their localities.

1

Political rhetoric frequently obscures subtle but important changes taking place in the social life of nations, and the formulaic description of most opponents of the Second Empire by the imperial police as "reds," "socialists," and "exalted demagogues" has occasionally been allowed to hide the moderate aims of many of the most popular anti-Imperial leaders. Karl Marx, in his despair over bourgeois support of the Napoleonic dictatorship, so eloquently expressed in *The Eighteenth Brumaire of Louis Bonaparte*, identified the notables as among the most ardent supporters of the regime. In more recent times, scholarly assumptions about middle-class support of the empire in the work of Theodore Zeldin and others have had the same effect, tending to ignore the political evolution of the bourgeoisie under the dictatorship.[1] Even the current interest in labor politics has helped distort modern perceptions of the period. Despite the valuable contributions of labor historians, the overall effect of their work has been to downplay through neglect the role of middle-class opposition to the empire. As a result, it would seem hardly credible that a large republican element existed among wealthy manufacturers and that members of this group were among the most enthusiastic participants in the overthrow of the Second Empire. In fact, the conversion of the bourgeoisie to the republic, completed in the 1870s, had already begun in earnest under the empire and was the most important development in the politics of the period. Following the establishment of the Third Republic, the industrial elite remained one of the most influential groups in political life and was for the most part loyal to the regime until its demise in 1940, despite the first real challenge to the middle classes by the Popular Front government of 1936. In light of the fatal consequences of the lack of middle-class support for the German Weimar Republic in the 1930s, one can appreciate the importance of the genuine conversion of the French bourgeoisie to the republic in the nineteenth century.

Most historians of the Second Empire have concentrated on life in Paris, but the political conversion of the middle classes after 1852 was accomplished mainly in the provinces. Ultimately, the political convictions of Parisian journalists and lawyers were less important in the evolution of the nation than those of the provincial industrial elite. Provincial politics were in turn greatly affected by the prolonged period of economic growth that followed the establishment of the imperial regime in 1852.

Both the mechanization of artisanal trades and the development of new industries under the empire created groups of industrial entrepreneurs who helped transform political life. The imperial government assumed that, as the particular favorites of government economic policies, the new industrial interests would be among the empire's most loyal supporters. In fact, many members of this group came to lead the middle-class opposition to the regime and became influential republican leaders in the 1870s. This major paradox, which was recognized by contemporaries as one of the most important developments in the political life of the period, is the central concern of this book.

Some very valuable work has already been done in the study of the bourgeoisie for the period of the Second Empire, though this has concentrated mostly on changing investment patterns and other purely economic matters. The massive study organized by Adeline Daumard, *Les fortunes françaises au XIXième siècle*, the most notable example of these efforts, is a detailed examination of middle-class investments in the period.[2] This present work, however, goes beyond Daumard's work in attempting to link economic development with changes in political life.

It is striking that economic growth and the long period of prosperity after 1852 tended to weaken rather than strengthen government support among the industrial elite. More prosperous conditions created a political climate less threatening to middle-class property interests than that of the depressed 1840s. Manufacturers began to feel optimistic about the future of industrial development in France, and most of them were increasingly able to pay their workers higher wages than ever before. Police repression, at first believed necessary to prevent revolution, therefore came to appear increasingly outmoded. By the 1860s a number of successful industrial manufacturers, believing that France was ready for a restoration of unfettered parliamentary government, became leaders of the provincial middle-class opposition to the empire. Politically ambitious, they were also convinced that decreased government interference in local elections would allow them to capture offices held by more conservative rivals. Their commitment to a more liberal regime combined with personal ambition initiated a struggle with local and national conservative forces. Industrialists came into conflict first with the older provincial elites, who had traditionally occupied local offices, and later with the central government. By the last years of the empire members of this group who had achieved prominence after 1852 were among the most important leaders of the republican opposition.

The experiences of two expanding industrial centers, Reims and St. Etienne, demonstrate the process of the political evolution of the bourgeoisie. Reims, typical of many woolens manufacturing centers, began the mechanization of its artisan industry after 1860. The development of the steel industry in and around St. Etienne in the same period produced a new group of wealthy industrial capitalists. In both cities, successful modernizing manufacturers helped create coalitions of middle- and working-class groups which regularly defeated conservative candidates even before the fall of the empire.

Attempting to win political office through popular support, manufacturers began in the mid-1860s to demand an end to the government's authoritarian controls of working-class life. Believing that workers were no longer potential revolutionaries, the elite formulated a political program compatible with the establishment of republican government. Liberal industrialists called for parliamentary elections free of government interference and a ministry responsible to the legislature. The popularity of these demands allowed them to ignore most elements of the old radical *démocrate-socialiste* program that had threatened middle-class interests. Only demands for compulsory, secular education and the establishment of a people's militia survived the Second Republic into the 1860s. The elimination of unemployment (the *droit de travail*) and the proposed nationalization of banks and railroads were ignored by bourgeois republicans. Thus when the authoritarian imperial regime gave way to the liberal reforms of Emile Ollivier and the Third Party, the leaders of the middle-class opposition had already ceased to support the empire.

Under the Second Empire the most important leaders in the opposition came from the bourgeoisie. Ironically, the role of the middle classes in local political life had been enhanced by the dictatorship after 1852. Under the Second Republic, working-class organizations had reduced the influence of the middle classes, which formerly had dominated local political life. It was only after police repression had put an end to independent working-class groups that bourgeois power and influence were restored at the local level. The subsequent political dissatisfaction of elements within the elite was created by industrialization that began to transform provincial life after 1852.

The effects of industrialization on the fortunes of the manufacturers at Reims and St. Etienne, defined as the enfranchised voters under the July Monarchy, have been traced through the use of the *Mutation après décès*, the probate of wills maintained until 1870. This enormously rich body of material provides a detailed picture of the fortunes of the bourgeoisie who died under the empire. The *Mutation* indicates which members of the bourgeoisie were wealthy enough to have been voters under the July Monarchy and hence members of the elite under the Second Empire. More important, it reveals the level of local investment in the mechanization of woolens production at Reims and the development of heavy industry in the Loire. Different levels of investment by various groups within local elites helped determine economic and political rivalries after 1852. Groups that were most closely associated with prosperous mechanized manufacturing tended to be more hostile to the empire than merchant employers of artisan labor who, faced with increased factory competition, were unable to pay good wages. This latter group felt obliged to continue to depend on the dictatorship to protect them from hostile employees. Consideration of the economic rivalries that emerged between industrial and mercantile maufacturers is thus of vital importance in explaining the development of liberal and republican opposition groups within the elite.

Relatively high levels of investment in factory industry by a variety of middle-class groups sometimes helped reduce political conflicts among the notables, as at Reims. In contrast, the relatively low levels of investment by St. Etienne's ribbon merchants in the development of heavy industry kept newer entrepreneurs economically independent of the older elite; the steel industry was ultimately financed with capital resources from outside the Loire. This difference contributed in part to the later political divisions between the two groups. By the 1860s, members of the new industrial elite opposed both St. Etienne's traditional merchants and the central government. At Reims, where the level of factory investments by merchant manufacturers was high, political life developed somewhat differently. The prosperity enjoyed by most elements in the woolens industry helped stimulate a liberal reaction to the empire. The government was obliged to find most of its supporters among mercantile interests in other industries, such as champagne manufacturing; these interests became the chief targets of liberal attack in the 1860s.

Economic development thus played a major role in the political struggle that took place among French provincial notables in the 1860s. Wealthy modernizing manufacturers, believing in the seemingly permanent prosperity created by the mechanization of industry, rejected dictatorship as the best means of dealing with labor unrest. Strengthened by their belief in a liberal future, they came into conflict with conservative mercantile officials of the previous generation who had failed to make the transition from the artisanal to the factory system. This created a generational as well as an economic and political struggle.

French governments throughout the nineteenth century had been faced with the problem of dealing with younger generations of politically ambitious men, and the 1860s were no exception. In the last decade of the empire a younger generation wished to fill the political offices of their elders who had rallied to the government in the 1850s. But the imperial regime faced an especially difficult problem. Economic changes had strengthened the hand of a younger generation of woolens manufacturers at Reims, whose entry into the business world during the period of mechanization had made them receptive to the new methods of production. The emergence of a new industrial elite at St. Etienne without ties to older mercantile groups demonstrated even more dramatically the changes brought about by rapid industrial growth.

The relative weakness of independent working-class political organizations under the Second Empire (in large part the result of police surveillance and controls), the transition from artisan to factory labor, and a weakening of traditional artisan organizations enabled dissident manufacturers to help shape the development of popular opposition to the regime. The emergence in the 1860s of a provincial opposition press, financed and controlled by liberals, also played an important role in directing local anger against the government and the local mercantile elite, while retarding the development of radical movements hostile to the interests of modern industry. Industrial dissidents at Reims and St. Etienne helped make both cities centers of antigovernment sentiment and prevented the development of popular movements hostile to capitalism—a role played by similar groups in provincial towns throughout France.

1

Two Towns and Two Elites

on the Eve of 1848

Provincial politics in France under the Second Empire have been neglected by modern scholars. The sudden fall of the July Monarchy, the drama of the June days, and the activities of the National Assembly all have focused attention on Paris. Interest in the development of Parisian politics under the imperial regime has further relegated to obscurity the very important political evolution that took place in provincial France after 1852. Sustained economic growth during the two decades that followed the establishment of the Second Empire created urban expansion and industrial development that fundamentally changed the economic and political life of many provincial towns. Previously autonomous regional economies became unified into a single national economy as the rapid growth of industry necessitated national sales of stock issues to finance development. Like the simultaneous development of the railroads, which created a national market for French goods, regional bourgeois economic interests were for the first time united into a national economic life.[1]

The Revolution of 1848 began a similar nationalization of political life which continued under the empire. After 1848 it became increasingly difficult for provincial elites to control local political life without also dealing with national political issues. As one recent author has said, "The nation state won a durable victory over local power holders and traditional particularisms."[2] Under the Second Republic these issues, which appealed to the new electorate created by the introduction of universal manhood suffrage, came increasingly to preoccupy provincial political life. A new politics of mass participation began to emerge under the Second Republic, a development that Louis-Napoleon was to use to advantage in the presidential election of 1848 and in the plebiscite that created the Second Empire in 1852.

But through the period of the Second Empire, the notables remained the most important local groups in the development of French politics and industry. This wealthy bourgeois group had previously enjoyed a monopoly of the suffrage because of the property qualifications for voting established by the July Monarchy. The control of political life had first been established by the Constitution of 1791, which created the distinction between "active" and "passive" citizens. Eliminated by the Constitution of 1793, the privileged bourgeois position had been restored by the Directory and maintained by Napoleon I. The Charter of 1814 further strengthened the political power of the notables by allowing them to control local elected assemblies as well as the Chamber of Deputies. This situation, which continued under the July Monarchy, was briefly threatened by the establishment of universal suffrage in 1848. But after their temporary eclipse under the Second Republic, the provincial notables regained local power under the empire. Their influence was strengthened in the 1850s and 1860s by the appearance of a new industrial leadership in their ranks.

For the working classes, the beginning of industrial development and the transition from artisanal to factory work marked a weakening of organized political activity. In the 1850s and 1860s a transition was made from the traditional artisan radicalism manifested in the revolutions of 1830 and 1848 to the new labor politics of the 1880s. But for the notables the establishment of the Second Empire, which coincided with the period of European economic prosperity that Eric Hobsbawm has called the "age of capital," enabled them to strengthen their economic and political position. They remained the directing element behind industrialization at the provincial level and the chief arbiters of provincial political life.[3]

Honoré de Balzac satirized the notables of the July Monarchy, Honoré Daumier caricatured them, and Marx chronicled the internal transformations that had begun to take place among them. The *Communist Manifesto* traces the transition from merchant elites who employed artisan labor to newer industrial groups whose introduction of "steam and machinery revolutionized industrial production. The place of manufacture was taken by giant, modern industry, the place of the industrial middle class, by industrial millionaires—the leaders of whole industrial armies, the modern bourgeoisie."[4] With the introduction of mechanized production under the Second Empire in such key sectors of the French economy as textiles and heavy industry, the difference on a provincial level between the older mercantile capitalists and the newer industrial elite became very important. The traditional business operations of putting-out merchants, dependent on the work of artisanal craftsmen, began to be replaced by factory labor concentrated in heavily capitalized manufacturing plants. A major contention of this book is that the provincial politics of the empire were pervaded by economic rivalries between industrialists and mercantile manufacturers at a town level. The success of industrial manufacturers in transforming local industry encouraged some of them to attempt to exercise greater influence in local political life as well.

The Second Empire was based from its inception on the support of those elements whose position in local politics under the July Monarchy was most threatened by the introduction of universal suffrage and working-class radicalism during the Second Republic. The government promise of full employment and the creation of the Luxembourg Commission in February 1848 had frightened many of the bourgeoisie. Even more threatening were the popular demonstrations in Paris in March and April, and the massive insurrection in June seemed to bring France to the brink of social revolution.

Despite the repression of workers' organizations in Paris through the summer and fall of 1848, the radical threat reemerged the following year with the appearance of the Comité démocrate-socialiste de Paris and its call for government recognition of the right to work, and for obligatory, secular education. The committee also demanded a limit on working hours, the nationalization of railroads, banks, and insurance companies, and the establishment of progressive taxation. These demands, popular among many smaller property owners, won the *démocrate-socialiste* leadership considerable support in large areas of France, including many provincial towns. In the legislative election of May 1849, 180 radical republican and socialist deputies were returned. Most *démocrate-socialiste* candidates were themselves from the middle classes and did not wish to threaten the ownership of private property. They did want, however, to make it easier to acquire some property, even at the expense of the wealthy.[5] But the abortive coup in Paris in June 1849, engineered by the radical republican leadership, allowed conservatives once again to act decisively against the growing threat from the Left. Workers' organizations and political clubs both in Paris and the provinces were dissolved by the police. For a second time the drift of artisans, shopkeepers, and peasants into the radical republican camp, which had increased in momentum in 1849, was stopped by the arrest of radical leaders in many provincial centers.

The repression of popular republicanism and the establishment of an environment favorable to property owners allowed the notables to reconsolidate their control of political life. Despite the partial industrialization of the work force after 1852, the new industrial interests that emerged within the local elites were more firmly in control of town politics at the end of the Second Empire than older mercantile groups had been at the end of the July Monarchy. But paradoxically, the new industrial leadership outgrew the authoritarian empire. By the end of the 1860s economic growth and political rivalries within provincial elites led to the creation of bourgeois political opposition groups which, made confident by years of social peace, were willing to undertake a new republican experiment.

Politically moderate industrialists were at the center of the new bourgeois republican coalition. They demanded parliamentary elections free of government interference and were willing to adopt elements of the old *démocrate-socialiste* program, including the establishment of compulsory secular education. As large-scale capitalists themselves, they could hardly oppose the expansion of industrial enterprise at the expense of smaller artisan producers, although they adopted some of the older slogans opposing "financial feudalism," directed against the largest Parisian banks during the period of the Second Republic. By identifying themselves with smaller provincial producers threatened by the supposed machinations of Paris stock jobbers at the imperial court, these major manufacturers were able to turn popular suspicions about the stock exchange and capitalist development to their own political advantage.

The strength of the moderate republican opposition was increased by the support of many influential Orleanists. Having already accommodated themselves to the imperial regime after 1852, members of this group by the 1860s increasingly supported the creation of a republic. A republican regime promised a freer parliamentary life and the opportunity for many leading families once again to play the influential role in national politics they had enjoyed under the July Monarchy. The industrial prosperity of the 1860s seemed to preclude any reemergence of the radical working-class political movements of the depressed 1840s. Orleanists had thus become a very adaptable political group, willing to accommodate themselves to any regime that provided social peace and parliamentary government controlled by bourgeois interests.

The republican movement was also strengthened by the adherence of formerly influential republican leaders from the period of the Second Republic. As men of property, few had arguments with the moderate program, and thus were willing to drop their more radical demands. Those few radical republicans who remained true to the old *démocrate-socialiste* program came increasingly to head political splinter groups with little real influence. The prosperity of the 1860s, combined with the enormous prestige enjoyed by major industrialists, helped win the support of many workers. A republican press subsidized by industrial dissidents also helped convince workers to support wealthy republican moderates. By the 1860s industrial manufacturers were able to create an influential bourgeois political coalition with considerable popular support. They believed they could reestablish parliamentary government in France without making any concessions detrimental to capitalist economic development.

The Notables of Reims and St. Etienne in the 1840s

To understand how industrialization and political life developed at a provincial level, it is best to look at places where economic and social change were clearly apparent. The rate of population growth is one indication of economic development, and some provincial centers were growing more rapidly than others. St. Etienne was one of the fastest growing cities in France. Its population increased from 49,614 in 1846 to 110,814 in 1872; only Toulon and Roubaix grew as rapidly. Reims, which did not grow as fast, was nonetheless similar to expanding provincial textile centers such as St. Quentin and Tourcoing; the development of its woolens industry contributed to a population increase from 43,905 to 71,994 over the same years.

St. Etienne and Reims were chosen for this study both because their economies underwent important changes in this period of industrial growth and because they experienced problems of urban expansion.

Both cities were the sites of important traditional artisanal industries. Reims was one of the oldest centers of the woolens trade; St. Etienne was France's most important ribbon manufacturing center. Both cities saw the progressive introduction of modern industrial techniques and capital operations. Heavy investment in the Reims wool industry permitted the introduction of mechanized production in the 1860s, which greatly strengthened the economic position of the city as a national center of textile production. It also created an economic crisis for the city's artisans, who were forced to adjust to factory work. At St. Etienne the introduction of modern production methods first in coal mining and later in steel also created a prolonged economic and political crisis. In both cities, these changes produced divisions within the bourgeois elite between industrial innovators and more conservative mercantile manufacturers wedded to artisanal labor. Rivalries between traditional mercantile manufacturers and the newer industrial interests dominated the political life of both towns under the Second Empire.

Expansion and industrial growth created similar problems at Reims and St. Etienne, but their respective elites chose different solutions to these problems. Although both cities were approximately the same size at the end of the July Monarchy—St. Etienne had about forty-nine thousand people and Reims about forty-four thousand—Reims was by far the wealthier of the two towns. The cathedral that dominated the city had been the site of the coronation of French kings since Clovis. The elegant residence of its archbishop, another scene of coronation ceremonial, also reflected the wealth of its clergy. The city had long been an important entrepôt for champagne wines. Surrounded by well-tended vineyards, merchants continued to store thousands of bottles of champagne wine in ancient chalk caves that were a relic of the city's Roman past. Reims's chief source of wealth, however, was its woolens industry. Wealthy manufacturers, from whose ranks the great Colbert had come, had competed with royal patrons to embellish the city. In addition to being one of the best paved and lighted towns in France, Reims boasted an elegant Hotel-de-Ville and a severely classical eighteenth-century *place* originally dedicated to Louis XV. Although the city remained surrounded by its medieval walls, which were not demolished until the 1860s, it continued to benefit from the generosity of new industrial interests after

1852 and was generally considered one of the most comfortable towns in France.[6]

St. Etienne had a very different history, being of little importance before the nineteenth century, when it grew rapidly as a center of mining and ribbon manufacturing. For centuries, iron deposits in the Loire region had made the city a minor center for the manufacture of *quincaillerie* (small metal utensils and tools). The concentration of skilled craftsmen in the area had first recommended it to the ministers of Francis I as the site for royal arms manufacture, and by the seventeenth century armsmaking had become St. Etienne's second artisan trade. Over the centuries its craftsmen successfully adapted themselves to the manufacture of guns, and in the eighteenth century the city received a royal monopoly for provisioning the army. This was extended under the First Empire and subsequent regimes. But it was the transfer of the artisan ribbon trade in the late eighteenth century from Montbrison, previously the most important urban center in the Forez, to neighboring St. Etienne that was responsible for the city's rapid growth.[7]

The city's weavers, the most innovative in the department, were the first to reap large profits by adopting new types of looms. But rising profits did little to produce the generous civic spirit common in older commercial centers such as Reims.[8] One reason for this was the absence of a large established elite. Many of the city's leading manufacturers were proud to have begun their careers as artisans and disdained what they considered bourgeois refinements. The city's rapid growth therefore resulted in a decline in the standard of living, a common phenomenon in early nineteenth-century manufacturing towns. As new housing was built to accommodate ribbon weavers along the extremities of the city's main street (the direction of urban expansion was dictated by the narrow valley in which the city was built), little attempt was made to deal with problems created by urban growth. Most houses were built without sewers, and the resulting seepage contaminated the Furan River, the city's main water supply. Although wealthy ribbon merchants built elegant residences outside the town, they were unwilling to subsidize public improvements. Flora Tristan, visiting in the 1840s, was unable to find a single park or monument of artistic value; even pavements were lacking, save at the town's center.[9]

The prosperity of both Reims and St. Etienne rested on artisanal production. The artisanal *fabrique de Reims* described by Claude Fohlen was similar to those for ribbons and small metallurgy at St. Etienne. It was "a unit of production possessing both an industrial and commercial character. The *fabrique* was a collection of merchants who bought raw materials or manufactured products such as thread, which they then distributed to their workers grouped in small workshops or at home, either in the city or the countryside. The city was the center of industry only in that it was the place in which many artisans lived and the center of commercial transactions between merchant employers and their workers."[10] Spinning, weaving, and dyeing both in Reims's woolens industry and in St. Etienne's ribbon trade remained overwhelmingly dependent on artisan labor.

The merchant employers of this labor force, along with local landlords and members of the liberal professions, were the traditional political as well as economic leaders of their towns. Typical of the urban provincial elites of preindustrial France, the notables dominated political life through their monopoly on the suffrage under the *monarchie censitaire*. Their control had first been established in the Charter of 1814, when the suffrage was limited to men thirty years or older who paid Fr 300 in direct taxes; tax qualifications for public office were even higher. Following the establishment of the July Monarchy, the maintenance of property qualifications for voting kept local and national political life in the hands of this elite.[11] The electoral lists of the 1830s and 1840s thus contain the names of a restricted group of voters who paid a minimum of Fr 200 in direct taxes.[12] These lists are indispensable for a study of provincial political life. They include most of the heads of households counted by social historians such as Adeline Daumard as "bourgeois" but are more inclusive of diverse elements in the city than the very small group of *grands notables* studied by André-Jean Tudesq.[13] The lists give the age and occupation of each voter, as well as a breakdown of his direct tax payments into four categories: the tax on real property, buildings, and land (*contribution foncière sur propriété bâtié et non bâtié*); the poll tax and the tax on furnished dwellings (*contribution personelle et mobilière*); the tax on businesses (*impôt des patentes*); and the tax on doors and windows (*contribution des portes et fenêtres*).[14] It is possible through the use of the electoral lists to create an economic profile of any provincial elite up to 1848, when universal suffrage was introduced and lists of wealthy voters ceased to be made. By this means the economic background against which political life was played may be assessed.

The wealth and economic interests of the elite helped determine local political hierarchies as well as the issues and character of provincial life. Table 1 shows the distribution of investments by the notables in 1848.[15] Manufacturers at Reims were most heavily concentrated in the woolens and wine trades; those at St. Etienne were most prominent in ribbon manufacturing. These figures are a clear indication of the importance of these traditional industries in the life of the towns. Analysis of the electoral lists according to categories of wealth shows that these established trades also had a disproportionately larger share of wealthier notables. In the occupational breakdown of the wealthiest quarter of the electorate at Reims, which paid one-half of the total taxes in 1847-48, the preponderance of the wealthy Reims woolens *patronat* is especially evident: 41 percent of the wealthier notables were woolens manufacturers as compared to 28.6 percent of the enfranchised bourgeoisie as a whole (Table 4). Ribbon manufacturers are similarly heavily represented among St. Etienne's wealthiest group. The importance of woolens and wine manufacturers at Reims and of ribbon manufacturers and small metallurgists at St. Etienne is evident both from their superior numbers within the electorate and from their greater wealth.

A more detailed analysis of the distribution of wealth can be made through a study of the taxes on business property and on real estate.[16] Of these, the business tax is especially important, because it helps identify the most important manufacturers within the elite. The 4.7 percent of the Reims electorate which paid this tax of Fr 500 or more (Table 2) was heavily concentrated in the woolens industry and included such important political figures as Victor and Charles Rogelet, two of the most influential Legitimist leaders in the city, and Antoine Barthelemy Villeminot-Huard and Edouard Henriot, both leaders of the liberal opposition. All continued to be important in political and economic life under the Second Empire. Two of the four electors who paid over Fr 1,000 were also woolens manufacturers: Armand Bertherand-Sutaine, another Legitimist whose party enjoyed the backing of several very wealthy manufacturers, and Félix Croutelle, perhaps the most important industrial innovator in the Reims woolens industry under the July Monarchy and an important economic leader under the Second Empire.

At St. Etienne, only 2.6 percent of the electors paid a business tax of at least Fr 500, indicating that with few exceptions ribbon-making involved smaller capital investments than did woolens manufacturing. Still, this small group of fourteen voters included many of the most politically influential ribbon manufacturers: Mathieu Passerat, Jean-Baptiste David, Denis Epitalon, and two members of the Balay family, all of whom were members of St. Etienne's small conservative Orleanist group. The man who paid the highest business tax at St. Etienne was not a ribbon manufacturer, however, but the entrepreneur of the government's arms factory, the Manufacture Nationale des Armes. As a government agent he also supported François Guizot's conservative policies.

The tax on real estate (Table 3) indicates the extent to which the bourgeoisie made more conservative and prestigious investments in land and houses and thus the extent to which it was composed of sedentary *rentiers*. One of the most striking differences between the two cities that emerges from a comparison of the electors at the end of the 1840s is the relatively higher concentration of landowners and *rentiers* at St. Etienne, both within the whole of the electorate (23.5 percent as compared with 18.1 percent at Reims) and among the wealthier electors (31.4 percent compared to 19.1 percent). Most of the *rentiers* and landowners at St. Etienne were also ribbon manufacturers. Seeking the prestige accorded to *propriétaires*, many had invested in land.[17] David Landes has discussed the national propensity of French businessmen to secure prestige through investment in land, a practice familiar under the *ancien régime*.[18] Thus Jules Balay, one of the wealthiest of the city's ribbon manufacturers and a landowner, styled himself Balay de la Berardière, an example that was followed by others.

The investment of local capital in land at St. Etienne, leaving less available for industrial investment, later made it difficult for the newer modernizing entrepreneurs in heavy industry to become integrated with the city's older families. Through the period of the empire the older manufacturing interests continued to invest chiefly in land or in their own businesses. The financial division between the older mercantile elite and newer industrialists contributed to political divisions under the empire. By contrast, Reims's woolens manufacturers were underrepresented among all categories of the *foncière*. Although some of the wealthiest Reims manufacturers such as Croutelle had major investments in land, most woolens manufacturers invested a greater portion of their capital in their own mercantile woolens businesses. They would later invest heavily in the mechanized manufacturing processes that began to be introduced under the Second Empire. The willingness of the Reims merchants to invest in factory production helped contribute to their financial integration with more innovative manufacturers, and helped produce a more unified political outlook within the elite.

Some manufacturers at Reims had been receptive to industrial innovations since the beginning of the century. Henriot *fils*, a member of a wealthy woolens family, had first adopted Jacquard looms for the manufacture of *nouveautés*, a new kind of cloth, under the Restoration. Under his leadership Reims soon became an important rival to Roubaix in its manufacture.[19] Other innovations such as merinos and flannels were also quickly adopted by the Reims *fabrique* and contributed to the prosperity of the city. The large-scale manufacture of merinos by the firm of Jobert-Lucas proved so profitable that it built the city's first mechanized spinning factory in 1812.[20]

The relation between innovation and increased profits was not lost on local manufacturers, and the first successful attempt to mechanize production encouraged others to follow.[21] By the late 1830s Croutelle, who had built the first mechanized weaving mill at Reims in 1838, had also begun to experiment with the spinning of shorter and cheaper carded wool fibers (*laine cardée*). It had been commonly believed that these fibers could be spun only by hand, and his eventual success was another important stimulus to local industry. The jury at the International Exposition of 1844 praised his working "toward this innovation with great perseverance despite the well-known failures of all those before him. At the risk of very costly research that might have proven useless . . . he has attained results of such importance that he cannot be given too much credit."[22] This innovative spirit, which entirely transformed the woolens industry at Reims under the empire, also proved very profitable. Application of the new methods soon made the firm of Camu fils–Croutelle one of the largest spinning mills in Reims; it employed more than 250 workers and produced an annual product worth Fr 1.8 million.[23] The firm soon rivaled the oldest and most prestigious artisanal houses at Reims.[24]

Croutelle's innovations were introduced into the new mechanized spinning mill of Lucas frères, which had also begun to surpass the traditional leaders of the industry. In the 1840s Lucas frères grew larger than the Croutelle factory, employing more than 360 workers and producing an annual product worth more than Fr 2 million.[25] Clearly, the future belonged to the large firms that were able to modernize their operations. By 1848, although most spinning at Reims continued to be done by artisans in the countryside, the city had sixty-three mechanized spinning mills capable of processing eight million kilos of wool a year.[26]

No similar mechanization of production was introduced into any of St. Etienne's traditional industries. Indeed, most of the local elite were hostile to modernization both within their own industry and in any other branch of manufacturing. During the 1840s, this conservatism found expression in the struggle between the local elite and the largest coal company in the region, the Compagnie générale des mines de la Loire. The attempt of the company to modernize its operations was greatly resented by the elite, who were suspicious of its Paris-based investors. They feared that the emergence of a new industrial group, outside of the closed circle of established local families, might pose an economic and political threat to the older notables. The struggle between the management of the Compagnie générale and the local bourgeoisie also presaged a more important conflict between leaders of the local steel industry and mercantile ribbon manufacturers under the Second Empire. Several major steel entrepreneurs later became the rivals of the older ribbon merchants and eventually leaders of the republican opposition. This later conflict was postponed, however, by the union of all segments of the local elite in the 1840s against the coal monopoly.

Under the July Monarchy, the ribbon trade still dominated the economic life of St. Etienne, and its leading merchants headed the fight against the Compagnie générale. Under both the July Monarchy and the Second Empire ribbon-making was the region's most conservative industry, but this had not always been so. It had first been revolutionized by the introduction of a new loom, the *métier à la zurichoise*, in 1765. This allowed the weaving of very elaborate ribbons, and made St. Etienne the leading ribbon center in the Loire.[27] By 1789 there were more than thirty wealthy manufacturing families in the city, among them the Neyron, Thiollière-Deslisle, and Praire, who continued to influence the life of the city under the Second Empire.[28]

In 1793 a member of the Thiollière family, Jean-Baptiste David, began to manufacture the large velvet ribbons that soon became another very profitable specialty.[29] By 1813, when St. Etienne began producing heavily for the American market, various members of the Thiollière family employed as many as a thousand workers. Other firms employed almost as many.[30] But as the merchant families grew wealthier, they also became more cautious. By the 1840s the old firms had come to value stability and security over rapid growth and further innovation.

The ribbon merchant elite had also become the center of bourgeois society. Like the woolens merchants at Reims, its wealthiest members had come to form an economically and socially unified group. Some merchant families had been founded by men from modest backgrounds. Denis Epitalon, for example, had been the son of an innkeeper; others had been established by men such as David, whose paternal grandfather had been councillor for the *baillage du Forez* in the seventeenth century. But both old and new families had become allied through marriage, creating a unified group that monopolized local political power under the July Monarchy.[31]

The director of the Manufacture Nationale des Armes, the wealthiest notable in the city, was closely associated politically with the ribbon manufacturers. The city's monopoly on military arms manufacturing, abolished during the Revolution, had been restored in the year VIII by Napoleon Bonaparte, and the post of official *entrepreneur* of arms had been established in the same period. A private manufacturer, he employed a large number of artisans whose work was controlled by government inspectors.[32] This was an extremely lucrative privilege; in 1811, when the Jovin brothers had the monopoly, they produced more than one hundred thousand muskets for the army and employed almost two thousand workers.[33] The regulations of 1844 retained the post of a single director to head the Manufacture, and even in peacetime the position of *entrepreneur* remained highly profitable. The Brunon brothers, who acquired control of the Manufacture Nationale in 1838, became extremely wealthy; Jean Brunon was the only elector who paid a *patente* of over Fr 1,000. Other arms manufacturers were limited by law to the production of hunting arms, creating under the July Monarchy and Second Empire rivalries between them and the head of the Manufacture.

While the ribbons and arms industries flourished under the July

Monarchy, *quincaillerie* was in decline, the victim of a shortage of capital that prevented the introduction of modern production methods.[34] During the late 1840s, most available capital at St. Etienne belonged to ribbon manufacturers, who invested only in their own businesses or in land. Later, under the Second Empire, this same lack of local investment obliged the rapidly growing steel industry to look outside of St. Etienne for capital and thus develop independent of the financial control of the ribbon-manufacturing elite.

The Structure of Local Politics and Political Issues before 1848

The voting restrictions of the July Monarchy allowed the notables to control local politics as completely as they did the economic life of the towns. Most workers grudgingly accepted the political as well as economic rule of their employers. The prestige enjoyed by the very rich allowed less wealthy members of the middle classes to accept the rule of the notables without too much rancor. It was generally assumed that a large fortune established its owner's right to play a role in national political life. The notables were thus able to create a political consensus within the middle classes and act as spokesmen for the bourgeoisie under both the Restoration and the July Monarchy. It was only in the last years of the Orleanist regime, when the development of industry put greater distance between larger and smaller manufacturers, that less wealthy members of the bourgeoisie could no longer identify with the conservative faction of the town elites. They were instead increasingly attracted to the liberal opposition, which promised an effective expansion of the franchise and protection for small businesses.[35] Some would even eventually join the *démocrate-socialiste* coalition under the Second Republic and denounce the rich as the enemies of small property owners.

The local notables participated in local government through the municipal council, which regulated local markets, schools, and poor relief, supervised voter registration, and was responsible for public works projects; they participated in departmental affairs through the *conseil général* and the *conseil d'arrondissement*. Under the July Monarchy the *conseils généraux* were also allowed to apportion taxation within the department and to represent local financial and business interests in negotiations with Paris. They also made recommendations to the prefect on departmental public work projects such as the construction of new roads, bridges, and railway lines. Similar functions within each arrondissement were filled by the *conseils d'arrondissement*.

The prefect, appointed by the central government, was the most important agent in the authoritarian, bureaucratic system first established by Napoleon I, and maintained under both the July Monarchy and the Second Empire, for the governance of the provinces. Prefectoral authority prevented intermediate elected bodies from playing a central role in running either the towns or the departments. As the chief representative of the central government, the prefect reported on local conditions to Paris and received the government's orders for the local administration. During elections, he was also the most powerful political figure in the department, using his prestige and influence with the electorate to support candidates favored by the government. Town government was also controlled by Paris through the appointment of the mayors and their assistants (*adjoints*), who dominated the locally elected municipal council and were answerable for their actions only to the prefect and the ministry.

Under the Second Empire, controls over locally elected officials were increased. Even municipal budgets were no longer drawn up by the local municipal council but were instead proposed by the prefect (usually in consultation with the mayor) and then presented to the municipal council for its approval. Similarly, the *conseils généraux* and the *conseils d'arrondissement* were stripped of their discretionary powers in the creation of the departmental budget. After 1855 the prefect alone drew up the departmental budget and was no longer obliged to act upon the suggestions of the departmental councillors. It was only in 1866 that the deliberations of the *conseils généraux* were made public and their power greatly expanded; as part of the liberalization of the empire they were allowed to participate actively in the apportionment of departmental taxation and once again to participate in creating the budget. The government hoped that their free operation would serve as a "primary school of liberty," in which the nation could learn about democratic procedures before the expansion of political liberties and a free exercise of the suffrage.[36]

Although the limited power of the councils was overshadowed by the broader powers of the prefect, who could appoint many local officials, the councillors played an important role in local political life. As A. J. Tudesq remarks in his study of the *conseillers généraux* under the July Monarchy, the councillors were often more important than the councils on which they served.[37] The economic power of the notables, combined with the prestige they enjoyed in their localities, resulted in their often successful rallying of public support against unpopular decisions of the central government. A recent study by Bernard Le Clerc and Vincent Wright has demonstrated the difficulties of the government in combating the influence of the elite over the local population even under the Second Empire, supposedly the period of the prefects' greatest power.[38]

The local notables also exercised an influence in national political life through elections to the Chamber of Deputies (and after 1852 to the Corps législatif). Even under both the so-called "Guizot system" of the 1840s and the Second Empire, when the central administration used the prefects to ensure the election of government candidates, the regime was careful to select its candidates from among figures acceptable to the notables. Sometimes candidates whose popularity was their only recommendation were chosen.[39] In this way bureaucratic interference in elections reinforced rather than weakened the elite's control of political life, especially under the Second Empire, when the prefectorial administration acted to ensure the election of notables to local and national office through universal suffrage. Prefectorial influence also helped elect men acceptable to the local notables to the municipal and departmental councils; mayors were chosen by the government from among those men best able to rally bourgeois support for the regime.[40] The central government and the local elite were therefore anxious to cooperate with one another. Notable candidates were eager for government support, which meant almost certain success in elections. The government was equally willing to support individuals nominated by the wealthy, who remained throughout the period of the July Monarchy and Second Empire the most influential leaders of bourgeois opinion.

Under the July Monarchy, woolens and ribbon manufacturers controlled municipal and departmental councils because of their dominant position within the restricted electorate, as well as the support they received from the national government. Yet even though the number of voters was relatively small, internal rivalries divided them into political factions. The electorate had developed differently at Reims and St. Etienne because of the previous histories of the two towns. Reims, with its many wealthy champagne manufacturers from the *ancien régime*, had a much larger Legitimist party than St. Etienne. Economic development, which affected the size of the electorate, also played an important role in local politics. St. Etienne had only 533 voters, or 1.1 percent of the total town population. Reims, a more prosperous town with many more middle-sized businesses and a slightly smaller population, had 927 voters, or 2.2 percent of its population (Table 1). This difference may seem inconsequential to a reader in an age of mass politics, but it helped create a more vigorous political life at Reims. A larger number of electors in the middling categories of wealth had a similar effect. The greater proportion of voters at Reims able to exercise political independence contributed to political divisions, while the greater distance between the wealthiest electors and the rest of the voting population at St. Etienne suggests that politics in this period was controlled by a narrower elite better able to impose its will on the majority of the voters.

Local offices at St. Etienne through the 1840s had as a result been almost totally monopolized by the wealthiest ribbon manufacturers. Antoine Neyron, a ribbon merchant, had been St. Etienne's first mayor, serving in 1790-91. Hippolyte Royet, another ribbon manufacturer, was mayor between 1819 and 1830. Jean-Louis Royet, a member of the same family, had founded the *Mercure seguisien*, the city's first important political journal, under the July Monarchy. Until 1848 the ribbon interests dominated the municipal council as well through such men as Denis Epitalon, Mathieu Duplay, Auguste Tézénas, Auguste Terme, Jean-Pierre Larderet, Joseph Vignat-Chovet, Jean-Claude Peyret-Gerin, L. Robichon, and Royet. The Chamber of Commerce, the labor arbitration board (*Conseil des prudhommes*), and the Tribunal of Commerce were also dominated by the same group. Two-thirds of the members of the Chamber of Commerce were ribbon manufacturers, as were all of its presidents save one.

The political control of St. Etienne by the ribbon manufacturers was thus never seriously challenged by any other wealthy bourgeois group under the July Monarchy. The steel industry, which was to provide the main political rivals of the older mercantile elite under the Second Empire, had not yet grown sufficiently for most of its members to develop political ambitions.

The industry had been founded under the Restoration. In 1817, the Holtzers, an Alsatian family that was later to acquire great economic and political influence, came to the Loire to work in the region's first small steel mill.[41] The Jacksons, who were also to contribute to the development of the industry, arrived from England that same year and joined another local firm. By 1820 the Jacksons had established their own business at Le Soleil, and in 1823 they owned fifteen smelting furnaces, a retort for making steel, two coke ovens, and a blast furnace.[42] Their company at first grew slowly because of the difficulty of tapping local capital resources, and the Jacksons continued to live modestly. The brothers, who were basically skilled craftsmen rather than financiers, worked long hours at their forges, assisted by French apprentices in a traditional artisanal relationship.[43] They and their wives lived in small houses on the factory grounds and, being English and Protestants, participated minimally in bourgeois social life.

Still other immigrants to the Loire were Hippolyte Petin and Jean Gaudet, who started a small steel mill in 1839; it was later to merge with the Jackson holdings during the period of the Second Empire and become one of the country's most important industrial firms.[44] Like the Jacksons, both were craftsmen who had worked for others before starting their own firm. Their first employer had been the Fonderies et forges Louis Frèrejean père, fils et cie, a company that had been founded by entrepreneurs from Lyons, and for a time had pioneered in the introduction of new techniques in the region.[45] In 1821 Frèrejean et Cie had become a limited liability company, a significant break with traditional family business organization in the Loire, where suspicion of limited liability remained strong.[46] But this structure enabled it to increase its capital resources greatly, and by 1822 it had begun operations at Terrenoire. In 1870, as the Compagnie des fonderies et forges de Terrenoire, la Voulte et Bessèges, it became the largest producer of Bessemer steel in the region and a major source of financial support for the political opposition to the imperial government.[47]

But most of these steel companies were to grow rapidly only after 1852. In the last years of the July Monarchy only the Jackson company grew enormously. By 1847 it was the largest iron and steel manufacturer in France, producing 910,000 of the total national output of 1,430,000 kilos.[48] The leadership of the rest of the industry in the period also remained, like the Jacksons, socially distinct from that of the older trades. Marriages between the families of leading ribbon manufacturers were common, but steel manufacturers were unable to make similar advantageous matches. Some, like the Jacksons and Holtzers, were Protestants, and most had not yet attained the fortunes that would have gained them entry into more established families. Most steel enterprises were for the most part still too small to encourage either lofty social or political ambitions in their owners. As a result, these new interests were not yet ready to play an independent political role in the city. The emergence of the powerful Compagnie générale, which threatened to control all local coal production, also helped to keep local manufacturers politically united. The Compagnie générale's size encouraged steel manufacturers to join with the old elite in opposing it, for although the coal monopoly was especially dangerous for the steel industry, which was dependent upon cheap coal, all elements of the local population felt threatened. Cheap fuel for heating had long been regarded as a right in this coal-rich region.[49] More important, the sudden appearance of wealthy outside investors seemed to threaten the control of the local elite over all aspects of St. Etienne's economy.

The foundations of the Compagnie générale had been laid in 1820, when the first large coal company in the region, the Compagnie des mines de Roche-la-Molière et Firminy, was established near St. Etienne by the marquis d'Osmond. Osmond and most of his associates were newcomers to the region, and their introduction of new techniques into an area where coal mining had previously been pursued by small local proprietors had immediately created fears of outside competition. One member of the local elite complained in 1825 that "one looked in vain to find mining concessions divided to the profit of the local notables."[50] Such complaints were premature, but when between 1831 and 1834 the price of coal fell, individual mine operators began to sell out to larger companies with the resources to introduce more efficient operations. In 1837, when profits fell again, a union of mining interests was begun with the creation of Compagnie générale des mines de Rive-de-Gier. A rival group, the Union des mines de Rive-de-Gier, was created the following year, and similar combinations took place at St. Etienne. The creation of the Compagnie générale des mines de la Loire in 1844 was the result of further mergers between the Compagnie générale des mines de Rive-de-Gier, the Union des mines de Rive-de-Gier, and several other concessions.[51]

By 1845 the new company, which was capitalized at Fr 64 million, was the first giant industrial firm in the Loire, dwarfing all other enterprises in the region. That same year, it absorbed the Société des mines réunies de St. Etienne and the Compagnie des houillères de St. Etienne.[52] This last acquisition was a major triumph for the Compagnie générale, for the St. Etienne company had been founded early in 1845 by Claude Palluat, a local banker, and other local notables in an attempt to resist the growth of the new concern. In 1846 the company continued to grow, producing 1,166,000 tons of coal, compared with 351,000 for all of the independent operators in the region.[53]

The need to offset the costs of modernization, which had led to the first fusion of the mines, forced the company to become increasingly dependent on outside capital. It borrowed first from the Paris-Orleans railroad group, controlled by the Parisian banker Bartholony, and later from the Crédit mobilier. The local elite's fear of outside capital is easy to understand. St. Etienne's traditional "bankers" had been men such as Palluat, a ribbon manufacturer who practiced banking as a sideline, or the Baron Corneille de Rochetaillée, a large landowner and mine operator, who had entered banking to qualify for admission to the Chamber of Commerce. The threat of powerful capitalists such as Bartholony to the financial control exercised by these local industrialists was obvious. Even greater was the fear that outside capitalists would ruthlessly exploit local markets in the Loire. The mayor of St. Etienne charged that "behind this monopolistic association was a vast financial conspiracy against the industry of the region." The Chamber of Commerce complained in 1846 that "in place of the former coal mine operators, tied to St. Etienne by the triple bonds of property, industry and family, such as the Neyrons, Jovins, etc. . . . magistrates and benefactors of their city, we see substituted a company that can give no moral guarantee, avid for gain, directed by agents paid proportionately according to the profits they produce, and thus stimulated by self-interest to oppress consumers to the greatest possible limit."[54] Even after such men as Laroche-André Thiollière, André Neyron, and the Jacksons became shareholders in the company, continued outside control kept local hostility alive.

The public believed mining should have been regulated for the general welfare, and the local newspapers, like the Chamber of Commerce, referred to the company directors as "hoarders" and conspirators in a new *pacte de famine*. Public outcry was further aroused when the company defied local custom and refused to sell coal at a reduced price in the immediate area of St. Etienne. Steel manufacturers felt especially threatened by the company's refusal to grant long-term contracts to heavy coal users. When in 1847 the company finally relented and offered longer contracts with progressive price increases, the fears of local industry appeared confirmed. Jackson, the spokesman for heavy industry, wrote that "what is expected is that the Compagnie générale will try to recover its capital outlays as quickly as possible at the expense of the metallurgical industry of the Loire. It has already paralyzed all progress, and the steel industry will be reduced to an agonizing and futile resistance. This is the unanimous opinion of all of our manufacturers."[55] As long as the old elite continued to fight the Compagnie générale, the interests of steel entrepreneurs remained united with those of the mercantile group. Once the common enemy that had brought them together was eliminated under the Second Empire, relations between the two groups deteriorated.

Even the unanimous condemnation of the local elite could not destroy a company enjoying the protection of the central government, however, and the notables were eventually obliged to look for new allies among the workers to defeat the monopoly. They began to use the threat of popular violence against both the Compagnie générale and the regime that supported it. Taking advantage of the tensions between miners and company engineers, which in the past had occasionally ended in bloodshed, they encouraged strikes among miners. The city's artisanal workers, most of whom were long-term residents, had little contact with miners, many of whom were newly arrived immigrants, and remained untouched by strike agitation in the coal fields.[56] Although miners' strikes in 1840 and 1846 were the product of independent working class organization and leadership, they thus became a useful tool in local political life.[57]

When the miners struck at St. Etienne in 1846, ribbon merchants

opposed the government's use of troops to protect the Compagnie
générale, and local newspapers lectured the company on its paternalistic duties as an employer.[58] The company in turn accused its opponents of encouraging communism and complained that the municipal
government as well as individual manufacturers had encouraged the
strike.[59] The local elite was so confident that the growing radicalism
among the miners would not affect either ribbon weavers or metalworkers that they even encouraged acts of violence against the company. The *procureur général* reported that "everyone excites the
workers to destruction . . . because it appears that the present disorders are a useful tool against the Compagnie générale" and cited cases
in which cabarets were paid by wealthy merchants to supply food to
the strikers.[60]

At Reims as well, elements of the elite would by the last years of the
July Monarchy use the threat of working-class violence against their
political and economic opponents. But unlike the situation at St.
Etienne, where local animosities were directed against an external
enemy, the elite at Reims was divided into several bitterly opposed
political factions. By the time of the banquet campaign of 1847, the
local liberal opposition was prepared to use workers against the
conservative notables who supported Guizot.

The Revolution of 1830 had initially replaced the oldest woolens
and wine manufacturers who were Legitimists and municipal councillors under the Restoration with an Orleanist manufacturing group
supported by anticlerical artisan workers.[61] Government-sponsored
attempts by the clergy in the 1820s to proselytize in working-class
neighborhoods had resulted in artisan riots, and the men who had
succeeded to local power in 1830 remained convinced that they
enjoyed popular support. But by the 1840s, the new ruling group had
become divided into conservative and liberal factions. The conservatives, led by Mathieu-Edouard Werlé, the general manager of the Vve
Cliquot-Ponsardin champagne company, included some of the most
powerful men in the city: Jean-Baptiste Plumet-Folliart, the director
of the local commercial bank; Le Roy-Myon, the conservative deputy;
Pierre Lecointre, a wholesale grocer later to become president of the
Chamber of Commerce; and several other rich manufacturers.[62] They
controlled most local offices and enjoyed government support during
national elections. Their opponents were divided between Legitimists

and a group of liberal Orleanists. Men outside of the wealthiest manufacturing circles, the leaders of the liberal faction were often smaller woolens manufacturers and members of the liberal professions. Two of their most important leaders, Nicolas Houzeau-Muiron and Léon Faucher, were also relative newcomers to the city.

Traditionally, local political influence was the patrimony of older elite families and was passed from one generation to the next, so that outsiders could rarely hope in one generation to acquire the same influence as members of the established group. Under the Guizot system the nomination of the government became equally important in achieving national office, for the regime provided its candidates with the support of the prefect and other local officials, as well as with campaign subsidies. Those lacking family and government connections tended to enter the liberal opposition, hoping to achieve through the creation of a popular following the political power otherwise denied them.

Houzeau-Muiron was able to win a seat in the Chamber of Deputies in this way in 1842. Having begun his career outside the city, he had subsequently established himself in Reims as a successful street-lighting entrepreneur, but his scheme to manufacture street-lighting gas from wool fat brought him into conflict with the city's conservative elite, who feared the cost of a major public works project. Obliged to seek political allies against the municipal administration, he won the support of the liberal *L'Indicateur de la Champagne* and eventually became a leader in the opposition. In 1842 he won a seat for Reims *extra-muros* by campaigning as a friend of innovation and progress and the opponent of a backward-looking conservative establishment. He received the support of all those elements of the electorate, both Legitimist and liberal, who resented the political domination of the conservative Orleanist group. But following Houzeau's death in 1844 and the strengthening of the Guizot system, it became increasingly difficult for the opposition to elect a deputy. It was clear that only an increase in the size of the electorate could ensure future liberal victories. Seeking their natural allies among the disenfranchised shopkeepers, smaller merchants, minor functionaries, and well-paid artisans distinguished from the working class mainly by the ownership of property, the liberals at Reims therefore began to demand an extension of the suffrage. They even attempted to use the threat of a popular rising to win concessions from the government.

They began recruiting working-class supporters for the electoral reform campaign of 1847. The importance of the campaign for the opposition was evident, for although the conservatives possessed about 350 votes within the limited electorate of the *régime censitaire*, they were highly vulnerable to any change in the suffrage. The liberal opposition had elected Léon Faucher in 1846. Like Houzeau, he was a newcomer to the city, an ardent supporter of free trade, and a self-proclaimed friend of industrial progress and liberal reforms.[63] But his victory had been secured only through a fragile alliance with the city's small Legitimist party. The liberals now hoped to create a permanent majority through an extension of the suffrage. In addition, many artisan spinners, weavers, and wool combers were susceptible to liberal paternalistic efforts on their behalf. Once the economic slump began in 1847, increasing unemployment encouraged working-class groups, along with shopkeepers dependent upon workers' business, to take a greater interest in politics.[64]

As early as 1845 the party attempted to attract popular support by encouraging various charitable schemes. When in that year Victor Considérant came to Reims to lecture on Fourierism, Villeminot-Huard, an important figure in the liberal opposition (he had made a fortune manufacturing machines for the new woolens factories), donated his house for the meeting. At a farewell banquet for Considérant liberals urged the government to establish workers' nurseries, shelters, and pensions, as well as apprentice schools for working-class children.[65] These demands were repeated during the legislative elections of 1846, when Léon Faucher's promises of higher wages, lower taxes, and cheaper bread led to the harassment of conservative leaders by groups of workers.[66]

Of course, the leaders of the liberal opposition were not all radicals or republicans, and they hoped to increase the suffrage only enough to ensure themselves a permanent electoral majority. Artisanal support was to be purchased as cheaply as possible with a few token gestures on behalf of woolens workers, as when at the end of 1846 Faucher proposed a voluntary subscription to aid the city's unemployed.[67] Dr. Maldan, the vice-president of the liberal reform committee before the revolution and an important republican leader after 1848, later confessed that he had not anticipated the disorders of 1848 and had accepted the revolution with considerable misgivings. Emile Dérodé, another important prerevolutionary opposition leader with family connections to the older manufacturing group, was later to say that before 1848 he had not even been a republican; conscious of the evils of revolution, he had never wished to overthrow the July Monarchy.[68]

Members of the elite in both towns thus seemed to believe that they could use the working classes against the central government without any threat to themselves or to the existing social order. This view was shared by many bourgeois liberals, who in the course of 1847 attempted to stir up popular discontent against the government through the banquet campaign. Until 1848 developments in both towns seemed to justify their assumptions. The failure of the miners' strike at St. Etienne to affect artisan ribbon weavers, or of the political demonstrations at Reims to develop into strikes, encouraged the belief that it was possible to avoid making any important economic or political concessions to workers.[69] The *Industriel* at Reims expressed the liberal view of the economic crisis in 1847 when it wrote that the working class of no other city in France had shown itself more peaceful: "This is to the eternal honor of the working class; and also to the honor of the fortunate classes. This is because the rich citizens of the town have understood that it is their duty to come to the aid of the workers . . . and that they have faith that moral force is sufficient to maintain order."[70]

The liberals thus remained confident during the electoral reform meetings at Reims in the summer of 1847 and continued to agitate among artisans against the regime through the early months of 1848. But as in the rest of France, the introduction of universal suffrage would shatter the political power of the notables. As working-class organizations grew, liberals found themselves first disregarded and then swept away by artisanal radicalism in 1848-49. The Revolution of 1848 and the establishment of the Second Republic thus marked a crucial turning point for subsequent political developments. Under the Second Republic the notables temporarily lost power, a development that seemed to require the establishment of new forms of economic and political controls to maintain middle-class supremacy in the towns.

2

Reims and St. Etienne
under the Second Republic
and the Threat of
Universal Suffrage

The revolution that began in Paris in February quickly spread to the provinces, where liberals attempted to repeat their successes of 1830. The 1848 revolution occurred, however, during a severe economic depression, and massive unemployment produced radical political demands from artisan groups. This made it increasingly difficult for moderate republicans to maintain their leadership of the revolution and created a struggle between notables and workers that temporarily ended the elite's traditional influence over the working classes. Conservative rule was not re-established until 1852.

Provincial life in 1848 traditionally has been assumed to have been quiet and basically conservative. Thus Marx in his writings on the Revolution of 1848 seems to believe that the Parisian "proletariat" was the only significant element working for the establishment of a truly democratic republic and that the sole role of the provinces was to elect the Constituent Assembly that suppressed the Parisian working-class movement and with it any hope for a democratic regime.[1] On the period following the election of the Constituent Assembly in April 1848, he wrote:

> Directly after the February days not only had the dynastic opposition been surprised by the republicans and the republicans by the Socialists, but all France by Paris. The National Assembly, which met on May 4, 1848, had emerged from the national elections and represented the nation. It was a living protest against the pretensions of the February days and was to reduce the results of the revolution to a bourgeois scale. In vain the Paris proletariat, which immediately grasped the character of this National Assembly, attempted on May 15, a few days after it met, to disintegrate again into its constituent parts the organic form in which the proletariat was threatened by the reacting spirit of the nation.[2]

But in fact, as recent writers have reminded us, the revolution occurred throughout France, not just in Paris.[3] Clashes in provincial centers between radicals, liberals, and conservatives were similar to those in the capital. The Second Republic generated more local support than was once believed, and the development of provincial politics in the 1850s is incomprehensible without an awareness of this fact.[4]

Although provincial opposition groups were at first surprised by the sudden collapse of the government in Paris, they were soon able to take advantage of the creation of the republic and quickly mobilized support among both liberals in the elite and workers to supplant local conservative administrations. In a number of industrial cities, including Lyons, Limoges, and Rouen as well as Reims and St. Etienne, the long economic crisis also encouraged elements within the working classes to develop independent political organizations. In addition, the combination of economic and political crises created an expectation of social reforms in centers of artisan production where traditional working-class organizations were strong. But in the first months of the republic only liberal members of the elite and the lower middle classes—shopkeepers and small merchants—were able to profit from the revolution. At both Reims and St. Etienne artisan groups in this period were still ready to act in support of the liberal opposition. Whereas the provincial political struggle in 1848 between liberal and conservative groups within the elite quickly became intense, provincial working-class groups formulated their own demands more slowly. As a result, the provinces in 1848 appeared more peaceful and politically complacent than they were to become in 1849.

Jean Lhomme has said that modern French society dates from June 1848, when Parisian artisans first demonstrated a social and political self-consciousness as members of a unified proletariat. It is certainly true that the Paris rising marked a fundamental change in the nature of French popular protest.[5] But the equally important emergence of working-class organizations in the provinces, which reached its highest development in 1849, has until recently been relegated to obscurity.[6] The immediate result of the June 1848 rising in Paris was the creation of a political alliance between conservative and liberal bourgeois political factions against the perceived threat of working-class radicalism. The long-term effect of the rising was the development of working-class organizations in the provinces. Roger Price has suggested that following the restoration to power of the *grands notables* in parts of France at the end of 1848, other politically organized groups, such as provincial artisans, were stimulated to oppose the growing conservative influence.[7] The republican movement in Paris might have been weakened by the repression following the June days, but the most important effect in the provinces was to strengthen radical workers' organizations.

The political power of the provincial working class began to fade only after 1850, when the effects of the second wave of police actions against workers' organizations began to be felt following the abortive Paris rising in June 1849. Price believes that because the notables continued to enjoy social and economic power, their political effacement following 1848 could only have been temporary; but there was nothing inevitable about the restoration of the notables at provincial manufacturing towns such as St. Etienne and Reims.[8] The rule of the conservative notables was restored only through the establishment of martial law. In 1851 the coup d'état that consolidated the restoration was accepted without violence at St. Etienne only because of the large garrison stationed in the city and at Reims because of the arrest of working-class leaders in 1849. There was more violence elsewhere. Overall, more than one hundred thousand men rose against the government, more than five hundred were killed, and twenty thousand people were convicted of rebellion against the state.[9]

The development of provincial politics under the Second Republic thus falls into two periods. The first began with the triumph of the liberals in February and ended with the combined liberal-conservative alliance in favor of Louis Cavaignac, the "hero of the June days," in the presidential election in December 1848. A second period began in 1849 with the emergence of powerful provincial artisan associations and ended in 1851 with the coup d'état of Louis-Napoleon Bonaparte and the restoration of the notables.

Reims, February to December 1848: The Triumph and Decline of the Liberals

The liberals at Reims continued to appeal to the disenfranchised for support right up until the revolution in February. In January 1848 Léon Faucher presented the Chamber of Deputies with a petition demanding electoral reform. *L'Industriel*, Reims's liberal paper, simultaneously attacked Louis Philippe's address to the Chamber, contrasting declining wages with his reference to the "progressive development of French industry."[10] When on February 25 news arrived of the king's abdication, the liberal opposition attempted to take advantage of popular disturbances in Reims to seize power. Agitators were encouraged by the unfriendly reception given Henri-Nicolas Carteret, the conservative mayor, by unemployed workers in the communal workshops. That night, a group of woolens workers attacked Croutelle's mechanized weaving factory, beat the factory manager, and demanded "the destruction of the machines and the head of M. Croutelle." When the National Guard arrived, the workers attacked several convents, sources of cheap female labor in competition with the artisans.

These incidents indicate that Reims artisans were chiefly interested in a solution to their economic problems. Whereas members of the middle-class opposition saw the revolution primarily as a means of achieving political office on the crest of an expanded suffrage, the workers saw it as a chance to improve their economic situation. This difference was the source of later conflict, in the terms of contemporary political rhetoric, between the demands of middle-class "liberals" and artisan "radicals." The former were content to establish universal suffrage and reaffirm civil liberties. The demands of artisan leaders for full employment, the reduction of rents and food prices, and the establishment of fixed wage scales went too far in challenging the free market system to which the liberals were committed for them to give the workers much support.

Wool combers were perhaps the most desperate artisan group. They had faced the threat of proletarianization ever since the beginning of the mechanization of wool combing in the 1840s. Since the time of the First Empire, mechanization in the woolens industry had been accompanied by Luddism and radical working-class political activity, and the beginnings of mechanization combined with the steady decline of wages in the decade before the revolution lent a terrible urgency to their protests.[11] Other groups of woolens workers were almost as badly off. Despite the relatively good diet enjoyed by Reims artisans in the 1840s, including good bread, wine, and *soup grasse* at least twice a week, Louis Villermé had found woolens workers in 1840 generally resentful of working conditions and the neighborhoods of St. Nicaise and St. Rémy scenes of drunkenness and despair.[12] As early as 1844 placards calling upon artisans to rise against their employers had been posted in the city; a typical pamphlet of the period, purportedly written by "a poor father with five children in need of bread and clothing," called for vengeance against Louis Philippe and local employers. Although wages for twelve hours of domestic or factory labor in that period had been barely sufficient for the survival of a working-class family, they had continued to fall through the rest of the decade. By 1848, woolens manufacturers began warning the government that wages could not be allowed to decline further without creating a revolt.[13]

The attacks on the Croutelle factory and the convents were thus motivated by economic grievances, but both incidents were used by the liberal opposition for its own political ends. Croutelle had been an outspoken opponent of electoral reform, and the convents were identified with the Legitimist party. The attacks were therefore doubly useful in intimidating the political enemies of the liberals as well as demonstrating the weakness of the conservative municipal administration. The day following the attack, the mayor's plea for order coincided with a proclamation from the opposition calling for the formation of a new local government supported by the National Guard and for the respect of property. This latter promise was necessary to persuade shopkeepers, who were otherwise inclined to support the republic, of the legitimacy of the new government. It was also consistent with the interests of the liberals who signed the proclamation. These included Jean Sentis, a woolens manufacturer, Emile Dérodé, a member of one of Reims's oldest manufacturing families and a lawyer well known for his defense of workers' causes, and Dr. Maldan, one of the leaders of the banquet campaign and spokesman for the city's liberal Masonic Lodge. Other leaders were Jules Mennesson-Tonnellier, a well-known bourgeois liberal, and Adolphe David, a woolens manufacturer and former St. Simonian.[14] The following day liberals continued to take advantage of working-class demonstrations, and fourteen liberal members of the municipal council demanded the establishment of a new municipal government. They were powerfully seconded by a delegation of workers from the various artisan trades in the city. Faced with a large crowd massed in front of the Hotel-de-Ville, the mayor acquiesced, and Mennesson-Tonnellier, Maldan, David, and Dérodé were named to head a new provisional administration. The municipal council was also expanded to receive several influential working-class leaders.[15]

The popular movement that overthrew the municipal government had emerged out of the network of artisanal organizations that had existed before 1848, when Reims had been an important center of mutual assistance societies. Mutual aid organizations or producers' cooperatives had become especially popular among artisans in many French cities under the July Monarchy, when, as Leo Loubère notes, "the word 'association' acquired the currency of a messianic formula."[16] At Reims, seventeen mutual societies had first joined together in 1843 under the leadership of a master weaver, Joseph Ferrand, to create a central fund for temporary assistance of its members. By 1848 twenty-one workers' corporations had joined this association, including those of the sheep shearers, wool combers and sorters, spinners, dyers, and cloth finishers, as well as carpenters, drivers, shoemakers, drapers, small retailers, metalworkers, masons, joiners, painters, stonecutters, tailors, barrelmakers, and even agricultural workers. Once universal suffrage was introduced in 1848, it took on a vastly increased importance by greatly facilitating the mobilization of artisans for political ends.[17]

The economic crisis that created the February demonstrations also led eventually to the development of a radical workers' movement and the subsequent decline of the middle-class liberals. Indeed, within a month of the creation of the new administration the aims of the artisanal association had already begun to diverge from those of the liberal elite. In March 1848 the first distinctly working-class political demands were made in Le Républicain, a small newspaper founded after the revolution by a group of shopkeepers and master artisans, which soon became the spokesman for the workers' corporations. Calling for the creation of a "popular democracy," the paper proposed an alliance of workers, shopkeepers, and small businessmen against the wealthiest capitalists and landed proprietors of the region. In March it told its readers that it wanted "the triumph of the democratic principle of popular sovereignty. If there are partisans of an aristocratic or bourgeois republic, their place is no longer in France." As the unofficial organ of the new working-class political organization of Reims, the Comité électoral de la démocratie rémoise, it reflected the artisans' growing radicalism. It demanded the immediate incorporation of all male citizens into the National Guard, the removal of the garrison from Reims, the end of the obligatory workers' good conduct papers (the *livret*), and the immediate lowering of rents and bread prices.[18] The Démocratie rémoise, representing between one thousand and fifteen hundred workers, was led by Ferrand and Jean-Louis Gonzalle, a former shoemaker, popular poet, and editor of *Le Républicain*. Eugène Courmeaux, a former Parisian lawyer and journalist, was one of the very few middle-class leaders of the organization. He had first been converted to socialism by Considérant in 1845 and since then had devoted himself to spreading socialist ideas. By 1848 he had become one of the most radical republican leaders in the city. Unlike most of the middle-class leaders, however, he was not interested in defending bourgeois interests and therefore made no attempt to reconcile the city's moderate and radical republican factions.[19] This task was undertaken by only one member of the moderate group, Simon Dauphinot, who, although a woolens manufacturer, was also a member of the Démocratie rémoise. Dauphinot, however, was unable to stem the growing hostility of artisans toward the provisional municipal government.[20]

Tensions also continued to grow between workers employed on public works projects and the new municipal administration. Clashes took place between the National Guard and workers both in March and April, when more than two thousand of the unemployed defied the Guard behind hastily constructed barricades.[21] In less than two months after the establishment of the republic, the question of a "social republic" had begun to split artisans from liberals. The new municipal leadership soon ceased to be the spokesman for the working classes, and liberal paternalism began to give way to repression. After the first clashes with the National Guard in March, the liberal Comité électoral républicain de Reims, headed by the leaders of the February revolution, Dérodé, Maldan, Mennesson-Tonnellier, and David, had issued a manifesto calling for the union of "all men of the former opposition, young men, and members of the working and impoverished classes." It reminded workers that "the first principle of the young republic, born on the barricades, was respect for property."[22] Faced with further disturbances in April, the administration tried a new tactic—it blamed the trouble on outside agitators, who it claimed were opposed to the true interests of the workers.[23] The elite hoped in this way to maintain the goodwill of artisans, but these efforts met with little success.

The Comité de la démocratie rémoise was relentless in its attacks on the administration. *Le Républicain* demanded to know the identity of the outside agitators and declared that "the people will no longer be the dupes of those who wish to exploit the political movement among the workers for their own immense *amour-propre*. Unlike the parvenu journalists who now only preach calm, union, and concord, we shall never forget our unfortunate brothers."[24]

The republican middle classes were clearly losing their influence over the workers. Similar developments took place in Paris. Alexis de Tocqueville in April saw "society cut in two; those who possessed nothing, united in a common greed; those who possessed something, in a common fear. No more links, no more sympathy between the two classes, everywhere the idea of an inevitable and close struggle."[25] Fearful of the growing militancy of the Démocratie rémoise and of *Le Républicain*'s suggestion that artisans should control local politics, the municipal government of Reims decided to act against the workers' committee. The councillors forbade it to meet and suppressed *Le Républicain*. The paper's last issue bitterly congratulated the liberals for having successfully eliminated the only authentic voice of the artisans in the city.[26] Although a third electoral committee founded by Courmeaux's friend Dr. Jules Bienfait attempted to reunite liberals and workers with slogans such as "Social reform as the end and the republic as the means" and "All Socialists are Republicans; all Republicans are Socialists," the liberal bourgeoisie and the workers' corporations had split. The two groups presented separate lists in the crucial legislative elections in April.[27]

The isolation of the notables from the new working-class organization weakened the liberal municipal administration. But although Mennesson-Tonnellier had opposed the suppression of *Le Républicain* and the Démocratie rémoise, the administration could have done little to appease working-class demands or reduce massive unemployment. The simultaneous introduction of the *scrutin de liste* into national elections, whereby voters supported an entire list of candidates rather than individuals, further weakened the elite. Whereas previously well-known notables had attracted working-class support, the new system made the ideological position of an entire list the most important voting criterion.[28] Workers running on working-class lists, easily identifiable as such, attracted the support of a majority of artisan voters.

The liberals were therefore forced to look to the rest of the bourgeoisie for support in the legislative elections in April. Their electoral list was similar to that of the conservatives, save for the inclusion of Maldan and David. They supported Léon Faucher, Dérodé, the most moderate member of the municipal administration, and Ferrand, who had come under the influence of the city's manufacturing interests. The local administration also tried to eliminate as many radical voters as possible. Because migrant workers were generally considered radical, the municipal government demanded birth certificates (ostensibly to verify date and place of birth) of all prospective voters. Migrant workers, who would have had to return to their place of birth to get such documents, were thus deprived of the suffrage.[29] Many workers who were able to vote supported the separate working-class slate presented by the Démocratie rémoise.

The division of the republican forces, along with the heavy conservative vote in the rest of the department, contributed to a conservative victory.[30] The election at Reims reflected a conservative mood prevalent in much of provincial France; frightened by workers' demonstrations in Paris in March and April, the provinces elected a majority of moderate republicans to the Constituent Assembly; fewer than one hundred radical republicans were returned.

While the beleaguered municipal council continued to view the demands of the artisan association with suspicion, the resurgent conservative party, encouraged by its victory, prepared for the upcoming municipal elections. Following the suppression of the June rising in Paris, the party leaders had become confident enough to challenge the appointment of the new radical members to the municipal council in February. They hoped that all "those electors who love order and detest usurpation" would force the liberal administration from office.[31] For a second time in three months the voters were presented with three lists: one drawn up by the conservative former mayor Carteret that included many of Reims's major woolens and champagne manufacturers; one presented by the liberal party with such wealthy manufacturers such as Edouard Henriot, Villeminot-Huard, and Lundy aîné, as well as the members of the local administration; and a third, working-class list.[32] The latter list included the most radical members of the bourgeoisie, Courmeaux, Bienfait, and Dauphinot, as well as several working-class leaders.[33] Once again the division between workers and liberals favored the conservatives, who won twenty-two of the thirty-six council seats.

Other factors contributing to the conservative victory included the apathy that had begun to overtake many workers following the first conservative gains in April. The traditional resentment of Paris among all classes in the provinces, combined with the Parisian revolt in June, also hurt the republicans, who were identified with the rising. Conservative propaganda convinced many provincial voters that the Parisian artisans who had participated in the revolt were a vicious mob, interested only in pillage and anarchy. It was claimed that if they were not stopped by the conservative "party of order," they would invade the countryside. In a panic reminiscent of 1789, rumors had begun to spread about an invasion from Paris into the surrounding departments; in late June it was said in Reims that Chalons had been sacked. Although these rumors had been refuted by the time of the municipal elections, the suspicion of Parisian "radicalism" that had produced them remained strong. Finally, the slow upswing of the economy and the disillusionment following the election of the Constituent Assembly drew many workers away from politics.[34] As a result, although Mennesson-Tonnellier won the largest number of votes in the municipal election, many of the most influential prerevolutionary conservatives were returned to the council. These included Lecointre, the president of the Chamber of Commerce, Carteret, and Werlé, the most important leader of the old conservative group, as well as such wealthy champagne manufacturers as Hippolyte Vivès, Victor Lanson, and Walbaum-Heidsieck.[35]

The constitution promulgated in November created a single-chamber assembly and a strong executive. The following month, General Cavaignac ran for the presidency against Louis-Napoleon Bonaparte. The Reims liberals, in disarray, joined forces with the conservatives to support Cavaignac; their joint committee was presided over by Mennesson-Tonnellier and Carteret. Many wealthy conservatives supported Cavaignac because he appeared to be a defender of order, while Bonaparte's politics remained unclear. The artisanal organizations at Reims that had survived the dissolution of the Démocratie rémoise supported Alexandre Ledru-Rollin. But both Cavaignac and Ledru-Rollin were overwhelmed by the support the city gave Bonaparte, who received over half of the ten thousand votes cast in the election. The majority of the workers at Reims apparently saw Louis-Napoleon as the heir of the revolution, and perhaps a Socialist, an illusion widely shared in France. Cavaignac's campaign appeared, however, to promise little except the preservation of the status quo.[36] Many workers preferred a Bonapartist dictatorship to the rule of the bourgeoisie as represented by Cavaignac.[37] The general was in any case hated because of his role in the June days.

By the end of 1848 the conservative party at Reims had thus reestablished its control of the municipal administration, and the city had given overwhelming support to the presidential candidate most closely identified with the conservative cause. But in December 1848 a new workers' organization replaced the disbanded Démocratie rémoise. Under new and energetic leadership, Reims's artisan community once again came to dominate local political life. Demands for a "social republic" were revived, and the conservative successes of 1848 were threatened by a resurgence of popular militancy.

St. Etienne, February to December 1848: From Liberal Victory to the Election of Bonaparte

At St. Etienne, as at Reims, a coalition of liberals and artisans overthrew the old municipal administration. On February 26, 1848, the mayor, Joseph Vignat-Chovet, was replaced by a committee of seven notables, including Hippolyte Royet, Jules Paliard, and Robichon, all of whom had been prominent leaders in the fight against the Compagnie générale. Two members of the formerly weak liberal opposition, Tristan Duché, a lawyer, and Dr. Soviche, were also chosen.[38] Eugène Baune, a *lycée* instructor and one of the original members of the Central Committee of the Lyonnais Society of the Rights of Man (which had played a major role in introducing republican political demands into the 1834 workers' rising), was at the same time named prefect of the Loire.[39]

Before the establishment of universal suffrage, the city government had been dominated by ribbon manufacturers, who, with several of the wealthiest arms manufacturers and *quincailleurs*, had remained immune to the feeble opposition of a few liberal lawyers, doctors, and smaller ribbon manufacturers. But the liberals were able to make use of the economic crisis and the establishment of universal manhood suffrage to improve their position. By 1848 artisan ribbon weavers and coal miners were becoming hostile to their employers as wages continued to fall. Doctors and lawyers, however, remained popular because of the free services they provided the poor.

In keeping with the spirit of reconciliation among all classes encouraged by liberals throughout France, the new city government called for the "union of all classes which make up a single family." Early in March, Duché invited three workers to join the administration's committee of seven. In response to the economic crisis, the local administration also created public works projects for the unemployed, hoping to appease workers who were beginning to create their own political organizations. Soviche, appointed the new sub-prefect, spoke for many liberals when he said he hoped to keep the new republic free of the excesses that had marred the Revolution of 1789.[40]

As at Reims, a workers' political organization, the Société populaire, was created within the first days of the 1848 revolution. Its titular leader, Pierre Chapuis, was a former ribbon weaver and cabaret keeper, but in this period it was controlled by Duché.[41] The society had been created to organize mass support for the new municipal government as well as the republic. But like the Démocratie rémoise, it soon broke with the liberals and became the center of independent working-class political activity.[42]

The greatest achievement of the society was the creation of a political union out of the previously antagonistic working-class groups in the city. Although such a union had been accomplished at Reims, at St. Etienne divisions between artisanal groups were particularly deep. Traditionally, the town's occupational hierarchy had divided silk ribbon weavers (passementiers) from the inferior velvet ribbon makers (veloutiers), and artisan armsmakers looked down on ouvriers quincailleurs. Members of all the city's artisan communities in turn considered themselves superior to miners, both because many were unskilled migrants from the countryside and relatively recent residents in the town, and because of their rough behavior.[43] The union of these groups into an association with more than eight thousand members in 280 organizations demonstrated the sense of political purpose and militancy that characterized St. Etienne's workers in the first days of the revolution.

The most militant members in the Société populaire were ribbon weavers, also the most numerically important group in the city. The principle of association, through which small-scale producers could defend their interests against the merchants, had been especially popular since the economic crisis of 1847. But the abuses that made ribbon weavers so hostile to their employers predated this crisis and included the refusal of merchants either to record the specific terms of contracts made with master weavers, or to weigh finished ribbons in the presence of weavers. Merchants were thus able to cheat their employees on the weight of the thread distributed and on their wages.

These practices had resulted in a series of demonstrations under the July Monarchy. In 1834 a strike to force merchants to establish fixed prices for ribbons had ended in a brief insurrection in which some artisans had seized the Hotel-de-Ville.[44] But violence was not the only response to the abuses of the putting-out system, for weavers had also attempted to create cooperative organizations in order to limit exploitation. In 1841 they had created a commercial association, the Société générale des passementiers, run by master weavers. The masters, who were themselves petty entrepreneurs owning three looms on the average, attempted to establish standard rate scales for all the association's members, hoping in this way to end the severe competition between artisans that kept wages down.[45]

The organization was also an important device for the political education of artisans. Like the Société populaire established in 1848, its leadership had included several members of the elite, including Duché and Laurent, vice-president of the middle-class committee for electoral reform. Members of the liberal opposition attempted to use the workers' organization, as they would again in 1848, to lead artisans from an interest in economic questions to support for liberal political demands. They hoped to create, in the words of the prefect, a "well-organized army of supporters upon whom the electoral committee could count when necessary." With a membership of more than eight hundred weavers and the possibility of recruiting many more, the Société générale posed a serious threat to the commercial and political power of the ribbon manufacturers. When at the end of 1841 an anonymous "Appel aux ouvriers" appeared, denouncing the poverty of the weavers and demanding the union of the entire working class, the administration decided to act. In December the society was dissolved and its leaders arrested.[46] The idea of a working-class union was not abandoned, however, and in 1848 Duché was again working to establish similar ties between workers and liberals through the Société populaire.

By 1848 the plan for a new workers' association was again taken up by master weavers. "The remedy of all present and future evils," one masters' group wrote, "is in association, which retains all the benefits of free competition with those of industrial concentration. Only association permits weavers to remain independent while providing the advantages associated with large-scale production."[47] The ability of master weavers to combine with their journeyman employees further strengthened their movement. The journeymen apparently never viewed the masters as "useless intermediaries," as they did the merchants. Journeymen could not accuse their employers, at whose sides they worked, of reaping unearned profits.[48] The union of masters and journeymen, like the union of the different artisan trades in St. Etienne, made the workers' movement a powerful force in local political life.

In April 1848 the former liberal opposition was again able to make use of artisan violence. Attacks on several convents by weavers protesting labor competition forced a change in the local administration. A large crowd appeared in front of the Hotel-de-Ville demanding the resignation of Royet, the conservative mayor who had been appointed by the local provisional government at the end of February to win the support of the majority of ribbon manufacturers. Now assured of artisanal support, the liberals no longer needed him. In a special election organized by the Société populaire, the entire municipal council was reorganized to eliminate all remaining members of the prerevolutionary conservative group. Liberals such as Duché and Auguste Terme were the only members of the old council to retain their seats, and the new council was filled with liberal professionals and master artisans able to escape at last from the political domination of the merchant oligarchy. Among the thirty-one new councillors were four middle-class members of the central committee of the Société populaire, several doctors and engineers, as well as a judge, a notary, and an arms manufacturer. None had ever previously served in local government.[49]

The reorganization of April 1848 was also a political victory for the leadership of the society. Seven of its members received positions in the administration.[50] The conservative *L'Avenir républicain* violently denounced the tactics that led to the remaking of the municipal council, but the liberal *Mercure seguisien*, reflecting the continued confidence of middle-class republicans in popular support, told its readers that it had accepted the changes in local government because it did not wish to endanger the union of all the parties of the Left. "One does not have to look to the Communists," the paper said, "to find cowards and egotists. . . . That has been the edifying spectacle of seventeen years of bourgeois rule. The bourgeoisie have created an association based on fictive capital to reduce the worker, whom they see only as a machine, to slavery. . . . The bourgeoisie fear conspiracies, but why conspire when the workers are free to raise themselves up through elections?"[51] The union of artisans and lawyers, doctors and engineers in the municipal government suggested by this and similar pronouncements continued through the legislative elections in April. By this time the elite at Reims had already broken with the workers' movement, but at St. Etienne the Société populaire nominated Duché, Louis Girard (a lawyer), and a ribbon weaver as its candidates for the legislative election. Although ten other workers, including Chapuis, also stood for election, the society continued to support its middle-class candidates. The merchant elite, faced with the seemingly invincible union of liberals and workers, could do nothing, and instead concerned itself exclusively with business.[52] Because of the greater economic differences and animosities between smaller manufacturers and the conservative oligarchy, the liberals at St. Etienne were able to preserve a liberal–working-class union longer than that at Reims.

The break between liberals and workers did not occur at St. Etienne until June. The local administration, torn between the political expediency of a workers' alliance and the need to maintain order, had elected to use the National Guard against striking mine workers in March. It offended radicals again on June 26, when it sent a message of congratulations to the National Assembly for restoring order in Paris. At the end of the month the council acquiesced to the central government's decree dissolving local radical societies such as the Société populaire.[53] The local administration had hoped to forestall the development of an independent workers' movement, which, as at Reims, had been forming through the influence of *La Sentinelle populaire*, a small socialist newspaper that had replaced *Le Mercure seguisien* as the spokesman for artisans and miners. The paper had attempted to expose the disparity between liberal promises and actual social conditions. Writing of the sudden dissolution of the Société populaire, *La Sentinelle* observed: "One cannot help feeling a little sad when . . . one compares present conditions with the hopes that inspired the February revolution. . . . The enemies of the people, who were terrified in February, now pursue their counter-revolutionary plans with impudence and audacity." Writing of the conditions of weavers and miners still subject to the laws against coalitions and forced to carry the *livret*, the paper ended with the refrain, "Poor sheep, yes, you have fine wool, and always they fleece you" (*Pauvres moutons, oui, vous avez beau toison, Toujours on vous tond*).[54]

As at Reims, 1848 ended with united bourgeois support for Cavaignac in the presidential election; even smaller manufacturers and shopkeepers in the Association républicaine joined the conservatives in support of the hero of the June days. Bonaparte, however, received most of the city's votes. The greater number of votes that Ledru-Rollin received at St. Etienne (twenty-seven hundred) was perhaps attributable to the stronger workers' organizations there; but the cooperation of broad elements in the middle classes with the merchant elite against the workers marked the beginning of the decline of liberal political power in the town.[55] When in 1849 working-class political organizations revived, liberal strength declined further.

Reims, 1849–1851: The Drift toward Restoring Order

Democratic sentiment remained strong at both Reims and St. Etienne despite the results of the presidential elections, and in 1849 artisan associations again became active in political life, challenging conservative and liberal notables for control of both towns. The elites ceased to enjoy undisputed influence over workers and in 1849-51 became more dependent on the national government to maintain their own rule.

The Association des corporations, founded by Agathon Bressy, an oculist, became the new center of working-class political power at Reims. A participant in the Lyons uprisings in 1831 and 1834, Bressy arrived in Reims at the end of 1848 and immediately began to organize all the workers' corporations into a vast association on the model of Lyons in 1834. The stated aim of the association was the creation of a politically unified working class, and its first meeting in December was attended by more than four thousand workers. In January 1849 *L'Association rémoise*, the organization's newspaper, began publication, giving workers a political voice for the first time since the suppression of *Le Républicain* in April 1848.[56]

The association was founded during a revival of working-class political activity following the conservative successes in the fall and winter.[57] A political reconciliation with the liberals had been effected by the resignation in February 1849 of Mennesson-Tonnellier from local government after he declared he could no longer resist the conservative majority in the municipal council.[58] The beleaguered liberals were thus anxious once again to have the support of artisans against the conservatives and were heartened by working-class demonstrations in support of the republic on the anniversary of the revolution.

Working-class support was especially vital for liberal candidates at Reims in the legislative elections in May 1849. The conservative political organization had been growing steadily in the department since the June days, and the liberals needed the votes of artisans to offset the conservative majority in the countryside. This threat was also mirrored in the press. Werlé, the local representative of the conservative Central Committee, had founded a newspaper, *L'Indicateur de la Champagne*, which had attacked "those doctrines so audaciously repeated aiming at the overthrow of society."[59]

But though *L'Association rémoise* joined *L'Industriel* in protesting the antirepublican as well as antisocialist policies of the new paper, the workers in the association were no longer willing to give their wholehearted support to the liberals.[60] The suppression of the Démocratie rémoise in 1848 had left artisans suspicious of moderate republicans. When in May 1849 the liberal organization Amis de la constitution proposed an alliance with the democratic socialists for the approaching legislative election, the Association des corporations demurred. Bressy explained that few workers were willing to support the former partisans of Cavaignac.[61] The working-class leadership was thus becoming the dominant partner in the liberal–working-class coalition, as was clearly demonstrated in the election. The eight candidates proposed by the association received more than six thousand votes out of nine thousand cast at Reims; conservatives Faucher and Carteret received only thirty-four hundred and twenty-six hundred votes respectively. The discredited liberals did even more poorly; Dérodé received only twenty-one hundred votes.[62] Within little more than a year after the establishment of the republic and universal suffrage, the Association des corporations had become the most influential force in local political life, superseding middle-class leaders of the revolutionary movement through 1848.

The liberal leaders had been in a precarious position since the founding of the Second Republic. Unlike the old Orleanist elite, which claimed the right to rule by virtue of its superior administrative and entrepreneurial ability, middle-class republicans could claim only to act as representatives of the workers. Men such as Emile Dérodé had risen to head the popular movement in 1848 because of their ability to voice artisanal demands. But as a more genuinely working-class leadership began to emerge, the precise role of these middle-class republicans began to be questioned. Although figures such as Eugène Courmeaux remained a part of the radical leadership to the end, sustained by socialist convictions, most middle-class republicans remained hostile to the economic demands of workers. The fundamental contradictions within the liberal–working-class alliance that emerged in June 1848 continued through 1849 and, combined with the growing strength of the Association des corporations, resulted in a fatal weakening of the moderate republican position.

The polarization of the electorate at Reims and the declining influence of the moderates was paralleled elsewhere in France. The number of conservative *grands notables* returned to the National Assembly in Paris increased, while the number of deputies supporting the republic was greatly reduced. The election of Louis-Napoleon as president had also shocked the moderates, who seem after December 1848 to have been torn between fears of a monarchist restoration and of popular violence. Their pleas for moderation in a climate of heated political rhetoric had little appeal. The emergence of the *démocrate-socialiste* party during the 1849 legislative elections, however, revealed a renewal of revolutionary sentiment in large parts of the country. Moderate republicans were unable to create a political alliance with either workers or conservatives, but working-class leaders and socialists developed a common program that included demands for full employment and the establishment of free compulsory education. Throughout France, the *démocrates-socialistes* received strong support from urban workers. Lille gave 63 percent of its votes to the list headed by Ledru-Rollin. The working-class neighborhoods of Lyons gave the radicals over 80 percent of the vote; they received 68 percent of all votes cast in the city.[63] Similar support was given by workers at Reims and St. Etienne.

The Association des corporations at Reims solidified its control of the electorate in this period by establishing a permanent committee, headed by Eugène Courmeaux, to encourage workers to vote for its candidates. The creation of a permanent democratic majority in the city posed a serious threat to conservatives, who were continuing to make gains in the rest of the department. The conservative departmental administration therefore decided to act against the Association des corporations much as the liberals had acted against the Démocratie rémoise. The abortive rising in Paris in June 1849 had been followed by demonstrations in Reims led by Bressy, Courmeaux, and Bienfait, who had demanded support for the insurgents in Paris and the immediate distribution of arms to the workers. Bressy's actions seem to have confirmed the central government's fears that the *démocrate-socialiste* leadership in Paris was planning a national insurrection to be carried out by radical organizations in the provinces. The result was the arrest of seventeen local socialist leaders at Reims at the end of June, and eventually their deportation. Bressy later died in Algeria, and Courmeaux and Bienfait did not return to France until 1860. Liberals were also frightened into silence. Dr. Maldan thereafter devoted himself entirely to the School of Medicine, and Emile Dérodé also retired from political life. The final dissolution of the Association des corporations took place in December.[64]

Commenting on the end of its parent organization, *L'Association rémoise* wrote: "One does not fool oneself; it is not only against universal suffrage, against the republic, against the constitution that war is declared—but against labor itself. The worker is to be maintained in eternal subordination."[65] The issue in which this article appeared was seized by the government, and the paper ceased publication shortly thereafter. In keeping with its campaign to weaken the political power of workers through changes in the voting laws, the regime continued its attack on provincial workers' organizations.[66] Artisanal corporations, some of which had established strike funds, were dissolved by government order at Reims as elsewhere in France.[67] As the *Association rémoise* foretold, the dissolution of the corporations soon resulted in a more arbitrary treatment of labor. Without organization, workers were powerless against employers, and although the announcement of wage reductions by a leading woolens manufacturer at Reims in October 1850 resulted in a strike, it soon ended with the workers accepting the reduced wage scale.[68]

The only apparent threat to the definitive restoration of the conservative Orleanists who had controlled the city under the July Monarchy was the coup d'état in December 1851. Although the declaration of martial law had temporarily removed the threat of popular revolt, Reims's merchant elite did not want a Bonapartist dictatorship, preferring parliamentary government under conservative leadership. One of the most often repeated conservative slogans during the legislative elections in 1849 had been the demand to be free of Parisian control, a theme that reemerged in 1851 at the time of the Bonapartist coup.[69] But without popular support, precluded by the deportation of Bressy and others, conservatives were unable to resist.[70] So great was the antipathy to the new regime among the elite that some workers supported the coup as a way of avenging themselves on the city's Orleanist manufacturers.[71]

The new government in Paris acted immediately to win over the conservative merchant manufacturers it considered its natural allies in its campaign against liberals and working-class radicals. In explaining the government's policy to the vicomte de Falloux, the duc de Persigny, the new minister of the interior, wrote that "we, who have no friends except below, if we wanted nothing but power, would have done two things: kept the salaries for M.P.s and allowed civil servants to sit in Parliament. We have done the opposite and given the legislature to the upper classes. We have openly chosen and supported our candidates, but from the highest ranks of society, from the great landowners, wealthy mayors and so on."[72] At Reims, this policy had the desired effect in some quarters, and Werlé, the leader of the conservatives, was soon won over.

Edouard-Mathieu Werlé had been one of the most important leaders of the prerevolutionary conservative Orleanist party. Although a German immigrant (he had come to Reims at age sixteen), he had spent his entire working life in the city. He began his career working for Vve Cliquot-Ponsardin and became a partner in the firm in 1831. Werlé first entered Reims society through his position in the company; he strengthened his role among conservative Orleanists by marrying Louise-Emilie Boisseau, a member of one of the oldest woolens manufacturing families. Politically ambitious, he had become a judge on the Tribunal of Commerce in 1838 and was president of the court from 1846 to 1850.[73] Like many French conservatives, he saw the possibility of a monarchist restoration made unlikely by the continuing split between Legitimists and Orleanists. He therefore supported Louis-Napoleon as the only alternative to revolution. A man of considerable energy and ability, Werlé soon made himself the leading spokesman for the new regime. He helped finance *La Concorde*, a newspaper established under government auspices to replace the suspended liberal and Legitimist press, and began to direct a campaign to win the support of the elite with lurid tales of an immense socialist rising prevented at the last moment by the coup.[74] Many notables, however, remained hostile to the new government. The Chamber of Commerce refused to support Bonaparte, and for the first time since the revolution Mennesson-Tonnellier, an outspoken liberal, was lionized in local salons.[75]

The government continued to appease fractious elements among the notables during the 1852 Corps législatif election by withholding its support from Werlé, who was unpopular among many of the bourgeoisie. Despite his efforts on behalf of the Bonapartist cause, Werlé's arrogance, combined with his sycophantic courting of the regime, had made him a political liability. The government therefore chose Pierre Soullié, a conservative, who owed his popularity to his initial opposition to the coup.[76] The ministry correctly assumed that he would eventually come to support the government, but this did little to strengthen its position in the city, for Soullié's lately acquired Bonapartist sympathies only reduced his popularity. Only forty-four hundred men participated out of more than eleven thousand registered voters. The official candidate received thirty-three hundred votes.[77]

By the end of 1852 elements within the middle-class Orleanist, Legitimist, and republican groups remained the government's most hostile opponents, although without working-class support they were unable to defeat the new regime's official candidates. The powerful coalition of artisan and bourgeois interests which had created the revolution at Reims in 1848 had been shattered by 1852 by middle-class fears of popular control of political life, and the imperial government was able to use this fear for its own ends. The conservatives who were restored to local power after the coup were favored by the regime only because they seemed most likely to support the new government. They had not exercised any real political influence over the local population since 1848.

St. Etienne, 1849–1851: The Republicans
Continue to Resist

At St. Etienne the old conservative ruling group was also restored, but resistance was stronger than at Reims, partly because of the nature of the city's economy. The great disparity of wealth between the richest ribbon merchants and the rest of the bourgeoisie had allowed the former to dominate the local administration under the July Monarchy. But having escaped this political tutelage under the republic, the middle-class leadership of the revolution made greater efforts to maintain its political alliance with the workers against the forces of reaction.

The period of political cooperation between conservatives and liberals during the presidential election of December 1848 was therefore short-lived. By the time of the legislative elections in May 1849 the republicans at St. Etienne had once again prepared their own list of candidates in opposition to the conservatives. But as in the Marne, the rural vote returned most of the candidates on the conservative list.[78] Republicans received a majority only in industrial centers and thus could only elect Duché. But within St. Etienne the conservative party remained weak, and the working-class leadership continued to sway a large number of artisan voters through giant political rallies.[79]

The issue of restriction of the suffrage, which emerged early in 1850, also helped maintain the political alliance between artisans, shopkeepers and smaller merchants. Although the new law threatened liberals by disenfranchising many of their supporters, small tradesmen felt even more directly threatened. The smaller bourgeoisie sought to forestall the loss of the political rights they had acquired in February, by supporting the republican cause and supplying copies of the republican press to artisan readers.[80] Démocrate-socialiste propaganda also appealed to the lower middle classes through its opposition to "financial feudalism," which it claimed "rendered dangerous and difficult the ownership of small capital," and helped keep many shopkeepers as well as artisans loyal to the republican cause.[81] Increasing government repression only fanned local radicalism, and in the summer of 1850, following the passage of the new electoral law limiting the suffrage, the *procureur général* wrote that workers at St. Etienne had become even more dangerous than those of Lyons.[82] Despite the introduction of the new law, which reduced the size of the electorate by three-quarters (from 12,747 to 3,254 voters), artisans and miners continued to hold meetings and remained ready to act to restore universal suffrage; the majority of the remaining voters also continued to support republican candidates.[83]

Although the government hoped to stem the growing workers' movement by appointing a new conservative municipal administration in September (municipal councils were elected, but mayors and their assistants were appointed by Paris), the artisans honored the republican deputies Duché, Baune, and Morellet with a giant banquet in October.[84] Hatred of the ribbon manufacturers was so great that even the use of blatant intimidation, such as soldiers' patrols in the cafes, was incapable of producing a conservative majority. Only nine hundred votes were cast in the municipal elections held in October 1850 out of a registered population of twenty-six hundred. Two democrats were elected to the council, while most of the remaining councillors save for two ribbon manufacturers were men of relatively modest means.[85]

Through 1851 the prefect complained that dangerous political societies, encouraged by widespread unemployment, continued to meet in cabarets. The administration claimed that many artisans were secretly arming themselves for a rising the following year. In April, when there were more than ten thousand unemployed workers in the city, rumors began to circulate of plots against the richest merchants, and demands were made for the reopening of the national workshops.[86] At the end of the year, four thousand votes against Bonaparte's second term and a large number of abstentions in the plebiscite in December 1851 showed that the government had still not succeeded in creating a friendly majority in the city. The presence of the army, however, prevented a popular rising following the December coup.[87]

The Bonapartist regime finally sought the support of the ribbon manufacturers, believing they were sympathetic to its aims. It was assumed, as at Reims, that the old conservative party was the government's natural ally in the campaign against bourgeois and working-class republicans. The ministry therefore chose Jules Balay, the head of one of the largest ribbon-manufacturing houses, as its official candidate for the Corps législatif in 1852; the conservative press recommended him both as an ardent supporter of Louis-Napoleon and an authentic representative of the city's industries.[88] But despite insistence that an industrialist, rather than the members of the liberal professions who had previously been elected to the Chamber of Deputies, was best suited to defend the needs of St. Etienne, most of the middle classes remained indifferent to the official candidate.[89] Workers were openly hostile, even though Bonaparte had restored universal suffrage. Ribbon weavers suspected that Balay had sent orders to England at the expense of local labor; miners disliked him because of his holdings in the Compagnie générale des mines de la Loire.[90] Less than five thousand votes were cast in the election out of a registered population of more than fourteen thousand. Balay received little more than two thousand votes, while Antide Martin, the radical workers' candidate, received more than three hundred despite government efforts to prevent his candidacy.[91]

The conservative list for the 1852 municipal election marked the political reemergence of many of the wealthiest members of the merchant group. Drawn up by a meeting of notables at the Hotel-de-Ville, it included such men as Vignat fils, André David-Colcombet, Jaure, the president of the Civil Tribunal, Jean-Jacques Neyron-Desgranges, Mathieu Passerat, the president of the Tribunal of Commerce, as well as Jules Balay and Christophe Faure-Belon.[92] The government supported the list, hoping to create a loyal political clientele within the manufacturing group. But it was unable to control the ensuing election, which resulted in a humiliating rout of the conservatives. Such well-known bourgeois republicans as Pierre Tiblier-Verne, Voytier, and Soviche received strong support, but hardly any of the conservative candidates were elected. Neyron-Desgranges, one of the city's most important ribbon manufacturers, ranked fortieth in number of votes received. Other great names in the ribbon trade, such as Jules Balay, Faure-Belon, and David-Colcombet, were sixty-first, sixty-second, and seventy-first.[93] The central government's appointment of a conservative mayor and attempted restoration of the merchant oligarchy turned the local population against the regime as well. In the plebiscite of 1852 anti-Bonapartist sentiment

among both workers and much of the middle classes resulted in only
fifty-four hundred votes in favor of the restoration of the empire out
of a registered population of more than fifteen thousand.[94]

At both Reims and St. Etienne the end of the alliance between
workers and liberal notables, which gave the latter brief control of
local political life in 1848, ultimately resulted in the restoration of the
old conservative elite. Yet the Second Republic had greater political
significance than merely to create a brief hiatus in an otherwise
unbroken period of conservative rule. The problems notables would
meet in maintaining local power should France ever become a true
republic were demonstrated. The opinions of the larger electorate
were shown to be decisive, and the appearance of distinct working-
class movements ended the influence of the notables.

The continuing hostility between merchant capitalists and artisans
in the political life of both towns prevented the survival of a liberal-
worker alliance necessary for the preservation of the republic. It was
not until the 1860s that new alliances were created between liberal
manufacturers and workers, made possible by changed economic and
political conditions under the Second Empire. The most important
economic change was the rapid expansion of mechanized manufacturing, which created a new group of industrial capitalists whose
relationship with workers was different from that of the merchant
group of the 1840s. When some of these manufacturers eventually
entered political life, they were successful in courting popular support and replaced the older mercantile elite as the arbiters of political
life.

3

The Elite and the
Economic Development
of Reims under the
Empire

The economic life of the bourgeoisie of Reims was affected in the 1850s and 1860s by the modernization of the woolens industry. The introduction of mechanized wool combing, spinning, and weaving changed the composition of the city's established manufacturing elite, forced many smaller artisanal manufacturers out of the market, and consolidated control of the industry in fewer hands. The transition from artisanal to factory production was painful for much of the city's labor force and altered the traditional relationships between manufacturers and their workers. The increasing prosperity of larger manufacturers and the relative weakness of workers' organizations encouraged the growth of liberal opinion among more successful woolens manufacturers.

Economic Changes in the 1850s

The mechanization of textile production, initiated in the English cotton industry in the eighteenth century, began very slowly in the French woolens industry. The low level of profit and the difficulty of mechanically spinning fragile woolen thread discouraged the introduction of expensive machines. Although a spinning jenny adapted to woolens manufacturing had been introduced into France in 1789, it was confined to the Amiens *fabrique* until the nineteenth century. A perfected self-acting mule developed in the 1840s, able mechanically to twist, stretch, and spin woolen thread in one operation, was similarly ignored at Reims until the period of the Second Empire. Mechanized weaving was introduced even more slowly. Despite the invention of mechanical looms by Edmund Cartwright in 1785, power looms were little used in the French woolens industry until the 1860s.

Mechanization required large capital investments for machines and factories, but heavily capitalized firms were able to undersell artisanal manufacturers. The first area to be mechanized was wool combing, a process that prepared raw wool for spinning. Attempts to mechanize combing, and thus replace the artisan combers who had previously separated the delicate fibers with oiled combs, were first made in the 1830s; the process was perfected through the 1840s by inventors such as Josué Heilman, Huntsman, and Hubner.[1]

Mechanical combing was first introduced at Reims in 1842 by the firm of Pierrard-Perpaite, and by 1849 the new Heilman mechanical combers permitted a wider application of the new techniques. By 1852 mechanized factories had been established by several important manufacturers, including Lachappelle and Levarlet, Walbaum, Sentis, and H. Givelet. There were sixty-three combing machines in the city when Isaac Holden, an English entrepreneur who had helped perfect the process, completed the construction of his giant combing factory in 1853.[2]

Competition from the Holden factory forced the remaining wool combers to modernize their operations. By 1859 Reims had 250 mechanical combers, each of which could process fifteen thousand to twenty thousand kilos of wool a year, although most of the smaller manufacturers were unable to assemble as large capital resources as the Holden factory.[3] Under the Second Empire Holden grew steadily, forcing smaller manufacturers out of the market. By 1869 it had become the largest wool-combing mill in France, employing more than twelve hundred workers on an annual payroll in excess of Fr 1.2 million, and producing 13,500 kilos of combed wool daily.[4]

The concentration of woolens production among a relatively small number of large firms, which began in wool combing, created rivalries within the elite. Further strains were produced by the subsequent mechanization of spinning and weaving. The effects of mechanization can begin to be understood through a study of the changing fortunes and investments of the Reims notables.

The disappearance after 1848 of the electoral lists that identified the notables and indicated the size of their fortunes creates a major problem in assessing the changes that took place within provincial elites after midcentury. Fortunately, the *Mutation après décès*, the probate of wills created by the law of 22 Frimaire VII (which required registration of the wills of all Frenchmen upon their deaths), provides detailed information similar to that in the electoral lists of the July Monarchy. Because these registers indicate the ages and occupations of the elite and provide detailed information on investments, they can be used to study changing patterns of wealth through the 1850s and 1860s.[5] But although the *Mutation* is an invaluable source, it does not show exactly which individuals listed in the register had sufficient wealth to have been voters under the July Monarchy. The group that corresponded in wealth to the pre-1848 notables can be traced, however, by estimating the size of the minimum fortunes recorded in the *Mutation* that would have carried a tax assessment of Fr 200 or more before 1848.

The size of the fortunes left by known electors was estimated by comparing the names of individuals who appeared on the electoral lists with those in the *Mutation* during the 1850s and 1860s. Fortunes in the *Mutation après décès* were assumed to include the combined wealth of a husband and wife, which was also a standard practice for determining tax qualifications for voting under the July Monarchy. Fictive credits, such as the remaining portion of a dowry owed to a husband by his wife, were not counted.[6] The linkages between the electoral lists and the *Mutation* were further checked by comparing the wealth of all adult males at Reims and St. Etienne who died in 1852 with the proportion of voters within the adult male population in 1848. The voting population of Reims in 1847-48 was about 2.5 percent of the total adult male population, so the level of wealth of the richest 2.5 percent who died in 1852 was assumed to represent the minimum fortune necessary to be considered a notable under the July Monarchy. At both Reims and St. Etienne this test yielded minimum fortunes of approximately Fr 20,000. The minimum fortunes of known notables in 1848 at death was also about Fr 20,000. Thus men aged twenty-five or older with estates worth at least Fr 20,000—765 men at Reims and 581 at St. Etienne—were chosen as representative of the group that between 1852 and 1869 would have been considered notables by the standards of the July Monarchy, and thus constituted the elite of the Second Empire.

Although the *Mutation* is useful in assessing the wealth of the elite, it raises problems because of the age differences between notables listed in the 1847-48 electoral lists, when many were still active in business, and those taken from the registration of wills, which contains a much larger proportion of older, retired people. A certain number of younger notables in the later years of the empire have thus escaped detection. The heaviest concentration of men on the 1848 electoral lists were in their forties and fifties, whereas the heaviest concentration listed in the *Mutation* were in their sixties. It is also difficult to interpret people's descriptions of their occupations after retirement. A large number of *rentiers* and *propriétaires* among formerly active businessmen would have made the occupations reported in the *Mutation* deceptive. But because the elderly were less likely to retire in mid-nineteenth-century France than they are today, most were still known by their professions until their deaths.[7]

The distribution of occupations among the rich at Reims under the Second Empire demonstrates the transformation brought about by economic change. Between 1847-48 and 1862-69, the number of woolens manufacturers declined from 29 to 20 percent of the total elite (Tables 1 and 5). It seems likely that this change was partly caused by the mechanization of wool combing. In the 1850s, when the demand for woolens was low, the market could not support the high prices necessary to keep smaller wool combers employing artisan labor in business. Heavily capitalized firms such as the Holden company were forcing less efficient manufacturers out of the market.

Yet despite the importance of large capital investments in the new mills, investment in other sectors of the woolens industry remained rare in the 1850s, partly because prices for woolens were low. Most manufacturers believed that increased mechanization would result in high factory overhead costs, leaving firms less able to adjust operating expenses to inevitable fluctuations of the market and increasing the danger of bankruptcy. Merchants employing artisanal labor could respond more easily to decreased demand by ceasing to distribute raw materials to their workers. This attitude, which was responsible for the slow mechanization in woolens throughout France, began to change widely only after 1860. The European cotton famine created by the American Civil War resulted in a greatly increased demand for woolens that made further mechanization profitable.[8]

Through the 1850s spinning, weaving, dyeing, and finishing continued to be divided among several hundred relatively small enterprises. Because spinning bobbins and looms used in cottage industry and small urban shops were inexpensive, textile firms could be established without large outlays of capital.[9] The essentially familial character of the French textile industry also discouraged the development of large firms. Entrepreneurs preferred small *sociétés en nom collectif* in which they were in business with their families and long-term associates and thus could preserve business secrecy. Such manufacturers, who often had begun their careers in the retail cloth trade, retained a shopkeeper's mentality. Their view of the scope of their operations was limited to a regional or even local level, rather than the national market.[10] Suspicious of new and untried production methods and unwilling to seek outside investments that would open their businesses to strangers, most local firms in the first decade of the empire had little need of outside capital.[11]

As late as 1857, an economic crisis demonstrated the vulnerability of heavily capitalized firms in a period of falling prices. Smaller merchant manufacturers ceased production, but factory owners were forced by high overhead costs to keep their machines running and thus were obliged to sell their products at a loss.[12] Before 1860 only the companies of Croutelle, Pradine et Cie, and Villeminot-Huard had built large mechanized spinning mills. Weaving remained even less affected by the new methods.[13] The few weaving factories in the city before 1860 were small and included Croutelle's mill, which had 177 mechanized looms, the Villeminot-Huard factory, Rogelet et Cie with 300 looms, Dauphinot frères with 100, and Pradine et Cie and Henriot frères, both with under 100 looms.[14] Such modest improvements in the 1850s could still be financed through local profits, and Reims did not yet need large amounts of outside capital such as was necessary for the development of the metallurgical and mining industries of the Loire.[15] Yet the occupational breakdown of notables at Reims in the 1850s suggests that even in the more slowly industrializing textile industry a significant concentration had already begun to take place. Because of the division of the Reims woolens market among a large number of small manufacturers, only a few large-scale *fabricants* had the funds necessary to undertake the risky investments involved in mechanization.[16] In the 1860s, when the pace of industrialization increased, they were able to take advantage of changing

conditions. The result was a further elimination of small manufacturers from the market and a greater concentration of control within a
narrowing elite.

Economic Changes in the 1860s

The period between 1860 and 1865 has been called the great
watershed in French economic development, when the first important
steps for the development of credit and mechanized production were
taken. In this period the new industrial sector of France's woolens
industry began to surpass traditional artisan manufacturing in importance.[17] These changes were typified by conditions at Reims, which
experienced an enormous demand for woolens because of the American Civil War and the ensuing cotton famine. Rising profits encouraged the *fabrique* of Reims to increase production through the
acquisition of new machines and furnished the local elite with the
funds necessary to buy them without much recourse to outside
investors. Industrial growth was further encouraged by the reduction
of tariffs with England through the Chevalier-Cobden treaty of 1860.
In addition to increasing the sale of fine French woolens to England,
free trade lowered the cost of English wool and machinery.[18]

The total value of Reims's woolens production rose from Fr 60
million at the end of the 1850s to Fr 75 million in 1862, when the first
effects of the cotton famine began to be felt. By 1867 profits exceeded
Fr 105 million, despite a 20 percent reduction in the price of cloth in
the same period.[19] This bull market stimulated the use of machinery
to increase production. Wool combing was made more efficient, and
the number of mechanical wool combers increased from 350 in 1861
to 500 in 1870. Mechanized spinning also expanded greatly; by 1866
more than 76,000 spinning bobbins were in operation in the city of
Reims and another 58,000 in firms owned by Reims merchants
throughout the department. The number of mechanized looms also
rose dramatically, from 577 in 1860 to more than 4,000 in 1870.[20]

Factories were increasingly concentrated around Reims, and contemporaries were struck by the rapid and dramatic decline of rural
industry because of competition from new mechanized plants and
refitted older factories. The concentration of woolens production in
centers such as Reims, Roubaix, Sedan, and Elbeuf marked the

decline in the 1850s and 1860s of more traditional manufacturing areas in the Midi, Dauphiné, and Berry.[21] Within the city of Reims large new weaving mills built after 1860 by Collet frères, Walbaum, Marteau, and Poullet continued to displace traditional hand-loom weavers.[22] With the mechanization of weaving the last traditional sector of the woolens industry had become modernized, and the pace at which labor was forced to adjust to factory conditions increased. Previously, displaced artisan spinners had been able to support themselves through hand-loom weaving; they were now obliged to enter the mills. Unemployment was much reduced as the number of workers employed in the woolens industry rose to more than forty-seven thousand in the boom year of 1866.[23]

Before the 1860s the need for capital investment had been limited enough to put little pressure on Reims's relatively modest credit market. After 1860, the profits of local industry became large enough to meet most of the demand for capital created by modernization, and local banks grew sufficiently to be able to finance industrial development.[24] The doubling of production of Reims's specialty goods, flannels and merinos, had given the industry more than Fr 100 million in profits, much of which was deposited in local banks. Accounts in the local branch of the Banque de France increased from Fr 67 to 79 million between 1861 and 1869; deposits in private banks rose in the same period from Fr 282 million to 474 million.[25] These profits remained in the control of the established manufacturers who were the majority of the banks' directors and thus helped keep control of the woolens industry in the hands of older families. Circumstances were different in St. Etienne, where the growth of heavy industry was not supported by the established ribbon manufacturers, and a new commercial banking system was created by steel interests. Traditionally, Reims's banks had been oriented toward commerce rather than industry, as was common throughout France, but in the 1860s the Reims bankers were able to meet the needs of modernizing entrepreneurs.[26]

In 1854 a new commercial bank, the Comptoir d'escompte de Reims, was established in the city with an initial fund of Fr 1.5 million raised by the local sale of three thousand shares; its board of directors included such important industrial manufacturers as Jacques Senart-Colombier, Louis Walbaum-Heidsieck, who served as the president of the Comptoir until 1859, and Henriot-Delamotte; Hippolyte Andrès, who had previously invested heavily in Croutelle's mechanized weaving factory; Simon Dauphinot, a leader of the liberal opposition, whose family later acquired important holdings in the mechanized Pradinc factory; Charles Rogelet, another important opponent of the empire; and Mennesson-Tonnellier, the republican leader.[27] The bank became the most common means by which local interests contributed to industrial development, and shares in the Comptoir d'escompte appear frequently in the inventories of bourgeois wills. Although investments were rarely as large as Senart's, whose shares were valued at more than Fr 106,000, bank stocks were on the average the largest single investment made by notables. Even Carteret and Soullié, the city's first two conservative deputies under the empire, participated in the industrial growth of the city; Soullié's shares in the Comptoir were valued at Fr 98,500.[28]

The importance of the Comptoir in financing industrial growth was reflected in its business transactions, which rose from Fr 120 million in 1855 to almost 300 million in 1869; deposits rose from Fr 1 million to over 6 million in the same period. The value of portfolio investments also went from Fr 1 million to almost 6 million, and the value of outstanding loans from Fr 400,000 in 1855 to Fr 2.5 million in 1869. Reflecting the profits that accrued from industrial investments during the 1860s, the bank's dividend fluctuated between 5 and 10 percent, reaching a high of 12 percent in 1864.[29]

Local bank investment was supplemented by another important innovation, the joint stock company. Before the 1860s there were few such companies in France because their creation required government approval, which was rarely given. But after 1863 the regime simplified the establishment of stock companies, which soon began to develop rapidly in all major sectors of industry.[30] The accumulation of capital for modernization was thus facilitated, and the integration of older manufacturing interests with industrial entrepreneurs furthered. The creation of Wagner-Marsan, one of the largest new joint stock companies, was illustrative of the shift from traditional to modern production methods. Financed through the sale of Fr 1,000 shares, the company began operations with seven thousand mechanized spinning bobbins and two hundred mechanized looms. Julian Turgan's *Grandes usines*, a nineteenth-century compendium of the world's most important industrial companies, described Reims as "one of the very few industrial centers where the creation of a giant new establishment such as Wagner-Marsan, equipped with the most recent innovations, is not seen as a threat to the interests of other establishments, and where the organization of the new firm is not stopped at all costs by the more or less well-founded fears of the manufacturers of the same product." At Reims, the more established firms seem not to have hesitated to supply advice and capital to the new firm. "Even those manufacturers who because of age or habit were hostile to the new methods also willingly invest their capital, finding the creation of such establishments an honor for the city."[31] Although perhaps excessively lavish in praising the investors, Turgan accurately portrayed the enthusiasm with which the notables of Reims invested their profits in the new mechanized factories.

The same willingness to invest also helped other joint stock companies, including Fortel-Villeminot, a large wool-combing factory with sixty mechanized combers, the Victor Rogelet company, and the Villeminot-Huard company. The latter, which was equipped in 1855 with five thousand spinning bobbins, was entirely refitted in 1866 with nineteen thousand mechanized bobbins financed through a stock issue.[32]

The economic integration of industrial entrepreneurs with more traditional woolens manufacturers was the most important result of the flow of business profits to commercial banks and joint stock companies. The problems faced by innovators in joining the economic elite in provincial France were frequently significant in the formation of dissident political groups. At St. Etienne steel manufacturers, unable to tap the considerable capital resources of established families in the region, eventually became the political rivals of the older group. Similarly, the growth of Reims's economy created a group of wealthy parvenus who could have represented a threat to the continued political control by established families. In the last years of the empire successful industrialists did begin to aspire to a share of local political influence, but because of financial ties to the older elite, they seem to have been less willing than St. Etienne's heavy industrialists to encourage working-class unrest and strikes. Consequently, an understanding of how this new group was integrated into the economic life of Reims is vital for an understanding of the politics of the period.

The electoral lists and *Mutation après décès* help identify the two generations of manufacturers whose economic and political rivalries dominated the period. The older generation, which had participated in political life under the July Monarchy, appears both on the electoral lists of that regime and in the *Mutation après décès*. A group of newer notables who entered the ranks of the elite after the creation of the 1847-48 electoral list appears only in the *Mutation*; these were the potential rivals of the established group. The most important element, however, was the younger members of established families, whose family names appear on the electoral lists, but who, because of their youth, do not themselves appear. These men, though tied to the older generation by familial as well as financial ties, also played a major role in the development of the liberal opposition. They were young enough to be receptive to the newer manufacturing processes and also able to tap the capital resources of older manufacturers. Examination of the economic interests of these three groups helps reveal the extent to which newer notables were able to integrate themselves into the economic life of the town.

Not surprisingly, a disproportionately large number of members of the older generation was concentrated in the woolens industry. A large number of the new rich entered the growing banking sector (Table 5). The large proportion of newcomers in banking, where they shared control of the increasingly important financial network with members of the old elite, is further emphasized by an analysis of the occupations of the richer notables (Table 6). Once again, the newly wealthy were heavily concentrated in banking. Although many also entered the woolens industry (23 percent), they never achieved the concentration of the older group (38 percent) or even of younger members of established families (36 percent). A fair proportion of the new elite also entered wine manufacturing (16 percent), which like woolens was expanding in this period, and construction (8 percent), prosperous because of the need for factories and workers' housing.

The relative integration of older families, who continued to control both the woolens industry and a large part of the banking sector, with the new elite in the city's credit institutions helped retard the development of autonomous and rival groups. The integration of newcomers was also furthered by their interest in new joint stock companies, which more than the banks permitted direct participation in both the management and profits of the factories that were becoming the dominant element in the woolens industry. Between 1860 and 1869 more than a third of the newcomers (38 percent) who appear in the *Mutation* invested in the new woolens mills (Table 7).

The emergence of large mills was only the most conspicuous change in economic life during the 1850s and 1860s. One other indication that the old world of the merchants was giving way to a more modern industrial one was the decline of the habit of acquiring wealth and prestige through the purchase of land. The elite had begun to forsake the passive role of *rentier* or *propriétaire* for a more active one in business affairs, and they were investing a larger portion of their income in business ventures, especially local woolens mills, railroads, and a wide variety of businesses throughout France (Table 10). Clearly the position of notables at Reims was becoming strengthened through an increasing geographical dispersion of their interests, a veritable nationalization of investments.[33] This trend, initially encouraged by rising prosperity, continued for the rest of the century.[34]

The potentially higher profits in private industry made government securities, long one of the elite's favorite investments, less attractive. As a result, the proportion of individuals investing in government bonds rose only from 21 to 23 percent between 1861 and 1869. These investors apparently were among the less wealthy members of the elite, who were perhaps less willing to risk their limited capital resources. Interest in newer industrial investments was much more widespread among wealthier notables. The proportion of the elite investing in local businesses rose from 17 to 25 percent (Table 10), that investing in French businesses outside the city more than quadrupled, rising from 5 to 22 percent, and that investing in railroads rose from 12 to 28 percent. Investors at Reims may therefore be divided into two categories: a group of less wealthy notables with modest investments in government bonds and the municipal utility companies that grew up under the empire; and a group of very wealthy woolens and champagne manufacturers who invested in railroads and private industry generally, thus aligning themselves with the modernization of the economy both at Reims and throughout France (Tables 8 and 12).

Smaller investors tended to be *propriétaires*, many of whom were retired people seeking a safe and steady return on their money. Their interests included the municipal gas companies of Paris, Marseilles, Metz, and Sedan, the Phoenix life insurance company, and the Suez

Canal company. They also bought the bonds of the Comptoir
d'escompte de Paris, the Crédit foncier, and the Crédit foncier
colonial. They invested in French, Austrian, and Lombard bonds, as
well as those of the Papal States and the new Kingdom of Italy. Large
investors tended to be wealthier woolens manufacturers. As a group
they had investments in most of the major railroad companies,
including those of the Est, Ardennes, Dauphiné, Ouest, Paris à Lyon
et à la Méditerranée, Orleans, Grand Central, Nord, Midi, and
Bourbonnais companies, as well as in such foreign railroads as the
Italian Sardinian, Roman and Victor Emmanuel lines, the Spanish
Madrid-Saragossa and Seville companies, and the Austrian railroad
system. Vve Cliquot's investment of Fr 760,000 in the Compagnie du
chemin de fer du Nord was unusual only for its size. Most of the
wealthier members of the Reims elite had similar investments, which
helped them maintain their economic position after 1866, when the
demand for woolens decreased and profits began to fall. The diversi-
fication of interests ensured their continued financial preeminence in
the city, while also furthering the trend toward the concentration of
local economic control among a relatively small number of wealthy
factory owners.

The important economic and political divisions that emerged at
Reims at the end of the 1860s did not result from a lack of integration
between the old elite and newcomers. They arose instead between
wealthier entrepreneurs who had the capital resources necessary to
mechanize production and smaller manufacturers who did not. At St.
Etienne the leading ribbon manufacturers supported the empire out
of fear of labor unrest caused by depressed conditions in their
industry. At Reims, only less wealthy woolens manufacturers were
faced with a similar crisis at the end of the 1860s. As the demand for
woolens decreased after 1867, merchant manufacturers found it
increasingly difficult to produce goods cheaply enough to compete
with the mills or to pay their artisan workers adequate wages. Factory
manufacturers enjoying economies of scale did not face the same
problems. As a result, smaller manufacturers were threatened by an
increasingly hostile work force as well as bankruptcy. Fearful of the
future, they looked to the imperial government to maintain their
position against an increasingly radical working class. Successful manufacturers, confident of the future, were willing to discard the imperial regime for a more liberal republic.

Developing Political Conflicts

Conflicts between artisans and merchants did not appear until the woolens boom ended when American cotton was again imported into Europe. Up to that time, prices for both inferior hand-woven wool cloth and the more regular machine-woven product remained high. Through 1866 the demand for Reims merinos and flannels continued to surpass the capabilities of factory production, and putting-out merchants made substantial profits by filling excess demand.[35] It was only after 1866 that the advantages of mechanized spinning and weaving were fully realized by industrial manufacturers, who were able to continue profitable production of cheaper factory goods, while falling prices forced the more traditional group into steady decline.[36] This period of falling artisan wages also caused increased labor unrest and created an additional threat to many smaller merchant manufacturers.[37]

The crisis of the less mechanized sectors of the woolens industry demonstrated a reversal of conditions since the 1850s, when factories were believed to prevent manufacturers from easily adjusting their operations to market conditions. The rivalries in the woolens industry between traditional and more modern manufacturers also shaped the debate at Reims after 1867 over the continuation of free trade. Hoping to preserve artisan industry, some merchants began to demand the creation of tariffs to prevent English imports and thereby help maintain high woolens prices. This idea created much hostility in industrial circles. The more mechanized manufacturers wanted to maintain free trade, use falling prices to undersell their competitors with cheap factory goods, and capture a larger share of the market. But the government's support of free trade did little to win the support of this group. Successful manufacturers felt secure enough to join their support of free trade with demands for greater political liberties and favored the restoration of parliamentary government. The empire's championing of free trade thus ironically made possible the reordering of the city's markets for the benefit of industrial interests in the opposition.

The local Bonapartist political establishment, led by the city's mayor and deputy to the Corps législatif, Mathieu-Edouard Werlé, increasingly supported smaller merchant manufacturers, hoping to rally bourgeois support against the liberal leaders who were their chief political rivals. Reims's Bonapartist party thus became a refuge for inefficient manufacturers who the imperial government had hoped would be eliminated by free trade. Their influence helps explain Werlé's opposition to the government's liberal reforms after 1867. His local supporters fully realized that the end of the laws against strikes and coalitions could further weaken their already declining economic position.

The advantages of free trade had been recognized by some woolens manufacturers as early as 1860, when it had first been imposed by the imperial regime. These manufacturers, who previously had feared the competition of cheaper English goods, came to realize that with prudent management French firms could successfully compete with foreign producers. They also discovered that free trade allowed more efficient manufacturers to increase their sales of French specialty goods such as merinos and flannels in England.[38] Only smaller manufacturers of cheaper flannels had trouble competing. It is indicative of the influence of this traditional merchant group that the Chamber of Commerce officially opposed the introduction of free trade in 1860.[39] The chamber chose Werlé, the Bonapartist leader, Louis Roederer and Edgar Ruinart de Brimont, a Legitimist leader, to carry its petition to the government.[40]

By the end of the 1860s, however, the influence of the political opposition in the Chamber of Commerce had greatly increased. While only Villeminot-Huard had represented liberal opinion at the beginning of the empire, liberal participation increased in 1863 with the inclusion of Jules Warnier and Simon Dauphinot. The latter succeeded the Legitimist Bertherand-Sutaine to the vice-presidency of the chamber in 1868. By 1870, liberals such as Auguste Walbaum and Jules Houzeau, the son of the opposition deputy under the July Monarchy, were also members. The growing influence of these men, who combined criticism of the dictatorship with support for free trade and factory industry, was also reflected in the election of Warnier and Dauphinot in 1867 as the city's representatives to the jury of the International Exposition. By 1869 the chamber had finally decided to oppose the abandonment of free trade.[41] Despite the fears of smaller traditional manufacturers, it rejected any action that would artificially raise the price of French woolens; the delegates from the woolens industry participating in this decision were once again Simon Dauphinot, Jules Warnier, and a third member of the opposition,

Frédéric Lelarge. The decision, though supporting a key government policy, was in fact a major victory for the opposition. Liberal control of the Chamber of Commerce continued under the Third Republic. In 1871 Dauphinot, Warnier, Houzeau, and Auguste Walbaum were elected to seats on the board; Werlé, the former mayor, ran thirteenth in the order of votes received. The following year Dauphinot succeeded to the presidency of the chamber, over which he presided until 1883.[42]

The Société industrielle was even more responsive to the new economic interests within the elite. Founded in 1833 and reorganized in 1857 to promote technical innovations in industry, it had become by the last years of the empire not only an important bourgeois social and business club but also a center of liberal political opinion. The society had first acted officially in town life in 1861, when it represented the entire Reims business community in commercial suits against outside interests such as the railroads. That same year it established a series of courses to popularize the works of Michel Chevalier, a proponent of free trade. Werlé had protested the classes in 1861 and again in 1866 on behalf of traditional manufacturers, claiming that the society used them to mount political attacks on the regime and that it had become a center of latent antigovernment sentiment as well as free trade doctrine.[43]

The beginning of the crisis in the woolens industry further strengthened the liberal opposition within the Société industrielle. Jules Warnier had became its president in 1860, replacing Villeminot-Huard, a moderate republican. Combining support for free trade with demands for broader civil and political liberties, Warnier had worked to create a political following among the bourgeoisie with the aim of displacing the political interests represented by Werlé. By the last years of the empire the society's other officers were also members of the opposition. Among these were the vice president, Victor Rogelet, a wealthy woolens manufacturer, and Charles Rogelet, a member of the administrative board. Liberals on the board included Auguste Walbaum and Isaac Holden, and both the secretary and vice-secretary were considered dangerous democrats by the prefect. Others on the board included Jules Houzeau and Dr. Henri Henrot, the brother of the democratic leader of 1848, whose free treatment of the poor made him a popular figure in the city.[44]

Through the efforts of these men the society began to reconstruct the liberal–working-class alliance that had been destroyed in 1848-49. As in 1848, members of the liberal professions, doctors and lawyers, helped win some support for the liberal program. But unlike the period of the Second Republic, the leaders of the liberal opposition at the end of the empire were not men on the periphery of the elite. They were among the most successful manufacturers in the city. Believing in the future prosperity of their industry, they were able to win working-class support with the promise of a new liberal regime compatible with capitalism and the free development of workers' organizations.

At St. Etienne, as the next chapter will show, the rapid development of heavy industry went even further in creating a new manufacturing group independent of the older merchant elite. In the Loire the recreation of the bourgeois–working-class political alliance tentatively begun at Reims had a fuller development, with greater consequences for political life.

4

The Elite and the
Economic Development
of St. Etienne

St. Etienne provides a clearer example than Reims of the tensions that developed under the Second Empire between merchant manufacturers and the industrial interests that challenged them. While in the 1850s and 1860s traditional manufacturers and industrial innovators coexisted within the Reims woolens trade, at St. Etienne the older and newer groups were in separate industries. Ribbon and arms manufacturing were the domain of the older manufacturing group, and coal mining and steel came increasingly under the control of newer interests. Economic and political rivalries between the two groups at Reims were reduced through investments by the older elite in factory production, a development facilitated by the relatively gradual pace of change in the textile industry. In the Loire, the economic sphere of the steel and coal industries remained separate from that of the ribbon merchants because of the low level of local investment. The need for capital eventually forced steel manufacturers to seek funds outside the region. The prosperity of the steel industry in the 1860s also produced a new liberal opposition group not found in the depressed ribbon industry. This diversity of interests along with the economic conservatism of the older bourgeois groups at St. Etienne helped create a more vigorous liberal opposition than at Reims. Unable to win government patronage in their pursuit of high office, several wealthy steel manufacturers joined the opposition in the hope of creating successful political careers. Industrial development in the Loire thus demonstrated more clearly than at Reims the importance of divisions within provincial elites produced by economic growth, and helped make St. Etienne one of the most important centers of middle-class opposition to the government in the last years of the empire.

Ribbon-Making and Small Arms Industries

The contrast between the modernizing industrial sectors of St. Etienne's economy and the more traditional manufacturing interests was heightened by the conservative business practices of the ribbon merchants, who resisted the industrial innovations that had transformed the Reims *fabrique*. Like the more traditional manufacturers at Reims at the beginning of the empire, few ribbon merchants recognized the advantages of mechanization. They continued to believe that heavy capital investment would make it more difficult to adjust production to meet fluctuating market demands. Their conservatism was in part a result of violent fluctuations of the ribbon market. Fashion demanded constant changes in styles and sizes, as well as the continuous invention of new and elaborate designs that could be woven only by highly skilled craftsmen. Mechanized equipment, which could have transformed production, required frequent and expensive retooling; merchants preferred to employ artisan master craftsmen, who were obliged to meet the cost of retooling themselves. These artisan ribbon weavers typically owned two or three looms. They worked on one themselves and employed either their children or journeymen on the others. Petty entrepreneurs, they were obliged to haggle constantly with merchants over the price of their work and the amount of time needed to complete it, resulting in bitter disputes between artisans and employers.[1] Lacking the powerful incentives to modernize production created at Reims by the cotton famine, ribbon *fabricants* continued to maintain the old artisanal system of production.

Ribbon-making nonetheless remained St. Etienne's most important industry under the empire. In the 1840s the industry employed thirty-two thousand workers and eighteen thousand looms, and under the Second Republic it accounted for most of the manufacturing wealth in the city.[2] The value of ribbon production in 1848 was Fr 45 million, compared with only 5 million in arms, 6.5 million in coal, 6 million in small metallurgy, and 8 million in iron and steel.[3] The ribbon industry continued to flourish through the 1850s, its most prosperous period, when the number of manufacturing houses increased from 258 to almost 300.[4] But the profitable conditions under which the trade might have modernized began to disappear in 1859, as European and American markets declined and the price of Chinese silk rose.[5]

Troubles in the industry were compounded by increased foreign competition, mostly from the expanding and more modern Swiss ribbon trade.[6] The value of cheaper Swiss ribbons entering France rose from Fr 3 million in 1850 to over 7 million in 1857.[7] By 1859 local manufacturers began to realize that this threat from highly mechanized competition was permanent.[8] Several smaller houses facing bankruptcy decided to begin voluntary liquidations.[9] But by the time the need to improve production methods had become apparent, the St. Etienne *fabrique* was in a poor position to meet the costs of modernization because of the weak market.[10] In 1863, when the ribbon trade appeared to be in precipitous decline, the prefect blamed conditions on the short-sightedness of the Chamber of Commerce, which had not warned of the technological changes taking place elsewhere.[11]

The future of the industry also seemed threatened by the introduction in 1860 of free trade with England. The Vignat brothers, who owned the only mechanized ribbon factory in the region, were already facing hard times before the introduction of free trade. They immediately petitioned the government for a Fr 1 million subvention to offset the added burden of English competition. At the behest of both the municipal and departmental governments, which feared that the failure of the factory would mean the end of all industrial progress in the city's silk industry, the government eventually gave the company Fr 500,000.[12] But even artisan industry was ultimately able to survive the competition, since the superior craftsmanship of St. Etienne's weavers allowed them to win English markets in partial compensation for the loss of American ones.[13] By the end of the decade the ribbon market had begun to improve, but the severe fluctuations of the 1860s left manufacturers more unwilling than ever to experiment with innovations.[14] The Vignat factory remained one of the very few mechanized ribbon factories in the department, and hand looms outnumbered mechanized ones in the Loire for the rest of the century.[15]

Armsmaking, St. Etienne's second traditional industry, was also based on artisan labor. Unlike the ribbon trade, however, it was

divided unequally between approximately eighty houses that manufactured hunting arms and the giant Manufacture Nationale des
Armes, the sole producer of arms for the French army. Small manufacturers had trouble raising funds to modernize their operations, but
because of large profits, the Manufacture Nationale was able to
mechanize production in the 1860s, much as the Reims woolens
industry had done in the same period. But whereas industrial modernization at Reims strengthened the position of liberal manufacturers in the elite, the special relationship that Félix Escoffier, the
entrepreneur of the Manufacture Nationale, enjoyed with the government prevented a similar development at St. Etienne. Instead, the
empire's preferment of Escoffier and the modernization of the Manufacture turned smaller manufacturers against the regime and
strengthened anti-imperial sentiment in the least mechanized sectors
of the industry.

Large orders from Turkey in 1855-56, from England in 1857, and
from Piedmont in 1861 furthered Escoffier's resolve to modernize
production in the early 1860s. Employing more than five thousand
workers, he was one of the most powerful men in the city. The
government considered Escoffier a model industrialist, who combined a belief in material progress and industrial innovation with
loyalty to the regime. He was eventually awarded the Legion of
Honor, and the official newspapers praised his attempts to mechanize
the Manufacture.[16] But despite the accolades of government and the
press, as well as his employment of a large part of the local work force,
he was very unpopular.[17] His receipt in 1866 of the exclusive right to
manufacture the chassepot rifle further increased the hostility of
manufacturers excluded from government orders, and his workers
resented his attempt to introduce machinery into his factories.[18] Their
traditional skills threatened, artisans became as hostile as smaller
manufacturers to the official entrepreneur. Escoffier's ties to the
imperial government convinced other *fabricants*, who hoped to receive
government contracts themselves under a new regime, to support the
liberal opposition. They were finally rewarded in 1870, when the
provisional government declared the manufacture of military arms
open to all armsmakers; a committee of seven local manufacturers
was appointed to distribute orders to firms according to their special-
ties.[19]

The difficulties involved with introducing more efficient production methods had a tragic effect on St. Etienne's oldest industry, the manufacture of metal tools (*quincaillerie*). Although small arms manufacturers were still able to use artisanal labor profitably, manufacturers of metal implements continued to suffer a decline begun under the July Monarchy. Unlike other industries, they faced strong competition within France, mainly from factories around Paris. Local manufacturers, who were simply putting out merchants, were both unwilling and unable to organize production more efficiently. Their answer to Parisian competition was to lower labor costs.[20] Reduced to desperate straits, artisan *quincailleurs* were unable to improve their methods. Constant pressure to lower prices resulted in an inevitable decline in the quality of their product, which further reduced the market for their goods.[21]

The Chamber of Commerce in 1850 could respond to the problem only by suggesting that the ribbon industry, then the richest sector of the city's economy, supply the capital investments necessary for the improvement of small metallurgy.[22] This plea went unanswered. The problems of *quincaillerie*, which continued under the Second Empire, were indicative of the general cautiousness of most of St. Etienne's notables in making investments outside their own businesses. Aside from the Vignat brothers and Escoffier, little attempt was made to modernize production in any of the city's traditional industries. When an occasional move to modernize was made, as was done by the Manufacture Nationale, the result was increased labor unrest and the heightened animosity of other manufacturers.

The effects of these traditional attitudes are reflected in the *Mutation après décès*, which shows that notables with interests in the traditional sectors of the economy suffered a relative decline in wealth during the period of the empire. Ribbon manufacturers constituted the largest group within the old elite (27 percent), and small metallurgists made up 6 percent (Table 5); these same two groups were also well represented among the wealthier members of the bourgeoisie, who were the most politically powerful group in the city, respectively 34 and 7 percent (Table 6). As at Reims, the notables under the empire can be divided into older and younger generations of established families, and newcomers. The decline of small metallurgy is reflected in the second generation in this occupational category (the merchant *quincailleurs* fell from 7 percent of the elite in 1847-48 to 3 percent after 1852 [Tables 1 and 5]). The continuing importance of ribbon-making was demonstrated by the proportion of younger members of established families in the trade (35 percent, Table 6). Ribbon *fabricants* continued to make up the largest single manufacturing group within the elite and provided the majority of the official candidates for the regime. But their declining political strength was related not only to the rapid growth of heavy industry but also to their own relative economic decline. The proportion of ribbon manufacturers in the elite fell, albeit less precipitously than that of *quincailleurs*, from 28 percent in 1847-48 to 19 percent under the empire. The decreasing vitality of ribbon weaving was also revealed in the growing number of *rentiers*, most of whom were members of older families who had renounced an active business career in favor of investments in land and houses; the size of this group increased from barely one-quarter (23 percent) of the elite in 1847-48 to almost one-third (32 percent) during the period of the empire. Investments of ribbon-makers outside their own trade remained almost entirely in land or houses. Because of the lack of diversity in their holdings, the periodic weakness of the ribbon market in the 1860s reduced their economic strength. The fortunes of wealthy republican dissidents were on the rise in the same period.

Still, most of the wealthiest members of St. Etienne's elite, those with fortunes of at least Fr 500,000 (Table 13), continued to be ribbon manufacturers or *rentiers* related to ribbon families. These two groups accounted for 85 percent of the wealthiest notables. They included Francisque David and Francisque Colcombet, the owners of the oldest ribbon manufacturing houses in the city; Joseph Vignat, the owner of the region's only mechanized ribbon factory; and Jean-Louis Royet, another manufacturer and an important political figure under the July Monarchy. Notables with fortunes of at least Fr 200,000 included Esprit Brunon, a former entrepreneur of the Manufacture Nationale, and several members of the Balay family, also ribbon manufacturers. One member of this family, Jules Balay, was the imperial government's candidate in the legislative election in 1852. Not until the 1860s did the wealth provided by heavy industry permit newer interests successfully to challenge the political power of the older notables.

Steel Manufacturing and Coal Mining

The political implications of the development of the steel industry did not emerge until the period of the empire. Under the July Monarchy, the most important new industrial interests in the Loire had been in mining, especially in the heavily capitalized Compagnie générale des mines de la Loire. After the dissolution of the Compagnie générale by government decree in 1854, steel manufacturing became the most dynamic sector of local industry and the source of important technological innovations.[23]

The modernization of the steel industry stemmed in part from previous attempts to improve the operations of the Compagnie générale through the concentration of production, elimination of smaller competitors, and the financing of development with national capital resources. These tactics, which frightened the local elite in the 1840s and 1850s, became common by the 1860s. The concentration of steel mills was also furthered by the need for greater economies of scale created by free trade. The government fostered bigness by placing its orders with the few large firms able to manufacture naval artillery and other military hardware.[24] The reason for disbanding the Compagnie générale was to win the political support of local traditional manufacturing interests, but from the late 1850s the imperial regime encouraged the development of large firms capable of introducing into French industry the modern techniques necessary to compete with England.

Industrial concentration in the steel industry had begun under the Second Republic, when in the hope of appeasing local opinion the Compagnie générale had introduced a system of privileged markets. Heavy coal users were thereafter assured a steady supply of coal at reduced cost, with a clear advantage to larger firms. The system was continued under the empire, and by 1853 all of the larger steel manufacturers—Jackson frères, Petin and Gaudet, the Loire and l'Ardèche company, Neyrand-Thiollière (the only large steel firm owned by older notables), and the Manufacture Nationale—benefited from it. The burden of price discrimination thus fell almost exclusively on small coal users and speeded their elimination.[25] It was significant both of the changing attitudes of the steel industry and of the success of the Compagnie générale in winning over the larger manufacturers that the Chamber of Commerce denounced steel manufacturers for giving up the fight against the company. The silence of the steelmakers had been purchased with special lower rates.[26]

Ties between coal mines and steel companies were maintained even after the dissolution of the Compagnie générale.[27] Because of the constant need to reduce costs, plans for a special mine-factory relationship were begun in 1855 between the largest steel firm, Jackson frères, Petin and Gaudet, and the Société anonyme des mines de la Loire.[28] Cooperation between steel and mining interests continued through the 1860s, when it was encouraged by the policies of the largest industrial bank in the region, the Crédit lyonnais. Henri Germain, the first general manager of the bank, had begun his career in 1854 as a director of the Montrambert coal company, one of the successors of the Compagnie générale, and through the period of the empire he worked hard to foster cooperation between coal and steel firms. In this way the local banking structure acted as a link between the two complementary branches of heavy industry.

The steel industry experienced a virtual revolution after 1852 in the application of new techniques. The German and English puddling processes had been introduced in the Loire by the Jackson brothers and other immigrant entrepreneurs. Under the empire, the region continued to lead in the introduction of new methods; the Bessemer process was introduced at St. Etienne eight years before its adoption by Le Creusot.[29] The use of Bessemer furnaces produced further concentration, and, as in the textile industry, a reordering of national production. Throughout France, less efficient producers dependent on wood and charcoal were eliminated in favor of those better adapted to the use of coal and coke. Traditional centers of ironmaking in Champagne and lower Alsace began to decline in favor of places adjacent to coal fields such as St. Etienne, Le Creusot, and Anzin.

The economic policies of the steel manufacturers were a primary cause of their growing split with the established elite.[30] The traditional attitudes of the French heavy industrialists, fearful of change and favoring small firms and a slow rate of expansion, were replaced by a desire to expand production, encouraged by a growing number of railroad and military orders. Industry ceased to be concerned about

quality and became obsessed with low prices and increasing economies of scale.[31] Traditionally, manufacturers had been expected not to
press their advantage to the detriment of their competitors. Typical
of this attitude was Adolphe Thiers's attack in 1840 on men who
"flooded the market with a mass of products, destroying old established firms, and ruining in days men who had been in business for
forty or fifty years."[32] This view, shared by most mercantile manufacturers, had scarcely begun to change under the Second Empire.

The growing social and political power of the industrial group was
for a long time concealed behind a modest style of life. Jean Gaudet, a
partner in Petin and Gaudet, the largest steel producer in the Loire
for most of the empire, had begun his career as a simple worker. The
Jacksons, too, had begun more as artisans than as entrepreneurs.[33]
Such men had left politics to older and wealthier ribbon-manufacturing families. But the old maître des forges, who was above all a crafts-
man, was disappearing by the 1860s. Once the steel industry began to
require large amounts of capital, especially to finance the introduction of the Bessemer process, a new style of entrepreneur, able to
solve problems of finance as well as production, began to appear.[34]
The need to tap national capital resources and the growth of a
national market also encouraged a new interest in political life.
Government policies concerning national defense, railroad construction, and free trade were of vital concern to heavy industry, and
manufacturers began to play a more active role in politics. At the head
of the liberal opposition to the empire, they eventually became the
most politically influential notables in the region.

Most steel firms had faced hard times in the 1850s, when they were
hurt by reductions of iron and steel tariffs. But the need to maintain
profits acted as a stimulus to improve efficiency. In 1853, the Jackson
company, already the largest in the department, was reorganized as
Jackson frères et Cie: Compagnie des forges et aciéries d'Assilly-Jack-
son, with a capitalization of Fr 6 million. More than Fr 5.5 million
worth of shares went to Charles and William Jackson. The rest was
given to Ferdinand Delahante and other directors of the Compagnie
générale des mines de la Loire, as well as to Jules and Francisque
Balay, the owners of the large ribbon-manufacturing firm Balay
frères et Cie.[35] The Jacksons attempted in this way to develop a giant
mining and steel combine that could increase production at reduced

cost and to use the capital resources of the established mercantile manufacturers. The introduction of modern financial and industrial techniques learned from the Compagnie générale thus continued to play an important part in the development of the steel industry, though the Balays' financial support of the Jackson company remained a relatively isolated phenomenon.

The first issue of common shares by the Jackson brothers was followed the next year by the creation of an enormous new company through the most important steel merger under the Second Empire. In 1854 the Jackson company, whose heavy capital equipment already included three blast furnaces, sixty-two coke ovens, and an elaborate forge powered by eleven steam engines, merged with Petin, Gaudet et Cie (founded at Rive-de-Gier in 1840), Neyrand Thiollière, and several other companies. The new company, Jackson frères, Petin, Gaudet et Cie, became the largest combination of steel mills and forges in France. It acquired the Jackson holdings, the Petin and Gaudet holdings at Rive-de-Gier and St. Chamond, and the Neyrand Thiollière forges at Lorette; the new company also received Fr 2 million in credit from the latter firm. The company issued forty-five thousand shares valued at Fr 500 each: sixteen thousand of them went to the Jacksons and to Petin and Gaudet, six thousand to Neyrand and Thiollière, and the remainder to other companies and individuals.[36]

Despite the size of the firm, which employed more than three thousand workers, it was at first unable to realize large profits.[37] Low prices and a limited demand for French steel, combined with the tariff reductions of 1853, continued to plague the industry. Other companies in the region also suffered from this prolonged depression; overall production fell to less than one-half of capacity. Seven of the department's thirty blast furnaces were idled. In addition to foreign competition, the industry was hurt by increasing labor costs, which had risen 40 percent between 1850 and 1855, and the high price of coal.[38]

The industry attempted to solve its problems by further concentration and greater economies of scale. This move was also necessitated after 1860 by the introduction of free trade. The real burdens created by the Chevalier-Cobden treaty, like those produced by the Compagnie générale's privileged markets, thus fell on smaller manufacturers least able to bear them. Government naval orders, which could have helped smaller firms, went mostly to the giants of the industry. The firm of Jackson frères, Petin et Gaudet received its first orders for campaign artillery and naval armor plating in 1855. After 1859 these orders increased greatly; the Terrenoire steel company also received large military orders in this period.[39] The government's encouragement of railroad construction provided yet another stimulus for industry; but with twelve thousand more kilometers of road to be built the regime was determined to force further reductions in the price of expensive French steel.[40]

The tariff reductions of 1860 enabled a few companies increasingly to dominate the steel market. Petin and Gaudet (as the company came to be called after the retirement of the Jackson brothers) employed more than eight thousand workers in 1860, produced an annual product worth more than Fr 30 million, and paid a 10 percent dividend to its shareholders.[41] Through the early 1860s it continued to receive large naval and railroad orders and by 1865 had produced the armor plating for twelve French frigates and three floating batteries, as well as for two Spanish frigates and three Italian corvettes. The company's forges, now a major employer of the Loire's skilled metalworkers, made the cannon for the armored frigates *Solferino* and *Magenta*.[42] In 1866, it received the privilege of exclusively manufacturing the barrels of the new chassepot rifle. In cooperation with the Manufacture Nationale, Petin and Gaudet produced more than 750,000 of these rifles before 1869, when other companies at last received similar orders.[43]

The giant rival of Petin and Gaudet, the Terrenoire steel company, also benefited from government orders. Founded in 1819 by the Lyonnais banker Louis Frèrejean as the Compagnie des fonderies et forges de la Loire et l'Ardèche, it had initially employed only sixty-nine workers. The company had expanded in the 1850s by absorbing a portion of the former Neyrand-Thiollière holdings at Lorette and establishing another plant at St. Julien-en-Jarez. By 1859 further mergers made it one of the largest steel firms in the region. Called the Compagnie des fonderies et forges de Terrenoire, la Voulte et Bessèges, it continued to grow through the period of the empire and by the late 1860s had surpassed Petin and Gaudet in the production of Bessemer steel, the industry's main product.[44]

Political Divisions within the Elite

Even with government support, wealthy manufacturers sometimes turned against the empire. Unlike Petin and Gaudet, who remained loyal to the regime, both Félix de Bouchaud, the general manager of Terrenoire, and Alexandre Jullien, the chairman of the board, were important financial backers of the opposition press during the last years of the empire. Antigovernment sentiment was even stronger among smaller manufacturers denied the official patronage given to Terrenoire or Petin and Gaudet. It is not surprising therefore that several of the most important opposition leaders at St. Etienne, including Jules Holtzer and Frédéric Dorian, came from one of the smaller steel companies, Jacob Holtzer et Cie. Although it had grown in the 1860s, Holtzer resented the lack of government orders.[45] Other small steel companies included the Compagnie des forges et aciéries de Chambon-Feugerolles, founded in 1852, and the Aciéries de Firminy, founded in 1854; this latter company employed 750 workers in 1861 and produced an annual product worth Fr 4 million.[46] The Compagnie des fonderies, forges et aciéries de St. Etienne, founded in 1865, also attempted to compete with the larger companies, despite the lack of government business. Military contracts began to be awarded to the Firminy, Holtzer, and other companies only in 1869.[47]

Tensions between railway and steel interests in the Loire also turned a portion of the new industrial leadership against the government. Although industrial growth had been made possible through the development of joint stock companies, the enormous capital resources of the Paris-based railroads frightened local industry. Manufacturers were especially suspicious of the Paris à Lyon et à la Mediterranée railroad (P-L-M), which served St. Etienne. It was widely assumed that Eugène Talabot, the railroad company director who also controlled much of the heavy industry in the Gard, would favor his own interests over those of St. Etienne with discriminatory rates.[48] In fact, P-L-M tariffs do not seem to have slowed the development of Loire industry. All of the steel firms in the region benefited from the Talabot system, which owned the iron mines near Bône in Algeria as well as the railway that shipped the ore to the industrial firms of central France; Terrenoire, Petin and Gaudet, Le Creusot, and Chatillon-Commentry were all served by the Algerian mines.[49] But because of the vulnerability in which the Talabot system placed

St. Etienne's industry, the liberal opposition repeatedly demanded that secondary railroad lines be built. The Chamber of Commerce made similar requests, but these went unheeded until 1869, during the period of political liberalization, when the influence of the P-L-M declined and the government approved the building of independent lines.[50]

The imperial government's decision in the 1850s to underwrite the P-L-M's bond issues further increased local hostility to the regime. Republican arguments of the 1840s about financial feudalism and demands for the protection of smaller property interests still seemed valid in the political rhetoric of the 1860s. Although the scale of local industry had changed, St. Etienne's manufacturers could still claim to be the victims of larger, anonymous capital associations. Talabot's position in the highest political circles made both him and the Bonapartist regime objects of deep suspicion to the local steelmakers. Thus although the decline of the authoritarian empire at the end of the 1860s threatened privileged companies such as the P-L-M, it seemed to further the interests of heavy industrialists in the Loire. The emergence into national political life of an industrial elite that included the directors of large steel firms such as Eugène Schneider at Le Creusot and Casimir Perier was an important development in the 1860s, and strengthened the political opposition in the Loire.[51]

Most industrialists remained outside of the closed circle of ribbon manufacturers. Unattached by the financial and familial ties that helped create common political interests at Reims, they were able to mount a vigorous struggle against the ribbon manufacturers who had been the political agents of the government since 1852. The difficulty that industrial interests had in attracting the investments of established groups was thus an important factor in the development of political life. David Landes has called attention to the problems "new men" faced when seeking financial support.[52] A comparison of the investments of the elites of Reims and St. Etienne reveals considerable differences in the ways provincial notables supported industrial growth. Established families at Reims seem to have been willing to invest in industrial development, but there apparently was much less inclination to do so among the older interests at St. Etienne.

Investments by the elite in industry at St. Etienne were well below those of Reims throughout the period of the Second Empire, and especially during the 1860s. The proportion of investors in French industries and railroads was 8 and 7 percent respectively at St. Etienne as compared to 22 and 28 percent at Reims (Tables 10 and 11). Investments in the newer sectors of the economy were made by only 9 percent of the elite at St. Etienne between 1852 and 1860 and 13 percent in the 1860s, despite the very rapid growth of heavy industry in this period; by comparison, 25 percent of Reims's elite invested in local industrial development in the 1860s.

The ribbon merchants of St. Etienne concentrated most of their limited investments in a few major railroad companies or in nonspeculative issues such as municipal bonds.[53] Established notables at St. Etienne may have been reluctant to invest in heavy industry in part because the most dramatic growth in the Loire took place outside of ribbon-making, the main business concern of St. Etienne's merchants; at Reims woolens manufacturers were investing in an industry in which they had traditionally been the leaders (Table 8). But the cautious attitudes of ribbon manufacturers may be contrasted with those of the liberal professions. Although not direct participants in the steel and coal industries, the latter group provided 18 percent of the investors in these businesses (Table 11). The status of most of these men as newcomers to the city may help explain why they were more receptive to new opportunities (Table 7). Coming from outside St. Etienne, they may have been less affected by the exaggerated suspicion of stock companies that characterized the highly provincial attitudes of local merchants.

Of course, not all members of the old elite were indifferent to industrial investment. Despite fluctuations in the ribbon market, ribbon merchants remained wealthy through the 1860s (Table 13), and some invested in the new industries. Antoine Neyron, whose family fortune had been made in ribbons, subsequently became an important coal mining entrepreneur and invested in local mines throughout the period. Claude Faure, another member of a ribbon-manufacturing family, owned shares in the Société anonyme des mines de la Loire valued at Fr 65,000. The most important investor in this group was Jules Balay. Although he never participated in the management of the new companies, as did the Neyrands and Thiollières, he was one of the major financial backers of the merger that created Jackson frères, Petin et Gaudet. At his death in 1862, Balay owned shares in steel companies worth more than Fr 300,000.

Members of the elite with large investments in both mercantile and industrial businesses were rare however. The great majority of ribbon manufacturers invested as did Jean-Baptiste David, a member of the most prestigious ribbon-manufacturing house in St. Etienne. A millionaire like Balay, he invested througout the period in nonspeculative issues such as the Banque de France or the Montpellier gas company, as well as in railroads. But he consistently ignored the possibility of investing in new local industries.

Most shares in the new companies were bought by investors outside of St. Etienne. The increasing willingness of the French bourgeoisie to purchase industrial shares all over the nation enabled heavy industry to grow without recourse to local capital. The isolation of the established merchants had been fostered in part by the steel companies' dependence on their own profits to finance growth; this practice was continued by most large firms for the rest of the century.[54] But by the end of the 1850s profits alone no longer provided sufficient capital, and the introduction of the Bessemer and Siemens-Martin processes forced the steel manufacturers to find new sources of funds.[55] One of the most important of these was a new bank, the Crédit lyonnais, that allowed the steel interests to bypass St. Etienne's relatively primitive banking structure. Local banks were controlled by ribbon makers and were frequently accused of discriminating against heavy industry.[56]

Since the days of John Law and his Mississippi investment company, banks in France had been objects of suspicion. Many traditional banks had for this reason preferred to call themselves caisses and refused to offer long-term industrial credits which they considered too risky. Thiers, the spokesman for the middle classes, had attacked the extension of easy, long-term business credits, which "made it possible for all sorts of incapable men, with neither ability or money, to start businesses."[57] Most French banks thus remained small and regional in their operations. It was only under the Second Empire that important new industrial banks, such as the Crédit mobilier, were begun.[58] The creation of the Crédit lyonnais in 1863 by steel manufacturers was another step in the attempt to fund industrial development through the use of national savings. The bank lent massively to heavy industry, almost a third of its available capital going to steel and coal manufacturers.[59]

Bank loans were protected by the creation of interlocking directories between lending institutions and major companies.[60] Jullien, the chairman of Terrenoire, and representatives of the Verdié company, Petin and Gaudet, and the Aciéries de St. Etienne were all members of the Crédit lyonnais's first board of directors.[61] The creation of the bank had been engineered by Henri Germain, who wanted industrial interests to control the region's financial network. Germain's role as the representative of local industry in the struggle with the P-L-M railroad reveals the importance of the ties between the bank and local industry. Despite the rhetoric of St. Etienne's Chamber of Commerce about the sanctity of smaller businesses threatened by the monopolistic schemes of financiers, the fight against Talabot by an equally powerful group of industrialists headed by de Bouchaud of Terrenoire, Henri Germain of the Crédit lyonnais, and Gustave Delahante, the former general director of the Compagnie générale, showed that whichever group won, the days of the political and economic preeminence of smaller traditional manufacturers were over.

The political position of the merchants was also weakened by divisions between them and the smaller bourgeoisie. The relative financial decline of the older notables compared with the rising fortunes of dissident manufacturers in heavy industry helped reduce the ribbon manufacturers' control of local political life. At the same time, the continuing concentration of much of the city's wealth among a small number of ribbon manufacturers created resentment among less wealthy bourgeois groups. At both St. Etienne and Reims most of the elite customarily made small loans to shopkeepers and artisans, establishing a clientele that was susceptible to the political influence of the notables (Table 12).[62] This relationship led the imperial government to believe the ribbon oligarchy could assure the political loyalty of many of the smaller bourgeoisie. The inability of the local conservative elite to exercise such control is indicative of very strong antagonisms which have to be explained. Most of the members of the middle class supported industrialists against the ribbon-manufacturing oligarchy, but for different reasons. Small armsmakers preferred the opposition because they resented the government's favoritism of the Manufacture Nationale. Their hostility extended to the ribbon merchants, who were the government's chief political agents. They also had other, more direct reasons for resenting the old elite. Many members of the bourgeoisie disliked the preponderant influence that ribbon manufacturers exercised in the municipal and departmental councils and in the Chamber of Commerce, while smaller ribbon manufacturers feared their more powerful competitors in the oligarchy. All these animosities contributed to a broad popular front against the traditional ruling group. Faced with political rivals as wealthy as themselves, and without the support of the city's less wealthy middle-class elements, the mercantile elite preserved its political power for most of the period of the empire only with the help of the prefect and police.

Government policies also helped increase hostility to the ribbon merchants. An imperial decree of 1852 stipulated that the electors of the local chambers of commerce be selected from among the oldest commercial houses in their localities, most of which at St. Etienne were ribbon-manufacturing firms.[63] Although the Chamber of Commerce represented the entire department and was the official voice of manufacturers in dealing with the government, other trades, including the steel industry as well as other artisan crafts, enjoyed only minority representation. During the first years of the empire, heavy industry had been represented only by Antoine Neyrand, who sat in the chamber between 1853 and 1856. Representation of the steel industry was later increased by the entry of Hippolyte Petin and Félix de Bouchaud, both of whom served between 1857 and 1866; de Bouchaud was president between 1860 and 1865. After 1867, representation was further expanded to include Lucien Arbel, the director of the forges of Rive-de-Gier, Edouard Janicot, the representative of the Aciéries de St. Etienne, Camille Thiollière, the director of the Forges de St. Chamond, and François Verdié, the director of the Société des forges et aciéries de Firminy.[64] But despite these additions, the chamber was dominated throughout the period by the ribbon industry, whose manufacturers generally occupied six to eight of its fifteen seats. Locally referred to as the *chambre des rubans*, the Chamber of Commerce was presided over by such important ribbon manufacturers as Auguste Faure (from 1857 to 1859) and Palluat (after 1865), while other representatives of the industry included Jean-Claude Vignat-Tézénas, Auguste Gerin, Grégoire Brunon-Nublat, Auguste Tézénas de Montcel, Pierre Girinon, Jean-Baptiste Duplay-Balay, the deputy, Christophe Faure-Belon, the mayor of St. Etienne, Mathieu Passerat, and Francisque David.[65]

The development of heavy industry in the Loire created a number of powerful entrepreneurs who were not tied either economically or politically to the established merchant elite. Some of these men later became the most important leaders of the political opposition. Their success, however, was dependent upon their ability to coordinate their demands with those of other groups. To be sure, the potential allies of these industrialists were chiefly other members of the middle classes who also favored a return to parliamentary government. But in an era of universal suffrage, the working classes continued to play a decisive role in elections. The political success of the opposition depended upon its ability to gain working-class support while avoiding a repetition of the events of 1848-49. The liberal leadership therefore attempted in the 1860s to mobilize artisan workers against their merchant employers while avoiding the reappearance of independent radical working-class organizations.

Industrial growth under the empire helped prevent workers' groups from playing a dominant role in the political life of the 1860s. Industrialization disrupted the unity of homogeneous artisan communities at Reims with the creation of separate artisanal and factory groups in the textile industry. The growth of a highly paid work force in the steel industry at St. Etienne also gave industrialists a greater influence over their workers than in 1848-49. Before giving further attention to the development of local politics, it is necessary therefore to consider the impact of economic growth on working-class life and organization in both cities in the two decades after 1848.

5

The Working Classes

The beginning of mechanized production affected the lives of workers even more profoundly than those of the elites because industrialization threatened long-established artisan trades and forced many workers to enter factories. The wages of artisans who attempted to continue to work outside the mills declined steadily. By the end of the 1860s, poverty and fear of proletarianization had radicalized many artisans. But the growth of mechanized industry also weakened the overall unity of the workers' movement, splitting formerly purely artisanal trades into distinct factory and artisan groups. Rapid urban growth also changed the composition of the working classes, and it became more difficult to organize newcomers than long-term residents into mutual aid societies and political clubs. Police repression further reduced the ability of workers to form cohesive organizations. It became more difficult to create a strong radical working-class movement, and, as a result, notables were able to maintain their influence over groups opposed to the empire.

At Reims, the development of factory industry split the unity of the artisanal woolens trades. At St. Etienne, the development of workers' organizations was complicated by the unequal introduction of new manufacturing techniques in different industries. Ribbon weaving hardly changed, and the old antagonisms between artisans and employers remained intense. Ribbon weavers maintained strong organizations and were the most radical element within St. Etienne's working classes. In contrast, the conditions in the steel industry left its workers largely untouched by labor unrest. Such differences became important in the 1860s, when the government began to loosen its controls over working-class life. With good working conditions in the steel industry industrialists could mount a political campaign against the government without fearing strikes in their own plants. They were also able to use the hostility of artisan ribbon weavers against their political opponents to create a strong republican party even before the fall of the empire.

Common Problems

Control of working-class organizations by the conservative elite at Reims had been facilitated after 1852 by government appointment of the presidents of workers' mutual aid societies. Though the members of the eleven societies that survived the Second Republic (the others had been dissolved by government decree in 1850) complained they did not want the alms of the rich, control was given by the administration to members of the municipal government. The local elite thus attempted to turn workers' societies into agencies of bourgeois paternalism. Werlé, the newly appointed mayor and director of the Vve Cliquot champagne company, was named president of the barrel-makers and champagne workers society. Two assistant mayors, woolens manufacturers Auguste Gilbert and Henri Lachapelle, were named to head woolens workers' associations.[1]

Further decrees in June 1853 gave the prefect power to nominate the presidents and vice-presidents of the Conseil des prudhommes. Charged with the mediation of labor-management disputes, this organization now began to prevent workers from making economic demands on their employers. Woolens manufacturers also took advantage of the restoration of the *livret*, the good conduct work book required for new employment, to impede the mobility of labor by refusing to surrender *livrets* to workers upon request. A veiled report of the Chamber of Commerce indicated that this new policy had created much hostility between workers and employers, but despite repeated complaints from the Conseil des prudhommes and the prefect, the Ministry of the Interior refused to act on the workers' behalf.[2]

These newly imposed controls, combined with the economic crisis in 1853-54, angered artisan workers. In 1853 the streets of Reims were filled with beggars, and even those workers who were able to find work could barely support their families. Placards appeared in the streets denouncing the emperor as an accomplice of the grain merchants and warning that "hunger justifies violence."[3] Fearing the uses to which the economic crisis could be put by members of the former liberal opposition, the imperial government increased its control of workers' organizations. After bringing an entire battalion of soldiers into the city, the government arrested ninety-one woolens workers belonging to a secret political organization. Among those seized was its organizer, a son of Bressy's former secretary Louis Lecamp, who had recruited almost two hundred members before his arrest. Alfred Lejeune and Simon Dauphinot, liberals in the elite friendly to the workers' movement, were also accused of belonging to the society. In June, sixty-two of those arrested were sentenced to prison terms of three months to four years.[4]

Following the trial, workers at Reims retreated from local political life until the late 1860s. During this period conservative bourgeois fears about "reds" also began to fade.[5] There were no working-class demonstrations in the city, either during the depression of 1857-58 or during the subsequent crisis of 1862. While many workers found relief through railroad construction jobs in the countryside, former radical leaders continued to be closely watched by the police.[6] So successful was the imperial government's control of workers during periods of depression that Dérodé, a former republican leader who attempted to take advantage of the crisis of 1857-58, was defeated in the Conseil général election in the heavily working-class third canton of Reims.[7] Most workers also remained unaffected by the appeals of republican propagandists during the economic crisis of 1862, and the majority of working-class voters supported the government in the legislative election of 1863. The number of abstentions was greater among the middle classes than among artisans.[8]

The elite simultaneously attempted to reconcile workers to the regime by launching several well-publicized paternalistic programs. The most important of these was the building of a retirement home (regarded as a model of its kind in France) and the construction of subsidized housing on the outskirts of the city.[9] Harmel, a manufacturer troubled by widespread atheism among workers, attempted to "organize the factory in a Christian fashion" and settled 150 workers in a model community at his suburban factory. Although benevolent in its intent, this "Christian manufacturing family" became a perma-

nent factory work force because the mobility of employees was reduced; the result was similar to that of the illegal retention of the
livrets.[10]

Other firms had less ambitious programs. The Holden company
provided subsidized meals for its employees, as well as an organized
picnic on the emperor's birthday, but most did little more than
contribute to the yearly banquet on the feast day of St. Louis, the
patron of spinners and weavers; this celebration usually began with a
mass in the cathedral and ended with a ball in the city's park.[11] Some
firms claimed that the construction of modern factories, which had
improved working conditions, had in itself greatly benefited workers.[12] Thus despite some real attempts to improve conditions, the
material hardships of working-class life remained largely unchanged
through the 1850s. Police surveillance of radical leaders, however,
and devices such as the *livret* remained sufficient to prevent any overt
hostility to the regime or local employers.

The government's success in maintaining a docile work force is
remarkable when considered against the problems facing artisans in
the 1850s. The displacement of many workers by the mechanization
of wool combing continued through this period. Before the 1850s,
there had been approximately ten thousand wool combers in Reims,
who sorted and cleaned wool before it was spun. The introduction of
mechanized wool combers, culminating in the building of the Holden
factory in 1853, destroyed this artisan industry. A single laborer could
produce 325 to 350 kilograms of combed wool a year, but a single
machine could produce 15 to 20,000 kilos. The resulting decline in
the price of combed wool greatly reduced the wages of these artisans.
Thousands were forced to live in the direst poverty, and depended on
charity to survive.[13]

In the 1860s the transition to factory production in other branches
of the industry had begun as well, but artisan spinners and weavers
escaped economic difficulties until the end of the woolens boom. By
1863 it was estimated that the mechanization of spinning and weaving
had greatly increased worker productivity, and factory wages, which
sometimes reached Fr 4 a day, reflected this change.[14] The boom also
vastly reduced unemployment through 1867. But wages for all
groups of workers except mechanics and power-loom operators remained low. Among the most poorly paid were the thirty-eight
thousand hand-loom operators who worked in Reims and its immedi-

ate suburbs and an even larger number of artisan spinners. In 1867 Louis Reybaud estimated that allowing for unemployment and accidents, the average daily wage for male artisan textile workers was Fr 1.50, Fr 1 for women, and 75 centimes for children. This meant an annual income of Fr 1,200 for a family of four with working children. Since rents were between Fr 75 and 100, and the cost of other necessities was equally high, minimum expenses were assumed by Reybaud to be Fr 3.25 per day, or Fr 1,188 per year. An annual income of Fr 1,200 left only Fr 12 to cover unusual expenses.[15] Clearly, workers had not benefited in the 1860s from the enormous increase of profits enriching their employers. The woolens boom, however, did ease the transition from artisan to factory industry by providing excess orders for artisan workers.

The real crisis for artisans came only after 1867, when the boom ended and increasing numbers of workers found themselves unable to earn even subsistence wages. Factory hands were also placed in a precarious position. Without job security in a weakening market, they faced the threat of reduced wages and sudden unemployment; they could be fired with only one week's notice.[16] But their employment was in the more modern sector of the industry whose future seemed assured. Factory workers could count on the continued existence of the mills, but the prospects for artisans were much more bleak.

Working-class organizations began to reemerge among both artisan and factory workers in the late 1860s, encouraged by worsening labor conditions and the government's growing toleration of mutual aid societies and strikes. Divisions between immigrants and long-term residents as well as artisan and factory workers made new organizations difficult to create and maintain, but even the local opposition continued to fear working-class radicalism. Liberal factory owners at Reims seem to have been more apprehensive about popular agitation in the economic crisis that began in 1867 than were the steel manufacturers in the Loire; this concern may have discouraged them from fomenting strikes against political opponents as did their counterparts at St. Etienne.

The prefect and municipal government at St. Etienne had been equally active in suppressing workers' organizations after 1851, but popular opposition to conservative rule remained stronger in the Loire. Despite government support of conservatives in the municipal elections held in September 1852, the liberal opposition received more than seventeen hundred votes as compared with only fourteen hundred for the official candidates. The prefect thereupon increased his control of the artisan communities and expelled all workers from outside the commune as vagabonds. Because many of the most militant workers were younger unmarried men from outside the city, this action severely reduced radical activity in the first years of the empire.[17]

By 1856, however, police harassment and the abuse of the *livrets* encouraged the development of new clandestine working-class organizations. The government discovered at least one secret society, the so-called "pères des familles." In anticipation of a revolution, the group had even accumulated a secret cache of arms.[18] As at Reims, the administration's answer to this presumed revolutionary threat was to continue the prohibition of independent workers' organizations. In 1857 local authorities refused to allow the reorganization of the ribbon weavers' mutual aid society dissolved in 1856. Although the society had no political aims and demanded nothing from the employers, "it was nonetheless assumed," the prefect wrote, "that the real purpose of the association was to create secret ties between its members allowing them to make collective demands on employers."[19] The regime thus used the threat of revolution to create economic conditions favorable to the middle classes. The administration assumed that local notables would appreciate its efforts against the mutual aid societies and support the regime.

The government also continued to use the police to assure the victory of its official candidates. The bourgeoisie was to be won over with favorable economic policies, but political conformity was to be imposed on artisans by harsher means. Polling officials routinely opened the ballots of workers, and St. Etienne's mayor declared known radicals improperly recorded on the electoral lists. The opposition press claimed that as late as the legislative election of 1863, these and other tactics had prevented more than six thousand workers in the city from voting. The regime also helped employers control the political opinions of their workers. The opposition complained of conservative employers marching their workers to the polls with the government's approval, as well as of the practice of mailing workers' voting cards to the directors of local companies, who then distributed them. Although citizens without voting cards were by law still permitted to vote, the local administration refused to allow them to do so.[20]

As at Reims, conservatives also tried to win working-class support through paternalistic programs, but the decentralized character of St. Etienne's ribbon industry limited these efforts to occasional charity drives in periods of depression. When a collection for unemployed workers was taken up by the curé of St. Etienne in 1857, his fund proved inadequate to meet the crisis. Relief efforts were equally ineffectual in 1861, when more than two-thirds of the ribbon workers were temporarily unemployed and many were forced to leave the city to find work elsewhere.[21] This failure of local charity also contributed to the hostility between artisans and their merchant employers.

The large mining companies in the Loire were far better able to create a systematic program of working-class assistance and could have been guided by the program established under the Second Republic by the Compagnie générale.[22] Similarly, at Reims, the greater resources of factory industry allowed for a greater degree of paternalism. But with increased police controls of working-class life after 1852, the St. Etienne companies showed little inclination to be generous, and paternalism never played a great role in mining. The four companies that succeeded the Compagnie générale after 1854 had each established an accident fund, although they provided fewer benefits under the empire than the Compagnie générale had under the republic. Contributions to the miners' funds (the *caisses de secours*) were made mostly by workers themselves through fines levied for infractions of company rules; because the companies were obliged to make up any deficits in the funds out of their own profits, it was in their interest to levy fines as frequently as possible.[23]

Even more conducive to labor-management hostility was the attempt to get the greatest amount of labor from the miners at the least possible cost. Mining accidents were frequent, and the *procureur général* suggested that careless company engineers were often to blame.[24] Armand Audiganne, writing in 1860, found that the companies "showed little sympathy for the suffering of individual miners . . . and saw the workers only in terms of profits. . . . The companies showed themselves lacking in all generosity and made contributions neither for pensions paid to disabled workers, nor to widows."[25] As a result, many miners sought relief in drunkenness, and angry confrontations with company engineers frequently threatened to develop into strikes.[26]

Despite the difficult living conditions of both miners and artisans, the repression of workers' organizations under the empire prevented them from taking an active part in political life. Although popular support for middle-class opposition groups continued to grow slowly through the 1860s, the prefect wrote in 1866 that most artisans were uninterested in politics, attempting instead to improve their situation through the creation of mutual aid societies.[27] When groups of workers at St. Etienne once again became active in politics at the end of the empire, these organizations played an important role in coordinating opposition to the government. The ability of various groups to organize was determined both by the effects of immigration to the cities and by the introduction of factory industry. These factors were to have a more important effect on political life than either paternalistic programs or government repression.

The impact of change on the working classes can be assessed in part through the *Successions et absences*, another death register maintained under the empire. It includes many smaller fortunes not listed in the inventories of the *Mutation après décès* and provides an assessment of the mobile and real property of workers at time of death. Like the *Mutation*, it can be used to survey wealth throughout provincial France, and a study of all adult males at both Reims and St. Etienne in the sample years 1852, 1862, and 1869 gives important insights into the economic life of the smaller bourgeoisie and working classes. As with the profile of the elite taken from the *Mutation*, the working-class sample contains a large number of older workers. It remains unclear to what extent workers retired or became indigent after retirement, and the number of indigent workers recorded in the *Successions et absences* is undoubtedly greater than that of workers at the peak earning period of their lives; also, many wage workers not badly off before old age probably accumulated very little property to leave at death.[28] The registers nonetheless provide some indications of the levels of poverty among various sectors of the working class and the degree to which artisan families were able to acquire some property.

The condition of artisan groups remains the key to understanding working-class politics under the empire. Before the development of modern trade unions in the 1880s, the level of popular radicalism was dependent not on the degree of factory work within any sector of the working class but on strong community ties. These were often pro-

vided by traditional artisanal organizations. William Sewell's study of
working-class political life at Marseilles reveals the typical division
between artisan and proletarian labor. He found the latter often
"impoverished, oppressed, frequently illiterate, without family ties,
unorganized, nomadic, and, to judge from their high crime rates,
personally disoriented as well." In contrast, artisans were "moderately
well paid, respectable, literate, organized, and rooted in the city of
their birth, and in a long standing urban corporate tradition." They
were therefore able to participate effectively in local political life
through their own organizations.[29]

Reims's greater wealth was reflected in the condition of its workers;
67 percent of adult male workers left no property under the empire,
as compared with 84 percent at St. Etienne (Table 14). More signifi-
cantly, the level of indigence among Reims's woolens workers, the
most important working-class group, was among the lowest in the
city; only 39 percent left no property. It is difficult to tell how many of
these were artisans and how many new factory workers. Presumably,
artisan workers were more likely to own some property, especially
tools, and perhaps part of a house in the city. Full employment among
artisans during the woolens boom and good factory wages were
responsible for the relative well-being of woolens workers. The effect
of the decline of wages, which started in 1867, begins to appear only
minimally in the *Successions et absences* by 1869. In contrast, two
important artisanal groups at St. Etienne, ribbon weavers and armsmakers, showed higher rates of indigence. Other groups of workers
were even worse off. Seventy-seven percent of the ribbon workers
and 75 percent of the armsmakers left no property, as compared with
84 percent of the working class as a whole.[30] This reflects the worsening conditions of ribbon weaving at St. Etienne in the 1860s and the
low wages paid in the arms industry.

The state of working-class organizations was another important
factor in the development of organized political activity. Whereas
woolens workers at Reims were divided between factory hands and
artisans, ribbon weavers at St. Etienne remained a relatively homogeneous artisan group. Although some were desperately poor, others
succeeded in preserving their limited resources. They possessed a
strong tradition of organization, which enabled them to act in concert
in the last years of the empire. At Reims, woolens workers were

slightly better off economically, but they were making a transition to factory work, which weakened their traditional organizations and made them less of a threat to the government than St. Etienne's weavers. Reims's giant woolens workers' union, founded in 1868, was numerically strong but internally divided, and differences between artisan and factory workers hindered the development of clear policy goals. St. Etienne's ribbon weavers faced no similar problems. They became the most radical group within the working-class community and played a major role in the creation of the city's commune in 1871.

The smaller bourgeoisie in both towns, shopkeepers and petty traders, also played a vital part in the development of republican politics under the empire.[31] They were more informed than workers about national political issues, and spread republican propaganda in shops and cabarets. The *Successions et absences* provides some information about this group as well. At St. Etienne smaller ribbon manufacturers and armsmakers comprised respectively 11 and 5 percent of the petty bourgeoisie (Table 16). Their resentment of the ribbon oligarchy made them as important as shopkeepers in strengthening the republican movement. The relatively low number of small-scale woolens manufacturers at Reims (5 percent of the total group) demonstrates the extent to which control of that industry had already come into the hands of the elite (Table 15). The notables at Reims were less vulnerable to the political rivalry of smaller competitors than were St. Etienne's merchants. In the Loire, smaller manufacturers and prosperous artisans in all of the city's trades played a greater role in the opposition to the ribbon weaving oligarchy.

Developments at Reims in the 1860s

The expansion of factory industry at Reims continued the disruption of artisan trades begun in the 1850s. The artisan community was also weakened by the entrance of a large number of new woolens workers to the town, as the city's population grew from 55,801 in 1861 to 71,994 in 1872.[32]

Women's jobs were the first affected, and a large number of female spinners and carders were displaced by the rapid shift to mechanized spinning. Weaving, which tended to be a man's occupation, was the

last affected.[33] Within several years, however, it too began to change
very rapidly. Some weavers benefited from the introduction of mechanization; operators of power looms earned Fr 4 a day. The situation
of this group, whose numbers increased from nine hundred in 1859
to twenty-seven hundred in 1862, seems to have been relatively good.
But hand weavers' wages rose only slightly.[34] Although the woolens
boom prevented the sudden dislocation of large numbers of artisans,
the decline of the artisan trades was inevitable.

Workers who secured factory jobs faced different problems, often
finding it difficult to adjust to new conditions. In 1861 a strike was
begun at the Villeminot-Huard factory after the company inau-
gurated a series of regulations punishing drunkenness and lateness.
In 1864, the attempt to improve factory discipline through similar
regulations started a strike at the Holden factory; in response to the
introduction of severe penalties for absenteeism more than seven
hundred workers walked off the job.[35] But strikes in this period were
rare; rising wages for some and full employment during the boom
kept most workers politically docile.[36] In 1864 the prefect reported
that small shopkeepers, who habitually read the democratic press and
loaned copies to their customers, were more dangerous to the government than woolens workers. He believed that only a new period of
unemployment and hardship would create renewed popular unrest.[37]

Strike activity and political agitation increased dramatically among
factory hands and artisans after the woolens boom ended in 1867.[38]
Although the introduction of mechanized weaving had initially
created unemployment among artisans, they had still been able to
find work after 1861; excess orders which factories were unable to fill
created full employment.[39] But by the end of the 1860s, artisan
weavers, of whom there were still several thousand at Reims, faced
real hardships. In 1869 they received the lowest wages in the city, far
below even the minimal standards of subsistence of the period.[40]
Many could find no work at all. Disaffection among this group
increased, a typical reaction of skilled workers whose jobs were being
eliminated by mechanization. It was thus only in the late 1860s that
the latent tensions created by mechanization of the industry became
apparent.[41]

The number of factory strikes at Reims also increased. Although
factory wages were usually well above those for artisan work, wage

reductions in response to declining woolens prices angered many workers.[42] They were willing to accept a reduction of hours but not of hourly wages, and ten percent wage cuts at Walbaum and at Wagner-Marsan in 1868 resulted in strikes.[43] Strikes were also encouraged by the liberalized law on coalitions first introduced in May 1864. Workers' combinations were for the first time made legal if created for the purpose of improving working conditions.[44] The rising cost of living was an additional cause of increased strike activity, and soaring food prices, combined with reductions in wages and hours, increased workers' worries about their future. Their interest in politics grew, and secret societies began to be formed for the first time since the early 1850s.[45] Relations between workers and employers also became less friendly after the strikes in 1867-68, although workers' meetings were held in 1868, in the words of the prefect, "in a most laudable spirit of moderation." They remained orderly through the early months of 1869, when workers still demanded only a reduction in hours commensurate with their reduced salaries and an end to the *livrets*.[46]

The strikes of the late 1860s marked the beginning of the reestablishment of independent working-class organizations at Reims. But attempts to unite all workers in a single society similar to those that had existed under the Second Republic were not successful. Growing divisions between factory and artisan workers were the primary cause of disunity, and the presence of a large number of recent immigrants outside of the traditional community also hindered cooperation. Most working-class migration to Reims had taken place in the 1860s. Immigrant workers thus had less time to assimilate into the local community by the end of the decade than had the immigrant ribbon weavers at St. Etienne, who entered the city in the 1850s. This division among workers may help explain why ribbon weavers at St. Etienne were better organized and more militant than the mixed artisan and factory population of Reims.[47]

Attempts to create a central mutual aid society at Reims began in the summer of 1868; but a year later workers were still divided into two factions over tactics. One, a moderate group, wanted improved wages but was hesitant to strike for fear of conflict with the government. The other, centered in the Société de solidarité et de résistance des travailleurs rémois et des environs, was as hostile to the regime as to employers. Its leaders worked hard to recruit supporters among spinners and weavers both in Reims and in the city's industrial suburbs, and by January 1870 the group was strong enough to win raises for its members by merely threatening to strike.[48]

The liberal opposition attempted to use the society to further its own political aims. The liberal newspaper *L'Indépendent rémois*, created in 1869 to convince workers that only a republic could provide the material improvements they demanded, now began to support the new mutual aid society.[49] Henry Thomas, the secretary of the society, had worked for Jules Simon in the legislative election in June of that year, and members of the bourgeois opposition encouraged workers to join the organization.[50] Liberals were thus confident of their ability to use the workers' movement to increase their own influence.

But the emergence of a truly radical working-class movement was incompatible with the aims of the middle-class opposition. In February 1870 Joseph Huard, the president of the society, attempted to strengthen the organization by joining it to the Association internationale des travailleurs, which by 1870 was claiming more than 250,000 members in France.[51] But this threat to the political leadership of the elite was soon reduced by dissension within the organization; Huard had not taken sufficiently into account the unwillingness of many members of the society to join a national union. When in March he suggested that a part of the local strike fund be sent to help silk workers at Lyons, he met with enough opposition to split the unity of the group.[52]

Radical denunciations of liberal as well as conservative employers followed the worsening economic situation in 1870. But divisions among artisan and factory workers, as well as within the Société de résistance, helped prevent the formation of unified working-class organizations that could have seriously threatened the leadership of the liberal elite. Despite frequent meetings of woolens workers through the spring and summer of 1870 and continued labor unrest, workers were not sufficiently organized or financially prepared to carry out long strikes. A strike against the Holden factory in May soon collapsed, and liberal manufacturers received sufficient popular support through the elections of 1870-71 to maintain their control of political life.[53] In May 1871, when Reims was under German occupation, the prefect feared the creation of a commune. The municipal and legislative elections, however, demonstrated the ability of moderate middle-class republicans to maintain their influence over the voters at Reims through the early years of the Third Republic.[54]

Developments at St. Etienne

The effects of industrialization in the 1860s were even more striking at St. Etienne than at Reims. The rapid development of steel manufacturing and coal mining in the surrounding region greatly increased the number of workers in heavy industry. The city's population grew from 78,189 in 1851 to 110,814 in 1872.[55] The ribbon industry was the least affected by the disruption this growth caused; its artisans seem to have had no trouble in organizing for political purposes. The influx of workers and the transition from artisanal to factory employment at Reims hindered woolens workers' efforts to create a unified political organization. But the migration of new workers to St. Etienne left ribbon workers' organizations relatively unaffected.[56] Charles Tilly believes the difficulty migrant workers experienced in integrating themselves into unfamiliar urban environments was a major factor in the development of popular protest. Working-class political organizations were easiest to create among long-term urban residents who had the community ties necessary for sustained action. New migrants remained outside traditional community networks and were only gradually assimilated into working-class organizations.[57] But most migrants to St. Etienne who entered the ribbon trade in the 1850s were already adept weavers and, having come from the countryside immediately adjacent to the city, were easily integrated into its economic life.[58] They also had a longer period to assimilate into the larger community. Despite their poverty, the ribbon weavers of St. Etienne were thus able to act in concert against their employers and the government.

The traditional character of St. Etienne's largest industry was not disrupted by mechanization either; the ribbon trade remained overwhelmingly dependent on artisan labor under the empire.[59] Master weavers believed that through hard work they could achieve the same levels of wealth as their merchant employers and vehemently opposed the introduction of mechanization.[60] Ambition and the need to accumulate capital drove many artisans to work as much as eighteen hours a day, often resulting in chronic poor health, which prevented them from working past the age of fifty.[61] Journeymen's fraternal organizations remained strong and helped promote political discussion. They also contributed to the underlying animosity between workers and merchant employers; similar organizations probably existed among artisan armsmakers.[62]

Apprenticeship in the ribbon trade began at age fourteen for boys and lasted from one to three years.[63] Between the ages of twenty and twenty-five they became master weavers, bought looms, and married. During the prosperous 1850s (when master artisans were earning Fr 100 to 125 per month per loom) many were able to buy an additional loom; some even built houses costing as much as Fr 10,000.[64]

Ribbon merchants had little contact with this closed artisan society. They preferred to deal with weavers through intermediaries (*commissionaires*), who chose which shops to employ and established terms of employment. These middlemen settled disagreements with master weavers or submitted grievances for arbitration to the Conseil des prudhommes; merchant manufacturers intervened only in serious disputes. By the late 1850s, however, falling ribbon prices led to frequent conflicts between artisans and merchants and made masters increasingly resentful of the contracts offered by the *fabricants*. Threatened with the forced sale of their idle looms, many weavers began to steal excess silk in order to survive.[65] This practice became so widespread by the end of the 1850s that the local authorities considered it a major threat to the industry.[66]

The petty materialism of St. Etienne's smaller ribbon merchants, who often cheated artisans on weights and wages, helped poison relations between manufacturers and workers and gave the merchant group increasingly more trouble in dealing with the problems associated with rapid urban growth. Most ribbon manufacturers remained at St. Etienne only long enough to make their fortunes. Without any solidarity among merchants, and in the absence of any feeling of civic responsibility, bad housing conditions and other problems remained unsolved. When Nicolas Heurtier, the mayor, proposed in 1851 that dangerous and unsanitary housing be improved through the efforts of private individuals and the municipal government, most manufacturers opposed the idea as an attack on private property.[67] The municipal council was unwilling to impose heavy costs on house owners and suggested that improving unhealthy housing should be an individual initiative.

The danger of this attitude was pointed out in an anonymous pamphlet published in 1852, which complained that "in a city at once so new and so prosperous, so busy and so rich, we have all the elements for a brilliant and enlightened society . . . but there is as yet properly speaking no society at all. It lacks . . . a center. The city also lacks many useful institutions. . . . We don't have a public hospital, but we have usurers. We have no public library worthy of serious attention, but we have cabarets where minds are degraded. . . . The lack of such institutions is unfortunate . . . for these are institutions of social peace."[68] It was in pursuit of "social peace" that Faure-Belon, one of the small group of wealthy manufacturers whose long-term residence in the city allowed them to dominate their peers, began an ambitious building program during his tenure as mayor between 1855 and 1865. Municipal expenditures on public works increased dramatically to finance the construction of new public buildings, but the most important problems created by the city's rapid growth remained unsolved. The Hotel-de-Ville and the Palais des Arts were completed, but, as at Reims, working-class housing remained dangerous and unhealthy.[69] The city established a Compagnie immobilière in 1856 to improve the old districts of the town by buying up and improving slum property, but its activities were limited. The mayor argued that too many improvements would drive up rents and force workers out of the city's center.[70]

Ribbon weavers had many reasons to become radical by the end of the 1860s. Relations with merchant employers, already bad, had deteriorated with the decline of ribbon prices after 1860. Poor housing conditions and the unwillingness to make any improvements created tensions between workers and the municipal government. Finally, the close ties between master artisans and their journeymen, combined with the distance between workers and merchants, made possible the creation of a unified artisan front against employers.

The first important workers' organizations under the Second Empire were producers' cooperatives. Popular socialist movements before the emergence of Marxism, such as those of Philippe Buchez, Louis Blanc, and Pierre-Joseph Proudhon, had all preached the idea of cooperation. These organizations would later help lead workers to a greater interest in radical politics. In 1863 a Société des rubanniers was founded by more than eleven hundred master weavers. They pooled more than three thousand looms to found a producers' cooperative that would allow the masters to escape from the exploitation of merchants and sell directly to the public; the society began production in 1866.[71]

The previous year the less wealthy velvet ribbon-makers had also become more militant. A coordinated strike of more than five thousand of these workers protesting the merchants' decision not to pay higher wages for new types of ribbons requiring more work stopped almost all the looms in the city. This success may be contrasted with the short-lived or abortive strikes that were organized in the wool industry at Reims.[72] The strike ended a month later with a compromise between the workers, who demanded a limit on working hours and prompt payment of wages, and their employers, who feared that a long strike would slow the recovery of the industry. Although the strike leaders were prosecuted by the government, workers' organizations continued to grow.[73] "The rule of the *patron*," the prefect wrote, "is submitted to today in the hope of taking revenge tomorrow."[74] Following the strike, a Société des secours mutuels des rubanniers et veloutiers was founded in 1866; and in 1867 more than eight hundred ribbon-dyers at St. Etienne joined the larger Association des teinturiers at Lyons.[75] By the end of the decade artisans were ready to take more direct political action and attempted to establish a commune as a solution to their problems. This however was preceded by the coal miners' strike of 1869, the largest since the establishment of the dictatorship.

By the mid-1860s the new interest in organization had begun to affect miners as well. Although this group included many migrants to the region, miners had a ready basis for organization in the coal fields and were continually provoked into union activity by the mining companies.[76] Because their work was so dangerous, they were especially concerned about accident funds and after 1866 began a campaign to unite all the funds of the various companies into a central one, hoping to retain their accumulated benefits when they changed jobs.

Demands for a united fund were combined with a desire to strengthen the role of the Caisse fraternelle des ouvriers mineurs, an

independent mutual aid society created in 1866, which also provided
an organizational base for strikes. The companies became alarmed,
and looked to the administration for protection, but the prefect
remained unconcerned. A short-lived strike at Roche-le-Molière in
1867 seemed to prove the weakness of the Caisse fraternelle. In
keeping with its new liberal policies, the government therefore decided not to dissolve it but appointed a new prefect, Castaing, with
orders to reconcile the miners to the regime. Castaing had previously
helped organize a central accident fund in the Pas-de-Calais and now
attempted to establish a similar one in the Loire. The mining companies opposed a central fund because they feared the greater mobility that such an organization would enable would weaken their efforts
to create a stable work force bound to individual companies; only four
companies (La Loire, Montrambert, St. Etienne, and La Peronnière)
therefore accepted the prefect's plan. All continued to refuse cooperation with the Caisse fraternelle.[77] Thus despite the best efforts of the
regime, the project for a central fund was defeated by the majority of
the companies. Castaing did, however, appease the miners by con-
vincing the owners to institute new benefits; a retirement fund was
added to the disability funds already existing in most companies.[78] By
continuing to court the leaders of the Caisse fraternelle, the prefect
believed he had prevented any further radicalization of the workers.
The strike in June of 1869 proved him wrong.

The membership of the Caisse fraternelle was unsatisfied with
Castaing's efforts. With more than five thousand miners in the organization, many of the rank and file believed they were powerful
enough to demand greater concessions and therefore continued to
call for a central fund under independent workers' control.[79] As at
Reims, the republican opposition encouraged workers' hostility toward the government. Michel Rondet, one of the founders of the
Caisse fraternelle, had campaigned for Frédéric Dorian, the republican leader, during the 1863 election. Ties between miners and republicans were further strengthened in 1866, when Jules Favre, a
republican leader of national reputation, was asked to represent the
miners during the reorganization of the companies' accident funds.[80]
Through 1868 liberal members of the municipal council also supported the miners' demands, hoping thereby to win popular support.[81] The struggle between the government and the opposition for
miners' votes was not finally resolved until the summer of 1869.

As late as the legislative election in the spring the leaders of the
Caisse fraternelle still hoped the prefect would force the mining
companies to accept a worker-controlled fund. When no major concessions were made, radical elements in the organization, possibly
connected with the Association internationale des travailleurs (Jullien, the director of Terrenoire, had been warned of such a connection by a Belgian industrialist), began a strike in June which soon won
the support of more than fourteen thousand miners.[82] Demanding a
central accident and retirement fund, a reduction of the working day
from eleven to eight hours, and an increased uniform wage, the
strikers closed the mines.[83] The prefect thereupon sent troops into the
basin, bringing to an end all hope of further cooperation between the
government and the miners.

The opposition acted quickly to take advantage of the prefect's
blunder, aided by a bloody incident in the coal fields. Frédéric Dorian
and Jules Holtzer, both liberals and directors of J. J. Holtzer et Cie,
had ordered their agents to disregard the boycott of local mines
during the strike and resume coal shipments. It is unclear whether
the Holtzer company assumed that Dorian's republican reputation
gave it immunity from the prohibition placed on local coal deliveries
or, as one writer has suggested, that Dorian and Holtzer in fact hoped
to provoke the strikers so as to embarrass the government.[84] In any
event, their action led to a number of arrests when miners attempted
to stop delivery. Attacked by a hail of stones when other miners
attempted to free the prisoners, troops fired on the demonstrators at
La Ricamerie. Thirteen strikers were killed, and many more were
wounded. L'Eclaireur, the republican paper financed by Dorian, immediately took advantage of the shooting to denounce the regime and
organized a collection for the families of the victims.[85] The republican
majority in the municipal council drafted a protest to Paris, and
seventeen of its members resigned when the mayor refused to support them.[86]

The following night the strike leaders were arrested; sixty-one were
eventually convicted and sentenced to prison terms. The government,
which hoped to maintain its influence over the moderate elements in
the leadership, acquitted some of the leaders of the Caisse fraternelle.
Those who were republicans, however, such as Rondet, or who were
supported by L'Eclaireur, received harsh sentences.[87] The republican
leadership continued its courting of the miners after the trial and

simultaneously eliminated the threat to its own claims of political leadership by discrediting the moderates in the Caisse; Renault, its president, had previously planned to run for the Corps législatif.[88] In the aftermath of the strike, the prefect persuaded the companies to establish higher wages and shorter hours and was able at last to create a central company-supported accident and retirement fund.[89] But the miners had been won over to the republican cause, and they received the news of the general amnesty of the strike leaders issued on the hundredth anniversary of Napoleon's birthday with hostility.[90] In November a ceremony over the graves of the La Ricamerie victims became the occasion for a large republican demonstration.[91]

L'Eclaireur continued to support the strike demands of other groups as well. The Legitimist newspaper La Loire, financed in part by directors of the Terrenoire company, also began taking the workers' part. Recognizing the success with which the republicans were using the strike movement, its editor supported the demands of ribbon weavers in the hope of creating a rival working-class following.[92] Only the local administration and its merchant supporters were unable to adopt a more generous attitude toward labor.

The ability of the opposition leaders, especially steel manufacturers, to support demands made by workers in other industries lay at the heart of the new labor politics of the 1860s. Labor relations in the steel industry were relatively untroubled. High wages helped keep steelworkers docile. Puddlers earned as much as Fr 12 per day, and skilled workers in foundries received Fr 4 to 5. Wages of other groups within the industry were also good. Their standard of living thus was very high for the region, and contemporaries were struck by the hardy, athletic appearance of steelworkers in contrast to the pale and often dispirited ribbon workers and miners.[93] The wives of some steelworkers also worked, thus making their families more prosperous than any other artisan group.[94]

Working conditions were also attractive, and most workers enjoyed considerable independence on the job. Even puddlers ran their own furnaces and were paid by the quality and quantity of steel produced. Artisan metalworkers also found freedom as well as high wages in the industry. Large projects, such as the building of warships, were usually divided into smaller jobs subcontracted to independent craftsmen who worked at their own pace.

Because of the wages and working conditions in the industry, steelworkers appear to have been generally impervious to radical propaganda. A "labor aristocracy," such as Eric Hobsbawm found within British industry after 1850, seems also to have begun to develop in the Loire. High wages, social security, and good working conditions were among the factors Hobsbawm used to identify this labor elite; all were present in the Loire steel industry.[95] Steelworkers also received many benefits only large companies could provide. These included accident and retirement funds, initially created by Jackson frères, Petin et Gaudet and copied by Holtzer et Cie, Verdié et Cie, and other firms.[96] Dorian built model housing for his workers and provided their children with free education.[97] By the end of the 1860s a decade of prosperity had prepared the industry for an even greater expansion of benefits. Following the example of the Compagnie générale, which had introduced profit-sharing under the Second Republic (when it had been opposed by the local authorities for binding miners too closely to the company), a similar scheme was introduced at Terrenoire in 1869. Management believed this benefit was in part responsible for the company's dramatic increase in production. Euverte, a company director, explained that "the principle of obtaining the most possible from the worker by paying the least possible, such as is followed by some of the coal companies, is erroneous. One should, rather, pay what is necessary to obtain the most possible."[98] By 1869 Petin and Gaudet also introduced a profit-sharing plan. The ability of the industry to encourage skilled labor through such schemes and to yield to infrequent wage demands without endangering profits helped prevent strike agitation. Workers were even occasionally willing to support their employers politically. Although steelworkers at Firminy and St. Chamond formed an independent mutual aid society during the last years of the empire, strikes in the industry did not occur until after 1870. It was only when skilled artisans were faced with technological changes that threatened job status that they began to organize to resist change.[99]

These conditions greatly helped industrialists in the opposition. Dorian was accused by more radical opponents of having led his workers to the polls both in 1863 and 1864 and of using them as political "shock troops" to disrupt radical meetings during the legislative campaign of 1869.[100] In the Conseil général election of 1866, a director of Terrenoire received more than eleven hundred votes from the twelve hundred workers in the plant. Although steelworkers were more likely to support their employers if they promised political reforms than if they supported the government, conservatives such as Petin and Gaudet also received most working-class votes during the Conseil général elections.[101] It was only in the period of political unrest after 1869 that support even for conservatives began to wane.

The Commune at St. Etienne and Its Aftermath

The implications of economic development, which allowed some industrialists successfully to court working-class support, emerged clearly in 1870. The level of strike activity continued to mount during the first months of the year. A cloth printers' strike began in April and was followed in May by a miners' strike at Rive-de-Gier; both were supported by the republican press. Despite the liberalization of the imperial regime and the promise of parliamentary responsibility, republicans continued to support Léon Gambetta's Belleville program. This program called for universal suffrage free of government interference, freedom of the press, the right of assembly and of combination, trial by jury for all political offenses, the separation of Church and state, and the elimination of the standing army in favor of a militia. The republicans also opposed the plebiscite held by the government in May 1870, which asked the voters to approve the "liberal reforms effected in the constitution since 1860." L'Eclaireur claimed that the result at St. Etienne, where more than fourteen thousand negative votes were cast (the highest proportion of any city in France), was a great victory for workers and the republican cause. Only five thousand voters supported the government's reforms. The paper also approved of the peaceful way in which antigovernment forces celebrated the victory. "The dignity of the democratic party proved," it wrote, "that the Republic does not stand for disorder and pillage, but for liberty, progress and *security*."[102] The liberal opposition seemed to be successfully avoiding the divisions that had weakened the republican coalition in 1848-49.

The first indication of potential violence appeared in August, when an unidentified band of armed men appeared in the streets after midnight; they were easily dispersed by the police. Although the purpose of the group was never discovered, L'Eclaireur was quick to call for the maintenance of order. The paper continued, however, to

direct its attacks against the administration. It criticized the recruit-
ment of the wealthy into the National Guard and claimed that the
government's arming of two thousand rich men had a bad effect on
an already agitated population.[103]

Despite the efforts of moderate republicans, an independent radical working-class movement, similar to that which had overturned
middle-class rule in 1848-49, began to reemerge in 1869. The Société
populaire, a small artisanal organization, had been founded in 1868.
The following year it presented its own list of candidates for the
election to the Corps législatif. *La Sentinelle populaire*, the press organ
of the society, immediately began to attack the method of choosing
republican candidates from among the wealthy. "In 1869," it reported, "Dorian had initially decided not to run again for the chamber, and so in imitation of the majority of the deputies, who treat their
office as a benefice, decided to choose his successor." The article
ended by asking: "Is St. Etienne a village peopled by ignorant serfs? Is
it a fief?"[104] By 1870 the society began to attract the support of ribbon
weavers and after the creation of the republic continued its attacks on
the moderate leadership. In November it demanded immediate municipal elections and denounced the Alliance républicaine, the middle-class organization controlled by Dorian and his political allies,
which had become the dominant political force in the city.[105]

The Société populaire again presented a separate list from that of
the Alliance républicaine during the legislative election of February
1871 and denounced "the *haute bourgeoisie*, which always allied itself,
after its political victory, with the enemies of the people." The society
claimed that "the so-called Alliance républicaine was born without the
support of the people, and thus is without any mandate save that
received in the antechamber of several pashas." *La Commune*, another
of the city's radical journals, called for a thoroughgoing social revolution and threatened the destruction of France if its demands were not
met.[106] But as in 1849, bourgeois republicans were unwilling to support demands for full employment, a minimum wage, or price controls on rent and food. Posters now began to appear calling for the
creation of a commune, for the resignation of the mayor, and for new
municipal elections.

Despite the obvious danger of such demands, the liberal elite
continued to enjoy broad working-class support, in part because
workers in different industries lacked political coordination.[107] Ribbon

workers, to whom most of the articles in *La Commune* were addressed, provided most of the supporters of the radical movement, but they remained isolated. There was, therefore, little danger of collective action among different working-class groups, as had occurred under the Second Republic.[108] The moderates retained their influence among both steelworkers and coal miners and were able to keep workers in the various trades divided.[109]

The success of the liberal strategy was demonstrated in the legislative election in February, when the majority of St. Etienne's voters supported the moderate republicans—Dorian received more than nineteen thousand votes, while the radical list received only six thousand. At the same time *L'Eclaireur* began to moderate its stand on social issues, fearing the further growth of the radical movement. It also fired Antoine Chastel, a ribbon weaver and member of the Société populaire, from its editorial board.[110] This action, however, only increased the distance between the liberal and radical camps.

La Commune now increased publication of broadsides against the middle-class republican leadership. It claimed that only the radical leaders of the Société populaire favored popular control of the city and the end of the exploitation of the working classes. "The bourgeoisie of *L'Eclaireur* and the Alliance républicaine," it wrote, "are no different from the conservative bourgeois supporters of *Le Mémorial de la Loire*, since all live at the expense of the workers, and all will unite against their emancipation. The Alliance républicaine has already begun making advances to the Orleanists behind the backs of the working class."[111] The paper warned that in the coming municipal elections "the White reaction would blend with the Rose reaction," as it called the moderates. In the midst of the growing inflation, *La Commune* told its readers that they were the white slaves of industry and could never hope to improve their conditions under the existing social order.[112] In an article entitled "The Inefficacy of the Strike," it explained that even if workers did manage to raise their wages through strikes, the rising cost of living would wipe out all their gains, leaving them as badly off as before.[113] The author's conclusion, that a fundamental change in the economic system was necessary to improve living conditions, was particularly threatening to the liberal elite.

The seriousness of the threat was not at first apparent even after the establishment of the Paris Commune. Under the leadership of a central committee composed of moderate and radical republicans as well as socialists, the leaders of the Commune had demanded only greater municipal autonomy, while also calling on Parisians to expel the German invaders from France. Liberals continued to play an important role in the city's government, and Dorian, the provisional government's minister for armaments, was one of the most popular figures in the capital. It was in this period that he emerged as an influential national leader. Then, while the government at Versailles was preparing to suppress the Commune by force, another commune was established at Lyons.

News reached St. Etienne of the Lyons commune on March 23 and marked the beginning of a brief period of intense radical activity.[114] The Central Committee of the Société populaire called a giant meeting to discuss the question of a commune. The society's local following had increased earlier in the month when it held a rally attended by more than sixteen hundred workers demanding the immediate expropriation of Bonapartist property and the extradition and trial of Louis-Napoleon ("Moustache III"). The leadership of the Alliance républicaine had wisely refused to have anything to do with this and similar meetings. On March 23 a delegation from the Central Committee demanded that the municipal council resign and that new elections be held. The council instead declared itself in permanent session and prepared to resist an armed rebellion. But by March 25 workers' demonstrations had become so threatening that seventeen municipal councillors resigned. The Alliance républicaine, however, remained adamant in its decision not to make any concessions to the Société populaire. When the remainder of the council announced that it would continue to govern, several hundred members of the society, supported by units of the National Guard, seized the Hotel-de-Ville and demanded the immediate establishment of a commune.[115] Nineteen remaining municipal councillors refused and were arrested, and the leaders of the Central Committee took control of the city government. The new municipal administration included Barthélémy Durbize, a bookkeeper and, like Chastel, a former member of the staff of *L'Eclaireur*, and Etienne Faure, a shoemaker, anarchist, and member of the Association internationale des travailleurs.[116] After the collapse of the Lyons commune, however, the Central Committee was forced to accept the promise of the municipal council to submit the question of a commune to a vote. They then evacuated the Hotel-de-Ville. The following evening a group of workers supported by members of the National Guard once again proclaimed a commune in the city and arrested the newly arrived prefect, who was murdered during the night; the Central Committee took control of the city's police force and promised new elections.[117] But when regular troops arrived from Lyons, St. Etienne's commune promptly collapsed, and the mayor and municipal council were restored to their functions.

The ease with which the commune was defeated suggests that its creation was not the expression of a majority of the working classes but rather of those ribbon workers who had supported radical candidates in 1869 and would do so again in 1871. The liberal *L'Eclaireur*, which during the brief existence of the commune had attacked these radical elements as the greatest enemies of democracy, immediately resumed its briefly usurped role as spokesman for the "people." It blamed events in the city on the National Assembly, rather than the artisans, claiming that the refusal of the deputies to declare themselves in favor of a republic had goaded the workers to violence.[118]

The liberals also attempted to regain radical support. Arrests of members of the Central Committee began in late March and continued through April. Liberals feared that the new prefect sent to the Loire was antirepublican and warned against new conservative plots to overthrow the republic. The Alliance républicaine therefore joined with the remaining leaders of the Central Committee to present a joint list in the municipal elections to oppose the prefect's candidates. These elections, held in May, produced another victory for the moderate republicans, and *L'Eclaireur* hoped that the central government would not impose a reactionary mayor on the city in the face of such unanimity. By June, the paper was even defending the idea of the commune. Rejecting rumors that it was connected with communism, it claimed that the rising had been inspired merely by a desire for municipal autonomy.[119]

It is clear that industrial development hindered working-class political organization during the period of the Second Empire. Even the establishment of the commune at St. Etienne, supposedly the most vivid assertion of working-class political strength, revealed important weaknesses within the city's artisanal community. Liberal elites both in the Loire and in France generally were therefore much better able to exert influence over the republican movement than they had been in 1848-49. The establishment of the Third Republic signaled the triumph of those politically moderate notables who, in the course of the 1860s, had come to head the republican opposition.

6

The New Politics
of the Elite at Reims

The mechanization of the woolens industry at Reims was accompanied by a protracted struggle between liberal notables and the Bonapartist dictatorship. Local political life during the first decade of the Second Empire had been totally controlled by Paris. Although the conservative party had been saved from the threat of popular rule, it was unable after 1852 to free itself from the political tutelage of the imperial government. Conservative leaders had hoped to regain the local influence they had enjoyed under the July Monarchy. Instead they found themselves under the control of the prefect appointed by the minister of the interior. Because they were incapable of creating any ties with workers' organizations, they could not act as spokesmen for popular interests but had to depend on government control of elections to achieve political office. In the 1860s, however, a liberal opposition group developed that was able to win popular support and to defeat conservative candidates. The triumph of the liberal elite in the last years of the empire marked the recreation of a genuinely popular middle-class political leadership for the first time since the establishment of the dictatorship.

The republican leadership from the period of the Second Republic provided one element of the new liberal opposition. This group was strengthened in the course of the 1860s by a younger generation of the city's leading republican families, and was joined by smaller entrepreneurs, liberal professionals, and shopkeepers who opposed government interference in local elections. But the most important new element in the liberal coalition was the growing number of manufacturers who opposed the government. The opposition enjoyed the support of younger manufacturers who had benefited both from the mechanization of industry and the introduction of free trade. These men believed that the prosperity created by modernization had eliminated the threat of a radical revolution, and they regarded the imperial government's controls of local political life as outmoded. They saw continued government interference less as a necessary source of security than as a threat to their own political independence. Confident of their ability to control their workers, they began to demand an end to laws against working-class organizations as a means of winning popular support. By the late 1860s they had also become adept at coordinating their program with the economic demands of a growing number of workers' mutual aid societies. Cooperation between the bourgeois opposition and workers' groups, combined with a loosening of government controls of elections, enabled the liberal elite eventually to become the most powerful political force in the city.

The municipal council was the first target of the liberal assault. The leaders of the opposition believed that the election of a liberal municipal council would be a political statement far more important than the limited powers exercised by the councillors, and they first began to seek municipal offices in 1865. Places in the Corps législatif, which promised a more important political role, were pursued by the wealthiest members of the opposition. The capital resources of manufacturers were used to create an opposition press which preached the need for reform and encouraged workers' support for the bourgeois republican cause.

Economic development in the 1860s played a major role in bringing about these political changes. But changes at Reims were more subtle than those at St. Etienne. Unlike the situation in the Loire, where industrial development created a new elite independent of an older mercantile group, the major established manufacturing families at Reims continued to provide the leadership for the opposition. Greater economic integration between newcomers to Reims and older manufacturing interests also helped prevent the development of a distinct new group of notables. In addition, family traditions played a stronger role in determining the leadership of republican and Legitimist factions under the empire. But the prosperity of the woolens industry in the 1860s did affect the political attitudes of the bourgeoisie. It was widely believed in manufacturing circles that mechanization had secured the city's future prosperity, and fear of social unrest was therefore greatly reduced. The result was increased middle-class support for liberals demanding a restoration of parliamentary life.

The important relationship between economic life and politics was illustrated by the role played by the Société industrielle. Originally conceived as a meeting place for manufacturers interested in the mechanization of industry, the society soon became a club for liberals, and its elected leadership combined support for free trade and industrial modernization with demands for a republic and free parliamentary institutions. In this way it helped transform the Orleanist sentiments of the majority of Reims's bourgeoisie. Although in the 1840s Orleanism had stood for a narrowly based electorate and an authoritarian ministry, by the 1860s it had begun to evolve into a liberal ideology compatible with universal suffrage. A growing number of notables were willing to tolerate free elections if they produced results favorable to bourgeois interests. Members of this group were not republican in that before 1870 they did not openly advocate the creation of a republic. After the establishment of the Third Republic, however, they easily accommodated themselves to republican institutions. These manufacturers were the political inheritors of those liberal Orleanists who, under the leadership of Léon Faucher, had opposed the Guizot system in the 1840s.

Their main opponents were the conservative Orleanist manufacturers around Werlé who had supported Guizot and subsequently rallied in the 1850s to the authoritarian empire. A good number of them were champagne manufacturers. Conservatives under the empire, they eventually became Legitimists through marriages into families of the *ancien régime*.[1] The Second Empire thus marked the slow division of Reims's Orleanist party into moderate republican and Legitimist elements, with the republican party being the main beneficiary. By the end of the 1860s they began to accommodate themselves to a new political alliance between entrepreneurs, members of the liberal professions, and broad elements in the working classes. Based upon demands for greater political liberties, their political program allowed them to defeat conservatives and control political life at Reims through the 1870s.

Political Life in the 1850s

The municipal council first created under imperial auspices in 1852 had contained many leading conservatives, including Lecointre, the president of the Chamber of Commerce, Werlé, Carteret, Aimé Richardot, and Theodore Belin, all leaders of the old conservative party, and manufacturers such as Walbaum-Heidsieck, Lanson, Vivès, and Andrès.[2] But once restored to power, some of these men, nostalgic for the parliamentary government that had existed under the July Monarchy, had attempted to establish their independence of the dictatorship. By the time of the November plebiscite they had become the government's most unyielding opponents, and eleven of the thirty new municipal councillors refused to adhere to the address pledging support for the regime.[3] By 1853, *La Concorde*, originally founded by conservatives such as Werlé to support the "Prince-President," had become so critical that the prefect closed the paper.[4] Members of the former liberal opposition, who before 1852 had borne the brunt of government repression, once again began to take heart and redoubled their efforts to organize the middle-class opposition. Former republicans worked to recruit new members for the Masonic Lodge, long a stronghold of liberal and republican opinion. Their attempt to resurrect a second lodge, though prevented by the administration, demonstrated the extent of their popularity.[5]

The principal reason conservatives gave the new regime even moderate support was fear of a renewed alliance between middle-class republicans and workers. The discovery that Henrot, Bienfait, and other republican leaders had distributed seditious pamphlets in the city reawakened concerns about working-class violence and thus strengthened the government's position.[6] The prefectoral administration was also obliged, in lieu of the development of a strong and influential Bonapartist party, to continue to support conservative Orleanists. The conservative-Bonapartist alliance was strengthened in 1853 by the discovery of a secret woolens workers' association organized by Lecamp's son, and it remained in force through the rest of the 1850s. In 1855, *Le Courrier de la Champagne*, the city's "official" newspaper, told its readers that the government had decided to support the council first elected in 1852. "This measure," it wrote, "adopted by the higher administration, attempts without impeding the independence of electors to prevent false protestations and unrealizable demands."[7] The election demonstrated the continuing dependence of conservatives on the government. Voting was very light, and although the old council was reelected, some councillors received as few as 862 votes; overall only 2,444 votes were cast out of a registered population of 9,258 voters.[8]

Hoping to increase its popularity, the imperial government chose Nicolas-Henri Carteret, a successful notary with family connections among the woolens manufacturers, as its official candidate in the 1857 legislative election. Long one of the city's most important conservative figures, he had helped found the *Journal de Reims* in 1838 and was mayor between 1845 and 1848. He had resigned after the establishment of the Second Republic, being in the words of one republican leader "too proud . . . and too imperious to cope successfully with the conditions of the moment." Carteret might therefore have been expected to support the restoration of conservative rule by the Bonapartist regime. But he had opposed the coup d'état while a representative in the Legislative Assembly and had become very popular in the city by refusing to support the restoration of the empire.[9] The government however was by this time so desperate to bring about a political reconciliation with a majority of the middle classes that it was willing to ignore its candidate's previous record of opposition.[10] Prefects in this period often asked Paris to support popular local figures in order to prevent the nonofficial candidacy of potentially successful dissidents.[11]

Although the government continued to depend on the support of only a small minority of Reims's bourgeoisie, these included many of the city's wealthiest manufacturers. Mathieu-Edouard Werlé, the leader of the conservative party under the July Monarchy, was the most important of these. By 1860 he was the most powerful political figure in the city.

Werlé's tremendous capacity for work had made him a successful manufacturer and political leader even before 1848. President of the Tribunal of Commerce until the establishment of the republic, he had been appointed acting mayor in 1850. But despite his administrative abilities, his German origin and cold, arrogant manner prevented him from becoming a popular local figure. The establishment of the Bonapartist dictatorship, however, greatly aided his political career by creating the conditions that enabled him to achieve high political office. He could devote his vast energy and bureaucratic skills to the regime without having to court the electorate and was rewarded with a series of appointments. Werlé was appointed mayor of Reims in 1852 and retained the post until 1868. In 1862 he received the government's nomination for the Corps législatif and was elected through the efforts of the prefect and police. Anxious to solidify his position, he arranged the marriages of his children into important families in the imperial party; his son Alfred married the daughter of Gustave Lannes, comte de Montebello, and his daughter Matilde married the son of Napoleon III's finance minister, Pierre Mange.[12] Through his influence in Paris Werlé became the most important political figure in Reims, able occasionally to act independently of the prefect. With the whole of the municipal administration under his control and powerful allies in the capital, he dominated local political life until the revival of the opposition in 1865.

The Development of the Liberal Opposition in the 1860s

The municipal elections in 1855 and 1860 took place without any serious challenges, and the entire council was reelected; Werlé and the members of his administration received the largest number of votes. The election also reflected the beginning of a reconciliation between the imperial government and elements of the city's middle classes.[13]

But the most significant event of this period was the economic changes caused by free trade with England and the American Civil War. The Chevalier-Cobden treaty produced new schisms within the manufacturing elite, as English competition put a premium on more efficient production. Pioneers in the mechanization of industry suddenly began to enjoy an advantage, while the mass of more traditional manufacturers, characterized by the *procureur général* as "prudent, circumspect, and the enemies of innovation," were threatened with elimination from the market.[14] The woolens boom after 1861 had an even more important effect on political life. It produced the prosperous conditions that convinced manufacturers that the Bonapartist regime was no longer necessary to prevent revolution.

Many younger manufacturers who were later to support the opposition favored free trade, seeing "in tariff reforms the beginning of a period of industrial development which would allow them to surpass the present chiefs of Reims industry."[15] Industrial development after 1860 strengthened the economic position of this group. It also increased their political influence, for the growth of factory industry created new means for employers to influence workers. Factory hands, organized under foremen, were more susceptible than artisans to political pressure. Industrial development also permitted the establishment of paternalistic programs, such as the provision of subsidized meals at the Holden factory, which allowed manufacturers to convince themselves that they could purchase the loyalty of their workers. Simon Dauphinot, a member of the liberal opposition since 1848, spoke for many factory owners when he addressed a meeting on the paternalistic duties of the industrial employer.[16] A number of manufacturers began to feel they could safely challenge the controls on political life exercised from Paris. Along with support for free trade, their demand for free elections divided them from an older merchant group still wedded to artisan labor and the dictatorship; this younger group increasingly supported the liberal opposition which was the leading advocate of both free trade and political liberty.

The development of political life at Reims was also stimulated by the extension of parliamentary liberties that began in November 1860. The Senate and Corps législatif were allowed to draft a reply to the address from the throne, and parliamentary debates were for the first time reported in the press.[17] The police measures that previously had reduced Legitimist, republican, and Orleanist opposition groups to powerless coteries were eased.[18] Public hostility to the government, though widespread, had been deprived of leadership. After 1860, the opposition began once again to take heart and increase its efforts to win local political office, although before 1865 it had little success.

The quiescent period of political life between 1860 and 1865 was in part a result of the woolens boom. The police also continued to play an important role in preventing popular as well as middle-class meetings. Following the suppression of their organizations in 1854, workers had ceased to play an important role in local politics; most radical leaders under the republic had either died in North Africa, like Bressy, or become supporters of the regime. Although artisans and some factory workers continued to remain restive, they were unable to act until further liberalization in the mid-1860s allowed them to organize. Working-class demonstrations did not begin until the beginning of a new economic crisis in 1867, providing a new surge of popular support for republicans.[19]

Middle-class opposition developed somewhat earlier, stimulated by resentment of government interference in local elections. In 1862, Werlé had been able to defeat the Legitimist candidate, Ruinart de Brimont, in a bitterly fought legislative by-election, but he had needed all the government support he could get.[20] Noting the way in which Brimont used the issue of government partisanship, the prefect reported that even a candidate with as much official support as Werlé was susceptible to a massive loss of middle-class votes.[21] Resentment of government interference also encouraged cooperation between Orleanists and republicans.

Through 1862 the sub-prefect continued to warn of the growing political frustrations of former Orleanists and their attempts to exploit popular discontent by adopting a moderate republican program.[22] Orleanism was thus forced to undergo great changes under the empire, becoming less the expression of loyalty to a particular dynasty than the desire to maintain individual liberties and regional independence.[23] By the 1860s it came increasingly to stand for the free exercise of parliamentary government in the style of England. Though still nostalgic for the July Monarchy, Orleanists were increasingly willing to accept a republic based on universal suffrage that promised a restoration of parliamentary government controlled by the middle classes. At Reims, this change was effected through the political activities of a younger generation of industrial capitalists who remained loyal to the Orleanist cause because of family traditions but who believed they could use free elections for their own political advantage. With the depression of the 1840s behind them and an apparently brilliant industrial future ahead, the younger generation believed that new accommodations could be made with workers without threatening the dominant position of the elite. In the 1860s the Orleanist label came to represent a pedigree, a sign of wealthy and conservative political antecedents, rather than a political program to restore the fallen dynasty. This change explains the ease with which many liberal "Orleanists" were able to make common cause with moderate republicans. Middle-class manufacturers were willing to support republican candidates because they appeared a reasonable alternative to Werlé and his authoritarian administration.

Not all of the new opposition candidates were members of a younger generation. Villeminot-Huard, the liberal candidate in the 1863 Conseil général election, had been a republican leader under the Second Republic and from a poor family. But like many of the younger generation he was a pioneer in the mechanization of industry. He was also the president of the Société industrielle, the bourgeois club devoted to the modernization of the woolens industry.[24] The prefect remained neutral in the struggle between Villeminot-Huard and Louis-Philogène Camu-Bertherand, the conservative candidate, for fear of arousing local hostility. But following the first inconclusive balloting liberal hopes ended when Villeminot dropped out of the campaign. He was replaced by Landouzy, the head of the School of Medicine, who was easily beaten; a physician, he lacked the prestige enjoyed by a major manufacturer such as Villeminot.[25] It was becoming clear that the reputations and influence of wealthy industrialists were as necessary as organized working-class support for liberal success.

The legislative election of 1863 was the last time Werlé was able to run unopposed. Because he faced no opposition, the prefect dispensed with the direct intervention of the police, telling the sub-prefect that he could "doubtless use them to watch men hostile to the government . . . but only with extreme caution." Still, all of the usual government measures on behalf of its candidate were observed: public meetings were forbidden, and the distribution of antigovernment pamphlets was stopped by the police. The prefectoral administration also paid the expenses of Werlé's campaign.[26] But the election generated little popular interest, and voting was light; the official candidate received only sixty-seven hundred votes out of a registered population of more than fifteen thousand.[27]

After 1863, rising profits in the woolens industry began to stimulate the political ambitions of some industrialists, and this too increased pressure on Werlé and the government. Although the problem of finding places for "new men" was a perennial one faced by French governments, the demands of the new generation after 1860 were particularly pressing, having emerged out of the greatest period of prosperity the city had known.[28] Many manufacturers, the *procureur général* wrote, were angered by their inability to exercise a political influence equal to their economic standing in the city. Attempts to influence the decisions of the national government through meetings or the establishment of political journals had been sharply curtailed by the prefect. The prefectoral administration's inability to find local offices for some manufacturers thus provoked resentment and drove some *fabricants* into the opposition. Among the most volatile members of this group were younger manufacturers, who were also among the most enthusiastic supporters of factory industry. "Knowing past revolutions only as history," the *procureur* reported, "they are encouraged by youthful ardor and inexperience to use political agitation to further their ends."[29] Combining support for free trade with demands for greater political liberties, members of this group began to support the opposition in greater numbers. They included some of the city's most important pioneering manufacturers: Wagner (one of the founders of Wagner-Marsan), Charles Rogelet, whose family had long been a leader in the woolens industry, and Edouard de Brunet, as well as Villeminot-Huard and Warnier. The latter two were also officers of the influential Société industrielle. By the late 1860s all the society's officers were active members of the opposition.

Warnier was the most politically successful of the younger industrial group. The son-in-law of Adolphe David, a leading manufacturer, and a republican leader in 1848, he was a supporter of both free trade and industrial modernization. He was also an eloquent exponent of liberal doctrines within a business community usually given to public reticence on political questions. Warnier used any available platform to expound his belief in industrial progress and the need for political reforms. A highly technical study for the Société industrielle on the newest chemical techniques for processing wool became in his hands a panegyric to science and the future prosperity of the textile industry.[30] As president of the society after 1860, he was able to find a larger audience for his ideas. Believing in progress, laissez-faire, and the free political institutions he regarded as a necessary corollary of both, he chose as his favorite theme the need to reduce government interference in political life. He claimed that business itself could make necessary concessions to labor to prevent social unrest. Confident of the ability of bourgeois employers to control their workers, he favored free exercise of the suffrage as well as elementary education, telling the society in 1865 that "in order to empty our prisons, we must fill our schools."[31]

Warnier eventually turned his attention to the larger electorate, developing a program of political reforms that gained the support of many workers. "An aristocrat by instinct, but a democrat through ambition," wrote the sub-prefect, "Warnier has already won a considerable reputation among the bourgeoisie because of his intelligence and ability, and is preparing himself for future political struggles through his courting of the working class." The local Masonic Lodge, headed by the republican leader Dr. Thomas, was also a center of liberalism. The son of a laborer, Thomas had studied medicine in Paris before becoming an anatomy professor at Reims's medical college in 1853. He had eventually been drawn into politics and by the 1860s was trying, like the leadership of the Société industrielle, to win popular support for a moderate republican program. The lodge also attempted to recruit many younger and newer manufacturers, thus hoping to develop an influential membership. Allied with veteran republican politicians such as Maldan and Mennesson-Tonnellier, liberal Masons began to spread republican propaganda among workers and small shopkeepers.[32] But fearful of adopting too radical a program, the leaders of the opposition were at first unwilling to specify the exact liberties they wished to conquer. They did not want to raise questions about wages and working conditions that might threaten profits, and therefore preferred simply to demand an end to government interference in elections.[33]

Werlé's political ascendancy, based on the support of the imperial government and the absence of any strong political party in the city, was first seriously challenged in 1865. The government's unwillingness by this time to interfere in local elections further weakened the mayor's position. The public had become so sensitive about government intervention that the prefect was obliged to take an increasingly neutral position.[34]

The opposition's first attack on Werlé came during the municipal elections, when the liberal opposition, laying its plans with great care, drew up its first list since 1852. It included manufacturers such as Villeminot-Huard and Jules Houzeau and prominent republican leaders including Adrien Henrot, Mennesson-Tonnellier, and Maldan. The liberals also included Legitimists such as Charles Rogelet and Henri Paris on their list, hoping to benefit from Legitimist popularity among portions of the working classes.[35] Le Courrier complained that the inclusion of well-known republican leaders gave the local election an undesirable political coloration, but the liberals, who wanted to turn it into a contest between Bonapartist and republican principles, continued to emphasize political issues.[36]

The combined efforts of liberals and Legitimists created the first major victory for the opposition at Reims. Werlé still received the greatest number of votes, but eleven members of the opposition were elected to the council, including the Orleanist manufacturer de Brunet and moderate republicans Villeminot, Houzeau, Maldan, Henrot, and Mennesson-Tonnellier. Three Legitimists, Rogelet, Paris, and Auguste Maille, were also elected; the latter two had done especially well in the working-class third canton.[37]

Although still dependent upon Legitimists for electoral support, the liberal opposition was soon able to acquire its own following. Legitimists had won votes through the distribution of coal and bread, but liberals attracted support by sponsoring democratic reforms. In 1867 they founded a local branch of the Ligue d'enseignement to promote the establishment of free compulsory lay education. Under the leadership of its board, a coalition of Orleanists and republicans that included Mennesson-Tonnellier, Maldan, Bienfait and Thomas, manufacturers Houzeau and Victor Diancourt, and Orleanist bankers Alexandre Auger and Camuzet, it began to spread republican propaganda as well.[38] Its energetic president, Eugène Courmeaux, a radical from the period of the Second Republic, was soon able to report a large working-class membership. It thus provided the liberals with a weapon equally useful against the government and their Legitimist rivals.[39] Recognizing the political purposes to which it was being put, Werlé had opposed the formation of the league, and had for a short time been able to prevent its public meetings. The *procureur général* had also warned against the spread of lay education, considering it dangerous because of the republican opinions of some of the teachers. But although Werlé finally eliminated all municipal subsidies for lay schools in 1868, he was too late to slow the spread of republican ideas. Liberals had already begun to receive an increasing number of workers' votes.[40]

Moderate republicans struck another blow at the administration in 1868 by creating a new political journal, an action facilitated by the new press law that eliminated the system of official warnings, suspensions, and suppressions that previously had controlled newspapers. The republicans thus broke the monopoly previously enjoyed by *Le Courrier de la Champagne*. They also bested the Legitimists, who had been planning an opposition paper since 1864.[41] The board of *L'Indépendent rémois*, as the new paper was called, included Camuzet and Auger, the Orleanists who had helped found t' e Ligue d'enseignement the previous year, and republicans Diancourt, Houzeau, and Thomas.[42]

The opposition was also aided by growing antigovernment feeling among even conservative notables. The new army law introduced at the end of 1866, which outlawed the purchase of substitutes for military service, outraged many manufacturers. This law, combined with growing fears about the government's Mexican adventure, encouraged conservatives to question other government policies as well. These stirrings gravely threatened the unity of the group around Werlé, which had previously provided the firmest support for the regime.[43] Among the most outspoken critics of the army law were Florens Walbaum, an important manufacturer, and Camuzet, one of the most important figures in the Comptoir d'escompte, who later supported both the Ligue d'enseignement and L'Indépendent rémois.[44]

Werlé's conservative program was becoming a danger to the government as well as to himself. A loyal agent of the regime, he had fought the opposition to the new army law, although doing so had cost him some support, and his increasingly autocratic manner threatened further losses. His attempt to retain the support of merchant manufacturers by opposing free trade was also deeply embarrassing to the government. The mayor hoped to win over the less efficient manufacturers least able to meet workers' demands for higher wages and so most in favor of a strong municipal government with broad police powers. Since both free trade and political reforms were basic government policies, Werlé's position weakened his standing in Paris. His disagreement with the regime to which he owed his appointment as mayor threatened to bring his municipal career to an end. By 1867 the sub-prefect warned the minister of the interior of the danger of supporting the mayor. Pointing to an article in the Parisian L'Epoque, which had reported that the municipal administration was creating "enmities which continue to grow geometrically," he predicted that the conservative leader would yet succeed in turning the entire population against the regime.[45]

Werlé's resignation in 1868 was received by the administration with relief. He had opposed the prefect's sanctioning of the Société de St. Louis, a woolens workers' mutual aid society, claiming it was merely a front behind which workers could establish a strike fund.[46] The prefect, however, wanted to court working-class voters before the legislative elections. Aware of the tensions in the woolens industry since the end of the boom in 1867, he thought the application of liberal policies might win artisans away from the republican opposition.

After Werlé resigned, *L'Indépendent rémois* hailed the new municipal administration, chosen from among the first five names of the council elected in 1865, as the beginning of a new period in the city's history. Simon Dauphinot, a republican, was appointed mayor by the Ministry of the Interior; Rogelet, a Legitimist ally of the liberals, was one of the four deputy mayors.[47] But the reconciliation with the regime was short-lived. There were still municipal as well as legislative offices to be won, and Dauphinot, the government's political appointee, soon replaced Werlé as the symbol of the despised dictatorship.[48] By the end of the year *L'Indépendent rémois* was attacking the new administration as vehemently as it had previously attacked Werlé's. It also began to criticize the Bonapartist system generally, commenting upon "the pitiful spectacle of the destiny of France being tied to the person of the emperor."[49]

Although continuing to demand political reforms, *L'Indépendent rémois* took a moderate line on social issues. Since the end of the woolens boom and the increase in labor unrest, the paper's middle-class backers were becoming uneasy about criticism of industrial conditions. The paper continued to support the right to strike in principle but told workers they should remain patient and moderate in their demands. "Workers who acted intemperately or who sought radical solutions to their problems," *L'Indépendent* warned, were as "blameworthy as manufacturers who refused to meet the just demands of labor."[50]

Through 1869 growing numbers of workers joined the potentially dangerous Société de résistance. But *L'Indépendent rémois* resolutely defended the local elite, and blamed economic difficulties on the interests closest to the imperial regime. The newspaper attacked large fortunes made through speculation and defended with violence, as at La Ricamerie. But it was also careful to point out that those fortunes were based on monopolies and sinecures distributed by the government. The fortunes of the notables of Reims, it emphasized, were acquired through hard work and astute business dealings. Disagreeing with Huard, the leader of the Société de résistance, who claimed that capitalists produced nothing, *L'Indépendent* said that "the intelligent application of capital was as necessary as labor for the preservation of national prosperity."[51]

Liberals were also anxious to win the support of shopkeepers who had earlier allied themselves with the radical movement.[52] They hoped thereby to divide the petty bourgeoisie from the Société de résistance, and thus reduce its influence. *L'Indépendent* therefore began to criticize the use of a restricted electorate of notables selected by the prefect to choose the Chamber of Commerce as a "vestige of the centralist, aristocratic spirit fostered by the empire." The paper suggested that the chamber be elected through a broader suffrage, so as to put the existing social order on a more democratic and stable foundation.[53] The combination of democracy and social stability, which was the essence of the moderate republican program, had great appeal for the city's shopkeepers.

The first split in the liberal coalition appeared in 1869, a product of the political reforms creating the Liberal Empire and of a growing fear of radicalism. The decision of a committee including Warnier, Auger, Thomas, Diancourt, and Henrot to support Jules Simon, a republican of national reputation, in the legislative election caused several moderates, including de Brunet, to come to Werlé's support.[54] Simon had long been a moderate republican and had voted with the majority in the Constituent Assembly in 1848. But after his election to the Corps législatif in 1863, he had distinguished himself as an outspoken critic of the empire. The prospect of an eloquent opponent of the regime haranguing the city's workers in a period of falling wages was too much for some Orleanists to accept.

Further defections took place over other issues. The prospect of a free parliamentary life under the Liberal Empire, combined with the repeal of the law of Sûreté générale of 1858 (allowing the arbitrary arrest of political dissidents) had impressed some members of the elite. The Corps législatif was for the first time given the right to propose laws, criticize and vote on the budget, and choose its own officers. Even more important, the ministers were to be responsible to the legislature. The government also promised to enlarge press freedoms by eliminating stamp duties on newspapers and to introduce jury trials for press offenses. Even the autonomy of local government was increased. Theodore Zeldin has suggested that the reforms were so popular that both the restoration of parliamentary rule and the preservation of the imperial dynasty seemed possible.[55] Certainly some liberal Orleanists, although never strongly attached to the regime, now began to find new reasons for supporting the empire.

These measures, however, also helped strengthen the opposition because it was now free to criticize the regime. The government's position in the city was further weakened by its support of Werlé in the election, despite his opposition to Ollivier's reforms. The candidacy of Jules Simon had forced the regime to support the former mayor.[56] But Werlé, though helped by the prefect and conservative champagne manufacturers Lanson, Vivès, and Roederer, won little support in the city. Many manufacturers and workers remained hostile, and *L'Indépendent rémois* spoke for many voters when it attacked his record on social and political reforms. It reminded its readers that Werlé had opposed the extension of the suffrage under the July Monarchy, which had "finally led society to the abyss," and that he continued to oppose the extension of secular education, an issue made popular by the Ligue d'enseignement.[57]

Werlé had by the last years of the empire become a political anachronism, defending society from a revolutionary threat few manufacturers feared. He continued to support political controls that maintained his own power at a time when most of the elite found them onerous. Liberals were able to create a much more attractive political program. They claimed that society could be preserved only by increasing political liberties, thus appeasing workers while satisfying the political ambitions of the elite. They were also helped by the inability of the conservative party and the government to create organizations necessary to win mass support. All the workers' mutual aid societies supported liberal or radical candidates, as did the Société de résistance and the Ligue d'enseignement. *Le Courrier*, in a feeble attempt to enlist popular support for Werlé, listed the gifts he had made to music societies, churches, and scholarships, but with little effect.[58]

The liberals' most serious competition came from the Legitimist candidate, Henri Paris; the prefect, too, feared that the party would win the majority of working-class votes in the election.[59] Paris was also popular among the middle classes, both as a supporter of the existing social order and as an enemy of the imperial system. Like the liberals, he favored the extension of local liberties, the abolition of the system of official candidates, and the establishment of ministerial responsibility.

Werlé won the election because of the conservative majority in the countryside, but liberals and Legitimists carried the city. (Simon received 8,400 votes in the department to Werlé's 18,000.) The two opposition groups received more than 6,300 votes, as compared with only 4,400 for Werlé.[60] More than 4,600 votes had gone to Jules Simon; Henri Paris got only 1,651.[61] After the election there were hostile demonstrations by workers in front of houses illuminated to celebrate the conservative victory. It was clear that moderate republicans had captured a majority of popular support in the city.

The growth of the Société de résistance created the first serious threat to liberal ascendancy because many of its leaders were as hostile to liberals as to conservatives. Until the fall of the empire, however, liberals and Legitimists continued to regard the imperial government as their chief enemy and never felt obliged to take a conciliatory line with the regime. Liberal opposition to the plebiscite of 1870 was intense, being organized both by *L'Indépendent rémois* and the Masonic Lodge; Thomas, the head of the lodge as well as secretary of the Société de résistance, used the issue of free education to urge workers not to support the government.[62] *L'Indépendent*, repeating its tactics of the previous year, made a special appeal to shopkeepers. In an article entitled "Le vote des commerçants," the paper reminded them of the dangers in which the empire placed them, externally because of the "armed peace" that threatened at any time to lead to war and domestically through the growth of government-supported monopolies that were already destroying small businesses.[63] The apparent inability of the government to create a coherent foreign policy since the collapse of the Mexican Empire also helped turn many middle-class voters against the regime.

Werlé loyally attempted to organize support for the government, but Dauphinot and the municipal administration did little to cooperate.[64] Many manufacturers were also hostile. But despite the unpopularity of the regime, the opposition enjoyed less success than it had anticipated. Less than half of the city's registered voters participated in the plebiscite, but the majority of those who did supported the regime.[65] The opposition in the aftermath of this setback once again concentrated on local political issues. Its attacks on the government moderated and, increasingly fearful of the Société de résistance, it attempted to divert attention from radical demands with a campaign to extend local liberties. "What is needed at the moment," wrote *L'Indépendent rémois*, "is the political education of the masses through municipal self-government, an end to prefectoral tutelage, and the right of the communes to elect their own mayors."[66]

The Liberal Revolution at Reims and the Transition to the Third Republic

The revolution at Reims that marked the final consolidation of power by the liberal opposition was sparked by external develop- ments: the Franco-Prussian War that began in July 1870 and the military collapse of the empire. The first French defeats in August were followed by working-class demonstrations at Reims against the local administration, and the opposition was quick to make use of these to win additional seats in the municipal elections held that month. Among the members of the opposition elected were Jules Houzeau, who received the largest number of votes, Henrot, Maldan, and Mennesson-Tonnellier, as well as manufacturers César Poulain, Victor Diancourt, and St. Marceaux; a member of the Tribunal of Commerce, St. Marceaux had distinguished himself by opposing the government during the plebiscite.[67]

A ten-member commission chosen to govern the city after the fall of the empire was controlled by men in the opposition, including Dauphinot, who was appointed president, Marteau, Charles Rogelet, Victor Diancourt, and Henri Paris. Liberals and Legitimists had also worked together to create a unified party of order during the transfer of power in September.[68] But in the months that followed liberals were able to use their greater popularity among workers to reduce Legitimist influence. In February 1871, moderate republicans elected three of their own number, Warnier, Thomas, and Dauphinot, to the National Assembly.[69] From that time on, the only two important political forces in the city were the newly dominant liberal group and the rapidly growing workers' movement organized by the Société de résistance.

The liberals' first clash with working-class radicals came during the municipal elections held in April and May 1871. A workers' commit- tee under socialist leadership, similar to that which had challenged bourgeois control of the city in 1849, presented a separate list of radical republican candidates. Courmeaux, who as president of the Ligue d'enseignement had great influence over artisans and factory workers, told voters to support only genuine republicans. This advice threatened to undermine support for several former Orleanists on the moderate list. But there was little real chance of a radical success in 1871. Workers were divided because of rapid economic changes in the previous decade, and the radical leadership had been heavily infiltrated by liberals. Unlike Bressy or Lecamp, strangers without local connections who had come to the city during the period of the Second Republic, Courmeaux was related to such influential moderate republicans as Henrot and St. Marceaux and was allied to liberal interests through the Ligue d'enseignement.[70] Thomas, secretary of the Société de résistance, also played a moderating role in radical circles. Finally, the Prussian occupation of the city, which began on September 4, helped prevent the establishment of a commune such as appeared in Lyons, Marseilles, and St. Etienne during the transition of power.

Both Warnier and Thomas, realizing bourgeois interests were protected, gave their support to the moderate republican list, and L'Indépendent rémois also confidently supported the moderates. These included Warnier, Diancourt, Marteau, and Poulain, as well as the banker Auger, and doctors Bienfait, Henrot, and Thomas.[71] Still conservative in tone, Le Courrier complained of the emphasis on politics in a municipal election. It stressed the importance of electing competent administrators rather than republicans of limited abilities.[72] But the liberals had made a shrewd tactical choice. Considering the tenor of national developments, they came out strongly on the side of republicanism and thus were able to consolidate their own power and successfully compete with the program of the Société de résistance. The establishment of the Third Republic, far from producing a social revolution, thus marked the triumphant culmination of the liberal political revolution begun in 1865. The power of the old conservative group was steadily eroded by a coalition of longtime republicans and liberal Orleanists, but bourgeois interests remained protected. Businessmen all over France similarly gave their support to Thiers's conservative republic as the best means of coming to terms with the republican movement while avoiding revolution.[73] The creation of the Third Republic forestalled discussion of social questions for almost fifteen years. In 1872 Gambetta told the nation that "there is no longer a social question," and in 1877 Thiers said, "One no longer speaks of socialism and that is good. We have been freed of socialism."[74]

At Reims, liberal-republicans easily defeated conservatives in the municipal elections of 1871. Only four candidates on the conservative list, which included men from the group around Werlé as well as Legitimists such as Paris, were elected. Among the victorious liberals were Poulain, Warnier, Diancourt, Thomas, Auger, Bienfait, Henrot, Courmeaux, Mennesson-Tonnellier, and Simon Dauphinot.[75] The post of mayor was given to Poulain, a partner in the large manufacturing company Benoist ct Cie; in 1872 he resigned and was replaced by Diancourt, another moderate republican manufacturer.[76] During the period of the Paris Commune the prefect feared a popular rising at Reims, and rumors circulated that Dauphinot's factory would be burned. But republicans won all of Reims's three cantons in the Conseil général election.[77] Bienfait won in the second, and Courmeaux defeated Paris in the heavily working-class third, thus marking the eclipse of Legitimist influence in the city.[78]

Le Courrier de la Champagne chided the middle classes for abstaining from the elections: "While the committees of workers and radicals march together to the polls . . . the bourgeoisie sleep. When danger comes, they hide themselves or run. . . . For the present the urgent need is for the Conservative-Liberal party to stir itself from its torpor."[79] But these political dangers hardly existed at Reims; the conditions that had created the social and economic crisis of 1848-49 had been fundamentally changed under the empire. Workers who had united under the Second Republic through artisan craft organizations were now divided between artisan and factory groups. Immigration further weakened working-class organizations. Although the Société de résistance remained a potential threat to manufacturers, internal divisions reduced its effectiveness. The real revolution of 1870-71 was not directed by workers against the elite but by a coalition of middle-class interests against the conservative Orleanists around Werlé.

The most important factor at Reims in the evolution of political life under the Second Empire was the transformation of Orleanism. The Société industrielle, at the center of the modernizing element within

the manufacturing group, played a vital role in this change. It became
a meeting place not only of the most economically progressive elements among the elite but also of those members of the middle classes
who most wanted to reestablish parliamentary government. The
elected leadership of the society, in vocal opposition to the authoritarian empire, played an important role in political life in the 1860s.
Although many opposition leaders came from republican families,
manufacturers without republican antecedents also began to support
the liberals. The slow change of the political climate in the city,
stimulated by economic development, allowed the latent hostility of
the majority of the middle classes to the Bonapartist dictatorship to
become in time a cautious acceptance of a moderate republic. At St.
Etienne, where there were fewer ties between merchant and industrial manufacturers, changes in the economy had more radical effects
on political life.

7

The New Politics
of the Elite
at St. Etienne

The relationship between industrial growth and the republican opposition is clearer at St. Etienne than at Reims. In the Loire heavy industrialists previously outside of political life came to dominate the local republican movement. They were able, with the support of workers and other middle-class groups, to reduce the political power of the ribbon-manufacturing oligarchy even before the fall of the empire.

Widespread hostility to the merchant elite had made it more difficult for the imperial government to reestablish conservative rule at St. Etienne than at Reims. Artisanal organizations remained strong, and many shopkeepers and smaller manufacturers continued to oppose the policies of the central government. Because most ribbon merchants did not take an active role in political life, it was impossible to create a strong local Bonapartist party. Although aware of the security offered by the destruction of workers' mutual aid societies, they remained unwilling to support the new regime actively.

The government's weakness had been revealed in the legislative election in 1852. Many middle-class voters declined to support Jules Balay, the government's candidate; others favored Benoît Fourneyron, a former conservative supporter of Cavaignac in the Constituent Assembly. Most workers were also hostile. Many opposed Balay both as a representative of the ribbon-manufacturing oligarchy and as one of the largest shareholders in the Compagnie générale.[1] With little support among either the middle classes or ribbon weavers, he was ultimately obliged to seek the help of the mining company, which pressured its employees to vote for him.[2]

Municipal Elections of the 1850s

The continued opposition of all classes to the Bonapartist regime was again demonstrated during the municipal elections in June 1852. The voters returned several former republican leaders but refused to support the administration's candidates chosen from among the merchant group. The government suffered an additional setback in November. Encouraged by the liberal opposition, more than half the city's voters refused to participate in the plebiscite approving the establishment of the empire; only 10,595 affirmative votes were cast at St. Etienne out of a registered population of 23,625.[3]

It was not until 1853 that the regime was able to exert sufficient pressure to elect its own candidates to local office. At Outre Furens, an industrial suburb of St. Etienne, the mayor openly checked workers' ballots.[4] At St. Etienne, citizens not appearing on the electoral lists of 1848 and 1851 were disenfranchised. Because town workers were among the most mobile elements in the population, this measure, like the residency requirements for voting established under the Second Republic, reduced republican support. As a result, only 2,456 votes were cast in the election, which reversed the results of the previous year and returned a municipal council more representative of ribbon-manufacturing interests than any since the establishment of the republic. Vignat fils, Victor Colcombet, André Merllié, Jean-Pierre Malescourt, Denis Epitalon, Brunon-Chalayer, and Auguste Faure were among those elected; only Philip-Thiollière and Neyron-Desgranges represented the interests of heavy industry. Faure-Belon, another ribbon manufacturer, was named one of the city's four deputy mayors. Men in the republican opposition such as Voytier, Soviche, Dubois, and Tiblier-Verne, who had been elected to the council the previous year, were eliminated.[5]

Conservatives were elected again in the municipal election of 1855. But despite government hopes that the councillors would be able to rally the support of their artisan employees, most workers remained hostile.[6] As at Reims, conservative victories could be produced only by eliminating all independent political organizations, and never represented any real support for the dictatorship from workers or most of the middle classes. Through the 1850s, however, the political power of the conservative party appeared to grow. In 1855 Faure-Belon was appointed mayor, and an additional seat on the Conseil général was filled by another ribbon manufacturer, Jean-Claude Vignat.[7] The following year the prefecture was moved from Montbrison to St. Etienne, giving the city's conservative party yet another advantage through its position and patronage in the new departmental capital.

The government also attempted, as at Reims, to increase middle-class support for the regime by warning of a continuing revolutionary threat to society. Arms discovered in the possession of the secret society, the Pères des familles, in 1856 seemed to demonstrate the potential for working-class violence, and the harsh sentences imposed on its leaders were approved by elements within the middle classes.[8] Even fear of a popular insurrection, however, was never sufficient to reduce the hostility of most shopkeepers and smaller manufacturers to the ribbon oligarchy, as became apparent in the legislative election of 1857.

The government supported Jules Balay for reelection. His most important qualification, *Le Mémorial de la Loire* wrote, was his ability to represent the city's ribbon trade. Balay employed more than fifteen hundred artisans, and it was generally assumed that he could count on their votes; with the help of other ribbon manufacturers, his election seemed assured. The official press therefore reproached the "men of the former liberal opposition, who through their positions in the city might better than any other group bring about the reconciliation of the old parties with the empire, but who instead continue to oppose the imperial government in a quixotic attempt to regain so-called lost liberties." Days before the election, the republican leadership, mostly middle-class professionals, decided to support Eugène Pelletan.[9] A Parisian writer and former follower of Fourier, he had no ties to the city. The result, however, was another rout for the government. Despite Balay's business interests, he received only 1,559 votes; Pelletan received 4,866.[10] In the eastern half of the city another republican, Sain, almost defeated Hippolyte-André, comte de Charpin-Feugerolles, the other official candidate.[11] The terrible weakness of the Bonapartist position at St. Etienne was again exposed, and the inability of the government or its few supporters to create a political clientele obliged the administration to maintain tight controls over public life.[12]

The business practices of ribbon merchants was one important reason for conservative weakness, for the rapacity of many manufacturers was a continuing irritant to artisan weavers. A few employers, such as Auguste Guitton, who worked in the administration of the city's hospitals, attempted to improve conditions. Auguste Gerin, who established the Hospital of the Infant Jesus and the agricultural colony for workers at St. Genest-Lerpt, was another exception. But most entrepreneurs lacked any interest in philanthropy and were even unwilling to distribute charity in depressed times, as did Reims's Legitimist party, or to provide the limited public assistance supplied by Werlé's administration.[13] This was in part the result of the continuous movement of merchants in and out of the city, especially in the 1850s, when many manufacturers left St. Etienne after making fortunes during the ribbons boom. The rapid turnover made it difficult for the government to create a stable conservative party with any sense of civic responsibility. The government's support of wealthy manufacturers such as Balay, who remained at the center of the elite, never provided it with a broader influence in the city.

Merchants remained immune to the hostility of artisan workers and middle-class dissidents as long as the government was willing to support conservatives with all the coercive means at its disposal. It was not until men from the new industrial group such as Dorian, the director of the Holtzer steel company, began to participate in local politics that the opposition saw some success. Until then, it lacked the funds necessary for a major campaign against government-financed candidates. In the municipal election of 1860, although the number of voters participating was very low, the largest number of votes went for the first time to the conservative mayor, Faure-Belon.[14]

Beginning in the 1860s, the rapid growth of heavy industry introduced new manufacturing interests into political life. The liberal opposition was also strengthened by the establishment in 1861 of a second political journal at St. Etienne. The paper was created, ironically, by Persigny, the minister of the interior.[15] A native of the Loire, he retained a special interest in the department and decided to increase the regime's popularity by allowing press criticism of the merchant interests that had previously dominated the city. He also hoped to create a Bonapartist consensus among broader elements of the middle classes by favoring increased press freedoms while reducing overt government support for the unpopular oligarchy. But the attempt to win support through attacks on the very men who owed their positions to the ministry was successful for only a brief time. By the end of 1861 Charles Robin, Persigny's hand-picked editor of the new liberal *Courrier de St. Etienne*, had begun to despair of increasing his paper's influence and attempted to improve circulation by attacking the mayor.[16] Faure-Belon reacted at once by demanding government protection.[17] Although both the prefect and the *procureur général*, who better understood the policy being pursued by the minister, initially refused to help, the mayor was eventually able to force Robin to pay damages through the courts.[18]

Embittered by what he considered the government's betrayal, Robin became increasingly estranged from the regime. He finally broke with Persigny during the legislative election in 1863 and vigorously supported the opposition candidates. The 1863 election thus marked the beginning of an alliance between a liberal newspaper and the opposition. When a similar union was created later in the decade, made possible by the liberalization of the press laws and the ability of industrialists to finance opposition journals, local political life was transformed.

Dorian and the Revival of the Opposition

Francisque Balay was one of the city's two official candidates in the 1863 election, having inherited government support as well as a large fortune from his uncle.[19] The other candidate was the comte de Charpin-Feugerolles. The opposition, which had begun to rally around the department's more progressive industrialists, supported Benoît Fourneyron and Frédéric Dorian. Fourneyron was the son of a surveyor. After attending St. Etienne's Ecole des mines, he worked for the Le Creusot mining company before becoming rich through the invention of a widely manufactured water turbine. Although a former supporter of Cavaignac, he was a popular figure in the city because of his opposition to the Compagnie générale.[20] Dorian had also attended the Ecole des mines and had subsequently started a sickle factory in the Haute Loire. His marriage to a daughter of Jacob Holtzer led to his becoming a director of the Holtzer company. Dorian's paternalistic treatment of his workers and support of liberal reforms had made him a popular figure among both artisans and the smaller bourgeoisie.[21]

Dorian was the first of a new generation of heavy industrialists, excluded from participation in political life since 1852, to challenge the older merchant group.[22] Previously, the government had rewarded them only with minor offices. In 1857, Alexandre Jullien, the chairman of the Terrenoire steel company, had been appointed mayor of Pelussin, Hippolyte Petin of Rive-de-Gier, Ernest Neyron of St. Chamond, and Jules Holtzer of Chambon-Feugerolles.[23] Jullien and Petin also sat in the Conseil général for St. Etienne. Jacques Claudinon, another industrialist, represented the mixed rural and industrial canton of Chambon.[24] Dorian had first been elected to St. Etienne's municipal council from Valbenoîte, an industrial suburb. Save for Dorian, all owed their offices to appointment by the government. In the 1860s, however, an increasing number ran as opposition candidates, hoping to use popular support to win major office without the support of the ministry.

As at Reims, industrialists entered political life for various reasons. Desire for the prestige of local and national office was combined with the wish to return to parliamentary government. High wages and peaceful labor relations in the steel industry convinced some industrialists that the need for continued police control of workers' mutual aid societies was over. Employers who, like Dorian, were committed to meeting the educational and housing needs of their employees were able to combine paternalism with demands for an end to government interference in elections. His program, which included support for secular education and workers' rights to organize and strike, was popular among both the middle classes and workers.

Liberal and republican industrialists were relative newcomers to the opposition, but they supplied it with considerable energy. The unique element they contributed, in addition to their prestige, was the money necessary to finance political campaigns. Theodore Zeldin believes that the emergence of these new candidates, men who virtually bought their seats in the Corps législatif through lavish spending on campaigns, was one of the most important political developments of the 1860s.[25] As money replaced government patronage as the means to achieve political office, older manufacturing interests were forced to give way before the greater resources of industrialists. Throughout France a growing number of successful manufacturers joined the opposition ranks. At St. Etienne, the combination of a popular political program supported by industrial figures and publicized by a well-financed opposition press allowed the creation of a coalition of dissident middle-class elements. The merchant elite lost its monopoly on political office and was obliged to share power with industrialists, smaller manufacturers, and liberal professionals.

In 1863, *Le Courrier* supported Dorian and Fourneyron as "liberal and industrial candidates" who best represented both the region's new industries and spirit of political independence. Praising Dorian as "a man both loved and respected for his liberal and independent spirit," the paper contrasted him with Balay and Charpin-Feugerolles, whom it claimed were pawns of the administration.[26]

The prefect vigorously attempted to reduce the opposition's support, asking several major industrialists heavily dependent on government orders to pressure their workers on behalf of the official candidates. The mayor also attempted to prevent workers without electoral cards from voting. Nevertheless, industrial centers in the first two electoral districts gave overwhelming support to the liberals. Dorian and Fourneyron received 4,074 and 3,700 votes respectively, while Charpin and Balay got only 759 and 785.[27] *Le Courrier* claimed that if the city administration had not opened so few polling places in the hope of limiting voting, the opposition would have done even better.[28] Balay eventually won because of his support in rural districts, but Dorian won enough votes to defeat Charpin. *Le Courrier* made much of the meager support St. Etienne had given one of its chief mercantile manufacturers, contrasting it to the popularity of a modern industrialist with "progressive liberal opinions."[29] The *procureur général* at first hoped that the new deputy, being allied to one of the region's wealthiest families, would draw away from the artisanal and shopkeeping elements that had supported him. Instead, Dorian soon made himself the leader of the opposition in the department. After 1863 he came increasingly to be the arbiter of local political fortunes, a role that had previously belonged to the prefect and the imperial government.[30]

Le Courrier, however, did not long survive the election. Faced with large deficits and increasing government pressure to close down, it ceased publication in 1864.[31] Robin said in the last issue that he had hoped to create an opposition party through a union of working-class voters with elements in the elite that could profit from the political eclipse of the ribbon manufacturers. He eventually came to realize, however, that a liberal pro-government party could never develop under the authoritarian empire. "The new liberal party," he wrote, "is neither a coalition of the old parties, nor a resurrection of the movements that had failed in 1830 and 1848. . . . Rather, the new liberalism, supported by the most diverse elements in the population, is attached to the principles of '89." But independent journalistic efforts were not sufficient to end the political rule of the old elite. Without the support of local notables, a maverick journalist such as Robin could do little to change political life. Local prejudices against an outsider were, as he finally realized, too strong to overcome. In one of his last editorials he concluded that "in certain large provincial cities, where there are only several hundred bourgeois families all connected by friendship and family ties, a journalist who takes an independent political position and imposes on himself the duty of fighting old prejudices, absurd ambitions and ridiculous vanities makes enemies on all sides, even among those members of the bourgeoisie he does not attack, because they all consider themselves threatened."[32] It was only when notables themselves systematically began to attack the local administration that it was possible to create a successful coalition of bourgeois interests. By 1865 republican industrialists had come to head such an amalgam of local elites and were poised to capture local government.

The efforts of *Le Courrier*, however, did contribute to the opposition by encouraging cooperation between liberals and artisan workers. In 1863 Robin had tried to persuade artisanal voters that support for Dorian and Fourneyron was a revolutionary act.[33] His efforts were to bear fruit in 1865. "What is overwhelmingly evident in the political life of this city," Robin had written in 1864, "is the need to act against certain men and the party to which they are allied."[34] Under the influence of manufacturers such as Dorian and Thomas Henry Hutter, a director of the Société anonyme des houillères de Montrambert et de la Berardière, diverse elements created a committee to choose candidates for the forthcoming municipal elections.[35]

The elections of 1865 marked a turning point in local political life. The established interests, whose representatives included Faure-Belon, Christophe Balay, and Brunon-Nublat, the president of the Tribunal of Commerce, as well as Jules Paliard and the baron Camille de Rochetaillée, were replaced by men who would control politics through the 1870s. Most of these were less wealthy members of the middle classes, smaller manufacturers, and shopkeepers with close ties to artisan workers. A few were modern industrialists who because of their greater wealth and prestige tended to be leaders of the opposition. Ten of the most influential of the new council members also belonged to the Masonic Lodge, which since the 1840s had been a center of liberalism. Among them were Jacques Clapeyron and Pierre Boudarel, a small ribbon manufacturer who became mayor of St. Etienne in 1871. Several others, including Benoît Crozet, the owner of a metallurgical factory at Le Chambon, Jules Chillet, a rubber manufacturer, and Hutter, represented the new industrial interests in the region. Two members of the council, Voytier and Tiblier-Verne, were also veteran republicans who had served on the council under the Second Republic. But while some had long political careers behind them, the composition of the new council suggests a generational as well as political struggle. Faure-Belon, one of the four members of the old council to be reelected, was sixty-three, but Boudarel was only twenty-eight, Victor Duchamps twenty-nine, Clapeyron thirty-six, and Chillet thirty-nine.[36]

Following the election, the government appointed Benoît Charvet, a coal dealer and one of the most moderate of the new councillors, as mayor; deputy mayors were also chosen from among the moderates.[37] But Paris was clearly disturbed by the election results and by the growing belligerency of the new council. The ministry therefore decided to hold new elections as soon as possible. By the end of the year it had forced the resignation of seven of the new councillors, including Chapelle, a liberal lawyer, and Boudarel. The *procureur général* reported with some anticipation that as soon as nine seats became vacant, new elections could take place.[38]

It was still not apparent by 1867 that the government could no longer win elections in the city. The minister of the interior that year supported Félix Escoffier, the entrepreneur of the Manufacture Nationale des Armes, against Dorian for one of the Conseil général seats from St. Etienne. From the government's point of view, Escoffier was an excellent candidate. He was an important manufacturer whose attempts to modernize the arms industry were in keeping with the government's plan to make French manufacturing competitive with that of England. He was also a major employer of local labor. The prefect thought that if only half of Escoffier's workers voted for him, he would win.[39] Escoffier seemed to the government a social and political moderate, equally opposed to republicans and Legitimists, qualities which the government thought would give him wide appeal among the middle classes. He told a group of electors that "we live in a time when industry is producing new marvels, and under a reign in which hard work and industrial merit are rewarded. Of course, there are some who regret the end of an age which shall never return or dream of new social upheavals; some imbued with ancient prejudices and a desire to see the return of divine right and the accident of birth the only source of nobility; others, implacable enemies of society, who wish to lower everyone to the level of brutes."[40] But Escoffier's views, reminiscent of Guizot's conservative Orleanism in its belief that the wealthy had a right to rule, did little to inspire support. Indeed, he was one of the most unpopular figures in the city. His attempts to mechanize production in the Manufacture Nationale angered many artisan workers, and his position in the arms industry was resented by other manufacturers. Most voters supported Dorian, the leader of the Union démocratique, which had organized the liberal victory of 1865.

Dorian won the election with 1,065 votes; Escoffier received only 947. But the baron Vital de Rochetaillée, the Legitimist candidate and nephew of a former municipal councillor, did much better than the prefect or the republicans had expected; he received 973 votes.[41] As at Reims, reduced government controls had helped the Legitimists, who became important rivals to the liberals. Rochetaillée and his party received most of their votes from the rural cantons and from urban voters who were influenced by the clergy. Like the republicans, they supported a popular political program demanding an end to government interference in local elections. Although the Legitimists' in the Loire never enjoyed the economic resources of Reims's royalist champagne manufacturers, they received considerable support through the political crisis of 1869. It was only when the program of administrative decentralization demanded by the party had been won and growing radical agitation frightened Legitimist leaders that the party ceased to court working-class votes. By 1870 Legitimists were no longer serious rivals to republicans in the city.

After 1867, awareness of the importance of working-class voters was clearly growing, and all factions within the elite competed for their support. The republican municipal council encouraged miners' demands for a central accident fund, and Legitimists attempted to follow their example.[42] Both liberals and Legitimists, profiting from the liberal press laws of 1868, also created new political journals with the financial support of figures in heavy industry. Since *Le Courrier de St. Etienne* had ceased to appear in 1864, the city had been left with only one newspaper, *Le Mémorial de la Loire*. Because of the small number of subscribers in the city, the prefect had opposed the creation of additional journals. He was convinced that a second political paper could survive only by fomenting unrest, as *Le Courrier* had previously attempted to do, and warned that a journal voicing working-class demands would find a large audience among artisans and miners.[43]

Dorian's financial support helped create *L'Eclaireur*. Because the official provincial press could count on government subsidies for the publication of legal notices, the opposition press, lacking this income, was heavily dependent on wealthy members of the opposition. Ten municipal councillors, among them Boudarel, Chillet, Clapeyron, Crozet, and Tiblier-Verne, as well as Antide Martin, the working-class leader during the Second Republic, joined Dorian in founding the journal. Boudarel, Clapeyron, and Dorian were also among the paper's first directors.[44] It supported the standard republican program, including the separation of church and state, free exercise of the suffrage, free compulsory lay education, restrictions on child labor, creation of a militia to replace the army, and the introduction of progressive taxation.[45]

The new Legitimist paper, *La Loire*, received financial support from Jullien and Carrete, both directors of Terrenoire. The company had previously supported the imperial government, and in 1864 de Bouchaud, a director, had run against Fourneyron as the official candidate in the Conseil général election. As late as 1866 the *procureur général* had praised the company directors for ensuring the political loyalty of their employees.[46] But by the late 1860s Terrenoire was less dependent upon government orders than previously, and the management began to attempt to establish an independent political following.[47] The paper also received funds from Rochetaillée and other wealthy landed proprietors who favored government decentralization such as Camille-Alfred de Meaux and the baron de St. Genest.[48]

The prefect immediately prohibited the sale of *La Loire* on the streets, hoping to reduce its influence. The cost of a subscription kept it out of the hands of most workers, who could only afford to buy individual copies in times of political crisis. Because of the administration's actions, as well as the conservative views of its founders, the paper originally had little influence in the city.[49] But as the prefect had predicted, *La Loire* soon began a vociferous campaign against the government to increase its readership, so that within months of its appearance he considered suppressing the paper.[50] The newspaper complained of the slowness of the transition to a more liberal regime and referred to the coup in 1852 as a tragic event in the life of the French nation.[51] The trial of its editor, Le Nordez, at St. Etienne in February 1869 provoked demonstrations throughout the department.[52]

The legislative election of 1869 thus took place in a highly charged political atmosphere and would mark the beginning of the definitive transfer of power to the republican coalition. It also marked the beginning of a struggle between the bourgeois opposition and the developing working-class movement.[53] In this period the republican and Legitimist newspapers continued to attack both the regime and each other, while the growth of workers' organizations further weakened the government's position. The largest workers' group, the miners' Caisse fraternelle, promised to support the regime if the prefect would extract concessions from the mining companies; artisan groups were less compromising. The political crisis for the empire that began with the election would not end until the regime's collapse. Radical agitation, however, continued well beyond the establishment of the provisional government and ended only with the destruction of St. Etienne's commune in March 1871.

The first radical threat to the bourgeois republican leadership emerged with Antide Martin's candidacy for the Corps législatif.[54] Martin had been a popular figure at St. Etienne under the Second Republic; he had easily defeated General de Grammont, the commandant of the state of siege, in the legislative by-election in 1849. He reentered political life in 1868 and immediately began to attack the middle-class leadership of the Union démocratique. The following year he warned voters that small numbers of wealthy citizens constituting themselves "grands électeurs" were trying to impose their own candidates on the general population and called for the creation of a republican organization controlled by artisan mutual aid societies.[55] The danger of a political movement led by artisans, which first appeared in 1869, continued to grow until the establishment of St. Etienne's commune in 1871. It was only after the collapse of the commune that members of the elite once again emerged as the undisputed leaders of the republican movement.

The radical threat had begun to frighten moderate elements in the opposition as early as 1869.[56] The announcement of Martin's candidacy, the first challenge to the notables' control of political life, had taken the leaders of the union completely by surprise. Their support began to erode almost immediately, when several radical members of the municipal council, including Chapelle, who had led the resistance to the municipal administration in 1868, went over to Martin. Martin also received the support of *La Sentinelle populaire*, a short-lived radical newspaper, which attacked Dorian as a capitalist exploiter who enjoyed large profits while simultaneously using the workers' movement to further his own career.[57]

Dorian, though the most important leader of the Union démocratique, had planned to retire from the Corps législatif and had chosen Martin Bernard, a venerable republican from the period of the Second Republic, as his successor. Although an adept politician, Dorian was not a good speaker and had never felt comfortable in the chamber; despite his forthright republican convictions, he had been chided by the radical press as "le grand muet" of the Left. He now felt obliged to act decisively and stand for reelection himself.[58] Bernard, a former typesetter from Montbrison, had neither the close connections with St. Etienne nor the prestige among the middle classes necessary to win. The subsidized republican press immediately came to his support. *L'Eclaireur* told its readers that for the opposition to be victorious it had to be united. It called Martin "un candidate liquidateur" and his supporters minor republican leaders without probity or influence. "Is Martin a democrat?" the paper asked. "We only know by his actions that he was an agent of destruction in 1868 and shall always remain so."[59]

The political program of Vital de Rochetaillée, the Legitimist candidate and nephew of Camille de Rochetaillée, posed another threat to the union, for it too demanded the extension of political liberties. Because the party was supported by *La Loire*, as well as landowning and industrial interests, its leaders expected to do well in the election.[60] The Legitimist danger was recognized by the radical and liberal press, and both attempted to draw workers away from Rochetaillée. The radical *Sentinelle populaire* complained that steelworkers at Terrenoire were being pressured by their employers to support the royalist cause. The liberal *Eclaireur* called Rochetaillée "the adopted child of the clergy whose privileges he would defend to the death" and claimed that Legitimist strategy was to win votes through the influence of the Church. The paper warned small manufacturers and artisans opposed to monopolies and special economic privileges not to be tricked by Legitimist promises. Only the creation of a republic, it said, could save small property owners from being destroyed by larger interests supported by the imperial government.[61]

The regime alone was unable to mobilize popular support for, having abandoned the use of police and prefect to help official candidates, it found that it could no longer influence voters. Religious institutions and working-class organizations were in the hands of Legitimists, liberals, or radicals. The government was therefore obliged to look once again to its only dependable political supporters, the ribbon manufacturers, who were among the largest employers of labor in the city. The prefect hoped that recent republican victories might frighten the merchants into greater political activity.[62] Although the manufacturers, in fact, exercised little influence over their workers or the mass of the smaller bourgeoisie, the government appealed first to Francisque Balay, the retiring deputy, and then to Faure-Belon, the former mayor, to represent it in the election.[63] Both declined to do so.

More than 18,000 votes were cast in May 1869 out of a registered population of 31,830; Dorian received 11,239 votes, Rochetaillée 4,908, and Martin 1,791.[64] The results demonstrated the continuing importance of groups within the elite in determining the outcome of local elections. Rochetaillée received his greatest support at St. Jean Bonnefonds and Rochetaillée, where he owned considerable properties, and at Terrenoire. The most significant result of the election, however, was the working-class support given to Dorian rather than Martin. Benefiting from his control of *L'Eclaireur* as well as his reputation as a wealthy and influential supporter of liberal reforms, Dorian was able to attract the majority of votes; most workers preferred a liberal industrialist to a radical of the Second Republic such as Martin.[65] *Le Mémorial*, St. Etienne's official journal, was disappointed with the election. It warned of the imminence of a Red revolution and saw local evidence of an emerging radical threat in the popular demonstrations that followed Dorian's victory.[66] But the liberal opposition was able to take a more sanguine view. Confident of its ability to control the workers, it remained relentless in its attacks on the government.[67]

The opposition continued to support strikes in the hope of further increasing its popularity. *L'Eclaireur* took the side of the miners against their employers in the early summer and continued to defend them after a strike began. It was also quick to attack the government for the La Ricamerie shooting, although it failed to mention that the incident occurred because of the Holtzer company's attempt to collect coal. *La Loire*, however, saw Dorian's complicity as the salient feature of the violence, and accused the republican leaders of deliberately creating an incident to embarrass the government.[68] The strike and the violence it provoked initiated a slow but definite change in the attitude of the Legitimist party to agitation, and it was in this period that Legitimists began seriously to reconsider their policy of supporting the workers' movement. They were becoming less certain that they could derive much benefit from encouraging independent working-class organizations. By the summer of 1869, *La Loire* hesitantly began to support the government. In the same period, the first steps were taken by its board for a reconciliation with the conservative party that was finally accomplished the following year.[69]

The disappearance of *La Loire* early in 1870 was one sign of the changing attitude of the party and marked the beginning of a period of cooperation between the government and several wealthy industrialists who had previously financed the paper.[70] *La Loire* claimed in its last issue that its task had been accomplished with the establishment of ministerial responsibility, a reference to the government's adoption of the plan of the 116 deputies of the so-called Third party. Under the leadership of Emile Ollivier, this group had begun to reestablish parliamentary government in France.[71] In May 1870 several of the paper's former backers therefore joined the ribbon manufacturers on the conservative local plebiscitory committee, which was headed by Euverte, one of the directors of Terrenoire.[72] But although various conservative groups in the city united against the republicans, their ability to influence the mass of voters began to decline. Except for the Legitimists, most conservatives did not know how to mobilize workers, having become accustomed to the administration acting on their behalf. The closing of *La Loire* ended the last chance of the antirepublican forces to exercise much influence over popular opinion. Moderate republicans, in contrast, had an active political organization developed through years of opposition to the government and gained support through 1870.[73]

Liberals continued assiduously to court the working-class vote through the last days of the empire. Until the split between the radical workers' movement and the moderate republican leadership in late 1870, *L'Eclaireur* consistently sided with workers against the administration. The paper claimed that the prefect was responsible for the miners' strike because during the election he had attempted to win votes for Charpin by encouraging the demands of the Caisse fraternelle. When he was subsequently unable to create a united accident fund, a strike became inevitable.[74] The paper also took full advantage of the shooting at La Ricamerie and, denouncing the army's role in the incident, started a subscription for the families of victims which continued until August.[75] Fifteen municipal councillors, led by Boudarel, Tiblier-Verne, and Clapeyron, demanded that the mayor request the immediate removal of troops from the city. The prefect then decided to suspend the council and replace it with a commission dominated by ribbon interests.[76]

La Loire supported this action and in its final issue denounced the defunct municipal council as a tool of the republican leadership. The leaders of the Union démocratique thus faced the combined opposition of both Bonapartists and Legitimists during the last months of the empire. But they demonstrated their ability to overcome them all during the plebiscite. The conservative *Mémorial* claimed that the republican refusal to support the reforms instituted since 1860 would lead to revolution and the plunder of the established interests. The antiplebiscitory committee replied that republicans alone were working to restore political liberties and that a vote against the government would further this end.[77] The committee included Dorian, Boudarel, Crozet, Clapeyron, Tiblier-Verne, and several other members of the suspended council. In the end, the opposition again prevailed. The electorate had been angered by the suspension of the council, and St. Etienne returned the highest proportion of negative votes of any city in France. A large number were also cast in the industrial centers of Chambon-Feugerolles, Rive-de-Gier, and St. Chamond.[78] Bourgeois republicans at first feared an outbreak of violence during the campaign but were relieved by the workers' peaceful conduct during the election, which proved, *L'Eclaireur* wrote, that "the new republic did not stand for disorder and pillage, but for liberty, progress and *security.*"[79] By the spring of 1870 liberal control of the city appeared complete. The extent of radical strength would become apparent only with the establishment of the commune that followed within months of the collapse of the empire.

The Third Republic and the Transfer of Power to the New Elite

The political influence of the older merchant group was only briefly restored by the commission established in June 1869; municipal elections in August 1870 returned the members of the council first elected in 1865. The government had hoped to increase the number of conservatives on the council, but only two were elected; Faure-Belon and Girinon, both ribbon manufacturers, won in the wealthy St. Charles electoral district.[80]

After the fall of the empire in September, a provisional municipal council, composed of most of the members elected in August, was created. Several radical working-class leaders were also brought into the council for the first time.[81] All conservatives, however, were excluded. The moderates welcomed radicals in the hope of preventing violence, and Tiblier-Verne's first proclamation as mayor was to demand respect for law and property.[82] The peaceful transition of power seemed to demonstrate the control of the middle classes over the popular movement. But despite the efforts of the provisional government to prevent the development of an independent artisanal political organization, radical sentiment continued to spread under the influence of the Société populaire.

The society, which had grown rapidly after the proclamation of the republic, had demanded immediate elections in September. This request was finally denied by the minister of the interior in November.[83] By that time, the first demonstrations by workers in favor of a commune had already taken place. When workshops for the unemployed were opened in December, the municipal government, fearing a rebirth of workers' organizations similar to those under the Second Republic, took steps to ensure that they would not again threaten middle-class control of the city; to reduce the amount of time available for political activity, unemployed workers were to be paid piece-work rates rather than a daily wage. The municipal government also depended upon the fifty-five companies of National Guards, formed shortly after the establishment of the republic, to quell any popular rising. Some elements of the National Guard, however, eventually supported the commune created in March.[84]

To contain the growing radical threat, moderate republicans attempted to win the support of the middle classes by assuring them that the republic was the only government capable of preventing further revolutions. During the legislative elections in February 1871 they campaigned in favor of a moderate, middle-class government, which they said would preserve both liberty and property.[85] In a pamphlet entitled *Plus de révolutions: Appel à la bourgeoisie*, the liberals asked the middle classes, who had created and then destroyed the first two republics, to support the new government. The bourgeoisie, it said, had both a political and financial interest in preserving the new regime because it provided the stability necessary to protect the social order.[86] Adding its own voice, *L'Eclaireur* warned that to vote for the old parties was to support men whose continued rule could provoke popular violence.

The Alliance républicaine, the new middle-class republican organization in the department, nominated Dorian, Boudarel, and Martin Bernard for the National Assembly. It also nominated Duchamps, the radical mayor of St. Chamond, in the hope of attracting the support of radical workers.[87] The radical Central Committee, connected with the Société populaire, presented a separate list supported by *La Commune*; this journal attempted, like *La Sentinelle populaire* before it, to draw workers away from the moderates in favor of a radical program demanding the end of the *livrets* and a government guarantee of full employment.[88]

Conservatives also presented a list which, like that of the moderate republicans, included several important industrialists.[89] Although Dorian, Holtzer, and Hutter remained leaders of the liberal movement, the Liberal-Conservative electoral list included Lucien Arbel, a director of the forges of Rive-de-Gier, and Alexandre Jullien, the chairman of the Terrenoire company.[90] General Louis Trochu, the president of the government of National Defense, Thiers, and Dorian were also included to convince voters of the party's sincere conversion to the republic. *L'Eclaireur* protested the linking of notoriously conservative figures such as Pierre-Auguste Callet (the editor of the new local Legitimist paper *Le Défenseur*, founded in October 1870) and Jullien with national republican leaders. Jullien supported the restoration of a monarchy and opposed the establishment of even a conservative Republic.[91] The salient feature of the electoral lists, however, was not the political attitudes of individual candidates but the emergence for the first time of a large number of local industrialists into national political life.[92]

Dorian won 19,245 votes in St. Etienne, and others on the moderate list also received large majorities. The conservatives got about 4,000 votes each and most of the radical candidates, such as Durbize and Durand, only 600.[93] Although the vote for Dorian was the largest in the department, the other seats went to Liberal-Conservative candidates, including Adrien de Montgolfier (an army engineer who later became a director of Petin and Gaudet), Jullien, Arbel, and Callet.[94]

Despite the relatively poor showing of the radical candidates in February, the influence of the Société populaire and La Commune continued to grow rapidly in the city through the early months of 1871, culminating in the proclamation of a short-lived commune in late March. The rising was easily suppressed by government troops, but the murder of the prefect initiated a new period of repression. Joseph Ducros, the new prefect of the Loire, suspended the National Guard and forbade all liberal political meetings.[95] Local liberals began to fear that the harsh measures taken by the government were the prelude to a new dictatorship. L'Eclaireur warned its readers to prepare for the suppression of local elected government and continued to urge the city's elite to support the republic. This plea was repeated during the destruction of the Paris Commune in May.[96] The duty of the elite, it said, was to fill the ranks of republican organizations with its own members, thus freeing the government from dependence either on the monarchist National Assembly or on the working classes. Only the bourgeoisie, the paper wrote, had the education and leisure necessary to prevent excesses by formulating a moderate political program.[97]

St. Etienne's conservative press, however, was encouraged by the government's actions after the rising. It blamed the revolutionary movement on the liberal opposition and hoped that government policies would result in a definitive restoration of conservative rule. Le Défenseur said the revolution had begun when liberal agitators roused the workers against the other classes in society, and Le Mémorial suggested that republican propaganda had rendered workers incapable of acting politically without violence.[98] The implication was that

France had to choose between anarchy or a return to authoritarian rule.

The virulence of the conservative polemics combined with the policies of Ducros encouraged cooperation between moderate and radical republicans, with the latter once again playing a subordinate role. Fearing new restrictions on the suffrage and a revival of the political power of the ribbon merchants under the patronage of the prefect, the Alliance républicaine and the remaining members of the Central Committee presented a joint list in the municipal elections in April 1871. They won thirty-two of the council's seats, while only four conservative candidates were elected.[99] Le Mémorial complained that in addition to conservative apathy many voters feared that Liberal-Conservatives were enemies of the republic, whereas the republicans were able to present their own candidates as moderates.[100]

In the aftermath of the commune, however, the republican triumph was precarious. The municipal council was again suspended by the prefect following a petition asking for leniency for the Paris insurgents.[101] As under the empire, the government appointed a commission made up of ribbon manufacturers, the only group willing to support its policies.[102] L'Eclaireur pointed to an additional motive for the suspension, "which was the wounded pride of rich men who, seeing that they could no longer govern the city under a truly democratic system, attempted to subvert the free exercise of the suffrage. But they deceive themselves if they believe that St. Etienne will long tolerate the rule of men who have gained office through usurpation and maintain themselves through base flattery of the prefectoral administration."[103]

The central government also attempted to reduce the influence of the Alliance républicaine and Central Committee through a mass trial of its leaders at Riom at the end of 1871. César Bertholon, Boudarel, Clapeyron, Crozet, Rolland, and Adrien Durand were among those accused of participating in the "moral complicity of the administrative authorities" that led to the creation of the commune.[104] Seven of the accused were sentenced to deportation but most were acquitted. They returned to St. Etienne where their influence in political life was undiminished. By May 1872 popular pressure forced the prefect to hold new municipal elections, which restored middle-class republican control of city government. Through the early 1870s the moderates solidified their position in the department.[105] In 1873 François Reymond, an engineer, defeated Faure-Belon, the conservative candidate, and succeeded Dorian in the National Assembly.[106] At the end of 1874 Etienne-Nicolas Moyse, a notary and also a moderate republican, was named mayor of St. Etienne; his council included Hutter and Fourneyron, who served as deputy mayor.[107]

The ability of moderate republicans to increase their political control in the department after 1870 demonstrated that the prefect's fears of social revolution were unfounded. In 1853 the restoration of the merchant oligarchy had filled a political vacuum left by the collapse of middle-class republican leadership in 1849 and of the workers' corporations in 1852. But the fall of the empire in 1870 revealed a new political coalition already in power. The most important element in this amalgam of elites was the new industrial group. Industrialists had both the funds to run electoral campaigns against the government and the prestige necessary to win widespread middle- as well as working-class support. They also brought an optimism about the future of industrial society compatible with the establishment of a free parliamentary system. Through their adoption of a republican program and their control of the opposition press, republican industrialists ensured the continuing political dominance of bourgeois interests at St. Etienne through the 1870s.

Conclusion

The evolution of French liberalism was the most important development in middle-class political life under the Second Empire and was facilitated by changes in the economy. With the rise of factory industry, a new group of industrialists had begun by the end of the 1860s to wage a successful struggle against their merchant competitors for national markets. Optimistic about their ability to provide good wages as well as high profits, these industrialists no longer feared a social revolution. As a result, they rejected Bonapartist dictatorship in favor of a republic they believed more compatible with prosperous times. The growth of anti-imperial sentiment in the industrial areas of France demonstrates this change. In 1852, the more heavily industrialized regions had put up less resistance to the coup than did the rural areas in the east and south.[1] But by the last years of the empire industrial areas were the most volatile centers of antigovernment opposition. This activity has frequently been interpreted to mean merely that many urban workers remained vociferous opponents of the regime. What is usually forgotten is that many members of the middle classes also vigorously opposed the empire and through the 1860s frequently became the leaders of anti-imperial coalitions. In Mulhouse and other manufacturing centers in Alsace, in the industrial departments of the center, and in Normandy, manufacturers such as those of Reims and St. Etienne joined the liberal opposition, bringing a new energy and vitality to the struggle for a republic. These groups were among the chief instigators of the political battles of the 1860s, and they remained dominant in their localities through the 1870s.

At Reims, the industrial boom stimulated the development of a cautious liberalism within the ranks of the notables. Successful manufacturers ceased to fear social revolution and became nostalgic for the parliamentary life that had been lost under the dictatorship. By the 1860s they no longer regarded the imperial regime as a necessary safeguard against revolution and began to oppose government interference in politics as an unwarranted curtailment of their right to govern their localities. At St. Etienne, the development of heavy industry also created a new feeling of optimism and a similar desire to break with outmoded government controls of local life. The hostility of wealthy industrialists greatly weakened the government's position in both towns, obliging the regime to look for support among more traditional manufacturers. Both St. Etienne's ribbon merchants and a number of Reims's mercantile woolens manufacturers had faced economic crises in the 1860s and were threatened by an increasingly hostile artisan work force. They therefore continued to depend on the government to prevent strikes. But successful industrial manufacturers rejected dictatorial methods and police controls. As a result, they were able to attract the support of workers as well as members of the middle classes in their pursuit of political office.

The entrance of new industrial interests into political life also changed the nature of middle-class opposition to the dictatorship. The republican opposition had formerly been dominated by members of the liberal professions, journalists, and other elements on the fringes of the elite. After 1860, leadership was increasingly shared with successful industrialists, who because of their wealth and influence were at the center of bourgeois society. They supplied the funds necessary to finance an opposition press and political campaigns. More important, their prestige among the middle classes drew others into the republican ranks. Industrialists were able to win working-class support as well by promising the abolition of the *livret*, the establishment of secular public education, and the free development of mutual aid societies. The 1860s thus marked the reemergence of genuinely popular political coalitions headed by wealthy notables, a situation unknown in France since the July Monarchy. The creation of a strong republican opposition during the last years of the empire was thus less a triumph of popular democracy than a reassertion of the influence of the elite after almost twenty years of powerlessness.

The success of industrialists in the opposition resulted in part from their ability to cooperate with other, less wealthy members of the bourgeoisie. Because of the sinecures and monopolies distributed to

Parisian speculators, Marx tended to identify Bonapartism with big business, but he ignored the fears of even the wealthiest provincial businessmen about the government's role in the economy. Even the enormous profits in the steel industry did not prevent St. Etienne's heavy industrialists from seeing government support of the P-L-M railroad as a threat to their own independence and security. Businessmen throughout France were similarly suspicious of the imperial regime's sponsorship of monopolies created for the benefit of Parisian financiers. The liberal press never tired of denouncing financial conspiracies hatched in court circles against local industry or of contrasting the machinations of Parisian stock jobbers with the honest practices of provincial businessmen. Republicans claimed that Bonapartism not only had deprived the provinces of their freedom but also threatened economic life through its support of Paris-based banks and railroads. The imperial regime, far from being the tool of industry, thus came to be regarded by liberal manufacturers as a danger to bourgeois interests.

Industrial dissidents also benefited from popular hostility to the empire. But despite universal suffrage, working-class leaders never achieved the influence they had enjoyed under the Second Republic and did not become the leading spokesmen for the opposition. Changes in the composition of the work force weakened working-class organizations and made them dependent on the leadership of the middle classes. The development of factory industry created divisions between artisans and factory workers. The immigration of new workers into previously homogeneous artisanal communities also reduced the ability of artisans to organize. Finally, police repression helped retard the creation of a popular political movement. Both the imperial government and liberals appealed to workers for support during elections, but years of police controls had greatly reduced their ability to play an independent role in political life. Instead, the major impact of economic change on politics was effected through the notables, who regained the preeminent position they had briefly lost under the Second Republic. Republicanism had become the best means by which the liberal elite could win and maintain political power. It was surprise at the reemergence of working-class radicalism into the complacent French political world of the 1860s, rather than any real revolutionary threat, that, as Eric Hobsbawm suggests, lay behind the ferocious repression of the Paris Commune.[2]

The lengths to which the middle-class opposition was willing to go to achieve popular support were, of course, determined by local conditions. Massive unemployment in the cotton towns of Alsace and Normandy in the early 1860s had left manufacturers occasionally hesitant about agitating against the government even after the end of the cotton famine. A similar decline in wages caused by a weakening of the woolens market in the late 1860s made some Reims dissidents cautious about adopting too radical a republican program. Although a liberal Orleanist group accepted the republic and supported the leadership of the Société industrielle against the conservatives around Werlé, it remained uneasy about strikes or the encouragement of radical demands on employers. But at St. Etienne, the role of dissident industrialists was less ambiguous. The leaders of the republican coalition were largely financially independent of the ribbon-manufacturing oligarchy, and both industrialists and liberal professionals were more willing to encourage strikes against the town's traditional leadership.

It is clear that industrialization strengthened the role of dissidents within the bourgeoisie and introduced an important new element into the republican coalition. Economic development thus helped contribute to changes in political attitudes under the Second Empire. The late 1860s provided a historical moment, when new industrial interests within the elite, as yet unchallenged by powerful working-class organizations, were able to combine with other middle-class groups to increase their influence in political life. They were able to serve as spokesmen for the republican movement, and in so doing they played an important role in assuring the creation of a socially moderate Third Republic acceptable to the French middle classes.

Chronology

Reims

1848
February   A republic is proclaimed in Paris following the abdication of
              Louis-Philippe.
              Popular disturbances begin at Reims.
              The liberal opposition calls for the establishment of a new
              municipal government.
March   *Le Républicain*, a newspaper dedicated to artisanal interests,
              begins to appear at Reims.
March-April   Serious working-class demonstrations take place in Paris
              against the government. In the same period clashes occur at
              Reims between the National Guard and unemployed work-
              ers.
April   The Comité électoral de la démocratie rémoise and *Le Républi-
              cain* are suppressed by the local administration.
              The Constituent Assembly elections at Reims result in a con-
              servative victory.
              General Cavaignac uses the army to suppress a popular rising
              in Paris.
July   The municipal elections at Reims result in a second major
              conservative victory.
December   The Association des corporations is founded at Reims.
              Louis-Napoleon Bonaparte wins an overwhelming victory at
              Reims as well as in the rest of France in the presidential
              elections.
1849
January   *L'Association rémoise*, the press organ of the Association des
              corporations, begins publication.
May   The candidates of the Association des corporations win the
              majority of the city's votes in the Legislative Assembly elec-

164

tions, defeating both the conservative and moderate republican candidates.

June   Ledru-Rollin's abortive coup in Paris results in further government suppression of workers' organizations in the capital.

Seventeen leaders of the Association des corporations are arrested by order of the conservative departmental administration following the Paris coup. The association was later dissolved by government decree.

1851

The use of the *livret* (the workers' good conduct book) is reestablished in France.

1852

A decree mandating government appointment of all officers of workers' mutual aid societies further reduces the possibility of independent working-class political action.

Soullié, the government's official candidate, is elected to the Corps législatif.

The prerevolutionary conservative elite is restored to the municipal council.

Edouard-Mathieu Werlé is appointed mayor of Reims.

1853

The Holden factory, the first large mechanized wool-combing mill in Reims, begins production.

La Concorde, originally founded to support the Bonapartist cause, is suppressed for being too critical of the government.

An imperial decree gives the government the power to appoint the presidents and vice-presidents of the Conseil des prudhommes.

1854

A new commercial bank, the Comptoir d'escompte de Reims, begins operations.

1855

The police arrest ninety-one members of a woolens workers' secret society.

The conservative municipal council is reelected.

1857

The economic depression of 1857 demonstrates the precarious position of factory owners, who because of high overhead costs must continue to manufacture and sell their goods at a loss.

The government chooses Nicolas-Henri Carteret as its candidate for the Corps législatif.

1860

The Chevalier-Cobden free trade treaty opens new markets
for fine French woolens in England and creates new opportunities for French manufacturers to buy cheap English textile
machinery. French manufacturers of cheaper woolens are
faced with the threat of very severe English competition.
The conservatives again win in the municipal council elections. Werlé and the members of his administration for the
first time win the largest number of votes.
Warnier becomes president of the Société industrielle.

1861

New penalties to prevent drunkenness provoke a strike at the
Villeminot-Huard factory.

1862

Woolens prices rise dramatically following the beginning of
the cotton famine created by the American Civil War.
Werlé defeats Ruinart de Brimont, a Legitimist, in the by-election for the Corps législatif, although Brimont was able to win
many votes by playing on resentment of government interference in local elections.

1863

Werlé is reelected to the Corps législatif without opposition.

May   Strikes are made legal.
August   A strike at the Holden factory begins after a system of new
                fines is introduced to enforce factory discipline.

1865

Eleven members of the liberal and Legitimist oppositions are
elected to the municipal council.

1867

The demand for woolens begins to decline.
A branch of the Ligue d'enseignement is founded at
Reims.

1868
March   Strikes begin at the Walbaum and Wagner and Marsan fac-
                tories following 10 percent wage cuts.
                L'Indépendent rémois, a liberal opposition newspaper, begins
                publication.
                Werlé resigns as mayor after a disagreement with the prefect
                over approval of a new workers' mutual aid society.
                Simon Dauphinot is appointed mayor.

1869

Werlé defeats Jules Simon in the Corps législatif election,
although the Legitimist and republican oppositions together
win a majority of the city's votes.

1870

January   The Société de solidarité et de résistance des travailleurs
             rémois et des environs, the largest woolens workers' mutual
             aid society, is able to procure raises for its members merely by
             threatening to strike.

February   The Société de solidarité joins the International.

March   The Société de solidarité becomes divided over the question of
             providing aid to striking Lyons silk workers.

May   A brief strike at the Holden factory soon collapses.

             The government wins a victory at Reims in the plebiscite
             asking approval of the liberal reforms "effected in the consti-
             tution since 1860," although most registered voters abstain.

July   The Franco-Prussian War begins.

September   A ten-man commission, made up of leaders of the former
             opposition parties, is appointed to govern the city.

1871

             Three moderate republicans, Warnier, Thomas, and Dau-
             phinot, are elected to the National Assembly.

             Moderate republicans and former Orleanists defeat Legiti-
             mists and former Bonapartist candidates in the municipal
             elections.

St. Etienne

1848

February   An executive committee of seven members replaces the con-
             servative mayor at St. Etienne following the proclamation of
             the republic.

April   Special municipal elections eliminate the remaining conserva-
             tives on the municipal council.

             A coalition of middle-class liberals and artisans defeats the
             disorganized conservative forces in the elections for the Con-
             stituent Assembly.

June   The municipal government thanks the National Assembly for
             restoring order in Paris.

             The local administration dissolves the Société populaire, the
             city's largest artisanal political organization.

December   Louis-Napoleon Bonaparte wins a majority of the city's votes
             in the presidential elections.

1849

May   Although the majority of artisan voters in St. Etienne are able
             to elect Duché, the conservative rural majority in the depart-
             ment defeats the other radical republican candidates in the
             Legislative Assembly elections.

1850

The most prosperous decade in the history of the ribbon industry begins.

The municipal elections fail to return a conservative council despite government efforts on behalf of the old merchant elite.

1852

Jules Balay is elected to the Corps législatif, although most voters in the city abstain.

The municipal elections result in another humiliating defeat for the conservative ribbon manufacturers and the government.

Only one-third of the city's registered voters support the reestablishment of the empire.

1853

French iron and steel tariffs are reduced.

The Compagnie générale des mines de la Loire establishes special lower rates for its largest customers.

1854

The Compagnie générale is dissolved by government decree.

Jackson frères, Petin et Gaudet becomes the largest combination of steel mills and forges in France.

1855

The conservative municipal council is reelected.

1856

The government uncovers a revolutionary secret society, the "pères des familles."

1857

Jules Balay, the government's candidate, is defeated in the city but elected to the Corps législatif by the conservative majority in the countryside.

1860

The imperial government introduces free trade with England.

Naval and other military orders begin to go to the largest steel firms in the region.

The ribbon industry begins to suffer the effects of the high price of Chinese silk and increased competition from abroad.

1861

More than two-thirds of St. Etienne's ribbon weavers are unemployed.

May

Le Courrier de St. Etienne, a liberal newspaper, is founded with the help of Persigny, the minister of the interior.

1863

A ribbon weavers' cooperative society, the Société des ruban-niers, is founded by more than a thousand masters to prevent a further decline of wages.

May

Frédéric Dorian and Benoît Fourneyron, both liberal candi-dates, win large majorities at St. Etienne in the Corps législatif elections; Dorian and Francisque Balay are eventually elected.

1864

Le Courrier ceases publication, a victim of government hostility and increasing deficits.

1865

A strike of five thousand velvet ribbon-makers ends in the introduction of shorter hours and other favorable condi-tions.

The municipal council elections return twelve new members, most of whom belong to the republican opposition.

1866

Petin and Gaudet receives the exclusive right to manufacture the new chassepot rifles in cooperation with the Manufacture Nationale.

A large ribbon weavers' mutual aid society, the Société des secours mutuels des rubanniers et veloutiers, is founded.

The mine workers' mutual aid society, the Caisse fraternelle des ouvriers mineurs, begins to demand one central fund for all miners in the region.

1867

Eight hundred ribbon dyers in St. Etienne join the larger Association des teinturiers at Lyons.

August

Dorian defeats Félix Escoffier, the entrepreneur of the Manu-facture Nationale des Armes, in the Conseil général elections. Baron de Rochetaillée, the Legitimist candidate, also receives more votes than the official candidate.

1868

Two new political newspapers, the republican *L'Eclaireur* and the Legitimist *La Loire*, are founded.

1869

The government authorizes the building of independent sec-ondary railroad lines in the Loire. Military contracts are for the first time given to smaller steel firms.

June

Fourteen thousand miners begin a strike, supported by *L'Eclaireur*, which ends in the shooting at La Ricamerie. The paper shortly thereafter takes up a subscription for the victims of the "massacre."

The municipal council is suspended by the prefect following

	criticism of the army's role in the shooting and is replaced by a commission dominated by ribbon manufacturers.
August	Several leaders of the miners' strike are sentenced to long prison terms.
November	The strike leaders are amnestied by the government to commemorate the hundredth anniversary of the Emperor Napoleon's birth.
1870	
	Petin and Gaudet and Terrenoire both institute profit-sharing schemes for certain privileged groups of workers.
January	Stating that its aims have been achieved with the government's new plan to increase local political autonomy, *La Loire* ceases publication.
	A cloth printers' strike begins at St. Etienne.
	A coal miners' strike begins at Rive-de-Gier.
	A larger number of negative votes are cast at St. Etienne during the plebiscite asking support for the liberal empire than in any other city in France.
August	Municipal elections return the council first elected in 1865.
September	The Second Empire is replaced by the Third Republic.
	The few conservative members of the municipal council are obliged to resign.
	The radical Société populaire calls for immediate new municipal elections.
1871	
February	Moderate republicans at St. Etienne led by Dorian easily defeat the radical candidates proposed by the Société populaire in the legislative elections. Only Dorian is elected, however; all the other successful candidates, members of the new Liberal-Conservative alliance, are able to win large rural majorities.
March	Communes are established at Paris and Lyons.
	A commune is proclaimed at St. Etienne. It promptly collapses after government troops arrive from Lyons.
March-April	The radical leaders of the Central Committee of the Société populaire are arrested.
May	Moderate and radical republicans win thirty-two seats in the municipal elections.
	The prefect suspends the municipal council and replaces it with a conservative commission dominated by ribbon manufacturers.
	The trial of the republican leaders begins at Riom.
1872	
	New municipal elections return the moderate republicans first elected in 1871.

Appendix

A Note on the Occupational Categories Used in the Tables

The notables have been divided into ten occupational categories: agriculture, mining, building, manufacturing, banking and insurance, transportation, dealing (shopkeepers, cabaret and hotel keepers, and petty entrepreneurs), public servants, members of the liberal professions, and proprietors (landlords); an eleventh category (unknown) has been added for individuals without specified occupations. Manufacturers in both towns, indicated in the column "Manufacturing" on the left in the tables, have been subdivided in the right-hand columns between the major manufacturing industries in each city: woolens and wine manufacturing at Reims and ribbons, arms, steel manufacturing and small metallurgy (*quincaillerie*) at St. Etienne; all other manufacturers have been listed on the right under "Other Manufacturing."

Among the individual occupations within each category are:

I. Agriculture: *cultivateurs* and *jardiniers*.

II. Mining: *mines directeur* and *mines ingénieur*.

III. Building: *bâtiment entrepreneur*; *bâtiment couvreur*; *maçon entrepreneur*; *plâtrier entrepreneur*; *peintre des bâtiments*; *travaux publics entrepreneur*; *construction entrepreneur*; *plombier*; and *architecte*.

IV. Manufacturing: See categories XI to XVII.

V. Banking and insurance: *assurance agent*; *banque directeur*; *banquier*; *comptoir sous directeur*; and *agent de change*.

VI. Transportation: *chemin de fer directeur*; *chemin de fer employée*; *chef du gare*; and *capitaine de vaisseau*.

171

VII. Dealing: *aubergiste*; *bijoutiste*; *boissons débitant*; *bois marchand*; *boucher*; *boulanger*; *chevaux marchand*; *cafetier*; *chapelier marchand*; *chiffon marchand*; *confiseur marchand*; *charbon marchand*; *charcutier*; *cordes marchand*; *cordonnier marchand*; *débitant*; *drapier marchand*; *droguiste*; *épicier*; *fruitier*; *fromages marchand*; *farines en détail marchand*; *habits marchand*; *hôtelier*; *libraire*; *liquoriste*; *lingerie marchand*; *maître de hotel*; *nouveautés marchand*; *papetier marchand*; *patissier*; *parapluie marchand*; *pharmacien*; *restauranteur*; *rouennerie marchand*; *sellier*; and *tailleur d'habits*.

VIII. Public Servants: *capitaine*; *cavalerie officier*; *colonel*; *colonel des gendarmes*; *réceveur des contributions directes*; *député au Corps législatif*; *réceveur des douanes*; *réceveur des domaines*; *brigadier des gendarmes*; *huissier*; *juge de paix*; *juge du tribunal civil*; *militaire*; *chef d'octroi*; *officier*; *directeur du prison*; *réceveur municipal*; *officier de santé*; *notaire*; *greffier*; *directeur des postes*; *instituteur*; and *armes controlleur*.

IX. Liberal Professions: *avoué*; *avocat*; *curé*; *ingénieur civil*; *médecin*; *professeur*; and *lycée professeur*.

X. Proprietors: *propriétaires* and *rentiers*.

XI. Other Manufacturers: *biscuits fabricant*; *brasseur*; *produits chimiques fabricant*; *chaises fabricant*; *chandelles fabricant*; *huile fabricant*; *navettes fabricant*; *peignes fabricant*; *parapluie fabricant*; *savon fabricant*; and *tapissier*.

At Reims

XII. Wool: *apprêteur*; *blanchisseur*; *cylindreur*; *commis*; *commerce courtier*; *commerce syndic*; *commerce voyageur*; *filateur*; *laine peignée marchand*; *laine laveur*; *négociant en laines*; *laine dégraisseur*; *laine marchand*; *laine fabricant*; *tissues commis*; *tissues négociant*; *tissues facteur*; *tisseur*; and *teinturier*.

XIII. Wine: *caves chef*; *négociant en vins*; *marchand des vins en gros*; and *vin marchand*.

At St. Etienne

XIV. Ribbons: *apprêteur*; *cylindreur*; *commerce courtier*; *commerce syndic*; *commerce voyageur*; *ruban fabricant*; *négociant en rubans*; *ruban commis*; *soies marchand*; *soie courtier*; *teinturier*; and *velours fabricant*.

XV. Small Metallurgy: *coutelier*; *ferblantier*; *quincailleur*; and *quincailleur marchand*.

XVI. Arms Manufacturer: *armes fabricant* and *armes entrepreneur*.

XVII. Iron and Steel Manufacturing: *acier fabricant*; *acier marchand*; *maître des forges*; and *fer marchand*.

The Working Classes

Workers have similarly been divided into categories, including agricultural workers, miners, artisans in the building trades, railroad workers, canal workers, and carriage drivers (in transportation), peddlers and shop clerks (dealing), day laborers (*journaliers*), and policemen and soldiers (public servants). They have also been divided according to the two cities' major industrial occupations: factory and artisan workers in Reims's woolens industry and wine trade; and artisan ribbon, arms, and metalworkers (there is no distinction in the *Successions et absences* between *quincailleurs* and workers in the iron and steel industry) at St. Etienne.

TABLE 1: THE TAX DISTRIBUTION OF THE NOTABLES IN 1847–48 ACCORDING TO OCCUPATIONAL CATEGORIES (PERCENTAGES)

REIMS

FRANCS	1	2	3	4	5	6	7	8	9	10	11	12	13	14	20	21
1,000–10,000	0	0	0	2	52	6	0	4	6	4	26	34	8	10	6 / 52 cases	4
500–999	0	1	0	2	58	4	3	4	8	2	18	41	11	6	18 / 167 cases	11
300–499	0	1	0	2	55	2	0	18	4	5	13	36	10	9	31 / 293 cases	20
200–299	0	1	0	3	33	2	1	32	3	4	21	17	2	14	45 / 415 cases	29
TOTAL	0	1	0	2	46	3	1	21	4	4	18	29	6	11	927 cases	64

ST. ETIENNE

FRANCS	1	2	3	4	5	6	7	8	9	10	11	15	16	17	18	19	20	21
1,000–10,000	3	0	3	0	52	3	0	0	3	3	33	37	3	6	3	3	7 / 35 cases	2
500–999	0	0	0	0	44	5	0	10	3	4	34	35	4	0	2	3	15 / 80 cases	5
300–499	1	0	2	1	50	3	1	17	2	3	20	35	4	2	4	5	35 / 185 cases	13
200–299	1	1	2	1	44	3	0	22	2	3	21	21	12	1	3	7	44 / 233 cases	16
TOTAL	1	1	2	1	46	3	1	16	2	4	23	28	7	2	3	6	533 cases	36

KEY: 1=Unknown; 2=Agriculture; 3=Mining; 4=Building; 5=All Manufacturing; 6=Banking; 7=Transportation; 8=Dealing; 9=Public Servants; 10=Liberal Professions; 11=Landlords; Manufacturing at Reims (A breakdown of column 5): 12=Woollens Manufacturing; 13=Wine Manufacturing; 14=Other Manufacturing; Manufacturing at St. Etienne: 15=Ribbon Manufacturing; 16=Small Metallurgy (quincaillerie); 17=Arms Manufacturing; 18=Iron and Steel Manufacturing; 19=Other Manufacturing; 20=Total within each city; 21=Combined total of both cities.
Significance=Distribution of means .05 (for all tables).

Source: Electoral lists of 1847–48 for Reims and St. Etienne; Departmental Archives of the Marne and the Loire, series 4M.

TABLE 2: THE BUSINESS TAX OF THE NOTABLES IN 1847-48 ACCORDING TO OCCUPATIONAL CATEGORIES (PERCENTAGES)

REIMS

FRANCS	1	2	3	4	5	6	7	8	9	10	11	12	13	14	15	16	17	18	19	20	21
1,000-10,000	0	0	0	0	50	25	0	0	0	0	25	_50_	0	0						4	1
500-999	0	0	0	0	88	10	0	2	0	0	0	_70_	8	10						40	4
200-499	0	0	0	1	81	3	2	12	0	0	1	_55_	15	11						313	34
0-199	0	1	0	3	24	2	1	29	7	6	27	11	2	11						570	62
TOTAL	0	1	0	2	46	3	1	21	4	4	18	29	6	11						927 cases	

ST. ETIENNE

FRANCS	1	2	3	4	5	6	7	8	9	10	11	12	13	14	15	16	17	18	19	20	21
1,000-10,000	0	0	0	0	100	0	0	0	0	0	0				0	0	100	0	0	1	1
500-999	8	0	0	0	84	0	0	8	0	0	0				0	_75_	0	8	1	13	3
200-499	0	0	1	0	62	7	1	28	3	0	1				1	_50_	1	2	5	138	36
0-199	1	1	3	1	38	2	0	14	3	5	32				3	19	8	3	6	229	60
TOTAL	1	1	2	1	45	3	1	17	2	4	23				1	27	7	3	6	381 cases	

KEY: 1=Unknown; 2=Agriculture; 3=Mining; 4=Building; 5=All Manufacturing; 6=Banking; 7=Transportation; 8=Dealing; 9=Public Servants; 10=Liberal Professions; 11=Landlords; (A breakdown of column 5): Manufacturing at Reims: 12=Woolens Manufacturing; 13=Wine Manufacturing; 14=Other Manufacturing; Manufacturing at St. Etienne: 15=Ribbon Manufacturing; 16=Small metallurgy (quincaillerie); 17=Iron and Steel Manufacturing; 18=Arms Manufacturing; 19=Other Manufacturing; 20=Total within each city; 21=Combined total of both cities; For both cities.

Source: Electoral lists of 1847-48 for Reims and St. Etienne; Departmental Archives of the Marne and the Loire, series 4M.

TABLE 3: THE REAL PROPERTY TAX OF THE NOTABLES IN 1847-48 ACCORDING TO OCCUPATIONAL CATEGORIES (PERCENTAGES)

REIMS

FRANCS	1	2	3	4	5	6	7	8	9	10	11	12	13	14	20	21
1,000-10,000	0	0	0	5	_17_	5	0	0	14	9	_50_	13	0	4	2	2
500-999	0	2	0	0	_25_	0	2	2	21	8	_40_	18	5	2	5	3
200-499	0	2	0	3	28	3	1	8	12	6	37	16	5	7	18	11
0-199	0	1	0	2	52	3	1	26	1	3	11	32	7	13	75	47
TOTAL	0	1	0	2	46	3	1	21	4	4	18	29	6	11	699 cases	

ST. ETIENNE

FRANCS	1	2	3	4	5	6	7	8	9	10	11	15	16	17	18	19	20	21
1,000-10,000	0	0	0	0	_35_	6	0	0	0	6	_53_	_23_	6	0	6	0	3	1
500-999	0	0	0	0	_20_	4	0	0	8	4	_64_	16	0	0	0	4	5	2
200-499	1	0	2	0	34	2	0	6	4	7	44	20	4	0	4	6	19	7
0-199	1	1	2	1	50	3	3	21	1	3	14	31	8	2	3	6	73	27
TOTAL	1	1	2	1	45	3	1	17	2	4	23	28	7	1	3	6	390 cases	

KEY: 1=Unknown; 2=Agriculture; 3=Mining; 4=Building; 5=All Manufacturing; 6=Banking; 7=Transportation; 8=Dealing; 9=Public Servants; 10=Liberal Professions; 11=Landlords; Manufacturing at Reims (A breakdown of column 5): 12=Woolens Manufacturing; 13=Wine Manufacturing; 14=Other Manufacturing at St. Etienne: 15=Ribbon Manufacturing; 16=Small Metallurgy (quincaillerie); 17=Arms Manufacturing; 18=Iron and Steel Manufacturing; 19=Other Manufacturing; 20=Total within each city; 21=Combined total of both cities.

Source: Electoral lists of 1847-48 for Reims and St. Etienne; Departmental Archives of the Marne and the Loire, series 4M.

TABLE 4: THE TAXATION OF THE WEALTHIER NOTABLES IN 1847-48 ACCORDING TO OCCUPATIONAL CATEGORIES (PERCENTAGES)

REIMS

	1	2	3	4	5	6	7	8	9	10	11	12	13	14	20	21
Total tax	0	1	0	2	56	4	2	6	7	3	19	40	10	6	27	249 cases
Business tax	0	0	0	1	77	4	1	14	0	1	2	53	13	11	42	392 cases
Land tax	0	2	0	2	27	2	1	8	12	7	39	15	4	8	33	308 cases
																927

ST. ETIENNE

	1	2	3	4	5	6	7	8	9	10	11	15	16	17	18	19	20	21
Total tax	1	0	2	0	48	4	0	8	2	3	32	36	4	2	2	4	26	140 cases
Business tax	1	0	1	0	66	5	1	23	0	2	1	47	10	2	2	5	46	246 cases
Land tax	1	0	2	1	30	3	0	4	4	5	50	18	3	1	3	5	34	181 cases
																		533

KEY: 1=Unknown; 2=Agriculture; 3=Mining; 4=Building; 5=All Manufacturing; 6=Banking; 7=Transportation; 8=Dealing; 9=Public Servants; 10=Liberal Professions; 11=Landlords; Manufacturing at Reims (A breakdown of column 5): 12=Woolens Manufacturing; 13=Wine Manufacturing; 14=Other Manufacturing; Manufacturing at St. Etienne: 15=Ribbon Manufacturing; 16=Small Metallurgy (quincaillerie); 17=Arms Manufacturing; 18=Iron and Steel Manufacturing; 19=Other Manufacturing; 20=Percentage of all the notables in 1847-48; 21=All notables; Business tax (patente); Land tax (foncière).

Source: Electoral lists of 1847-48 for Reims and St. Etienne; Departmental Archives of the Marne and the Loire, series 4M.

TABLE 5: THE CHANGING COMPOSITION OF THE NOTABLES UNDER THE SECOND EMPIRE ACCORDING TO OCCUPATIONAL CATEGORIES (PERCENTAGES)

REIMS

	1	2	3	4	5	6	7	8	9	10	11	12	13	14	20	cases
Old elite	1	3	1	3	50	3	2	17	5	3	12	30	4	16	25	192 cases
Notable names	5	5	1	3	38	3	1	14	6	6	18	21	3	14	36	277 cases
New elite	8	4	1	4	33	6	2	18	6	4	14	14	4	15	39	296 cases
Total	5	4	1	3	39	4	2	16	6	5	15	20	3	16		765 cases

ST. ETIENNE

	1	2	3	4	5	6	7	8	9	10	11	15	16	17	18	19	20	cases
Old elite	0	1	2	0	45	3	0	9	4	4	32	27	6	2	3	7	19	109 cases
Notable names	4	1	2	1	35	3	1	10	5	3	35	18	3	3	2	9	40	231 cases
New elite	6	1	2	1	34	2	1	15	5	5	28	19	1	3	2	10	41	241 cases
Total	4	1	2	1	36	2	1	12	5	4	32	19	3	3	2	9		581 cases

KEY: 1=Unknown; 2=Agriculture; 3=Mining; 4=Building; 5=All Manufacturing; 6=Banking; 7=Transportation; 8=Dealing; 9=Public Servants; 10=Liberal Professions; 11=Landlords; Manufacturing at Reims (A detail of column 5): 12=Woolens Manufacturing; 13=Wine Manufacturing; 14=Other Manufacturing; Manufacturing at St. Etienne: 15=Ribbon Manufacturing; 16=Small Metallurgy (quincaillerie); 17=Arms Manufacturing; 18=Iron and Steel Manufacturing; 19=Other Manufacturing; 20=Total within each city; For both cities: Old Elite=Notables listed both on the 1847-48 electoral lists and in the Mutation après décès; Notable Names=Notables listed only in the Mutation après décès, both with prominent local family names, and assumed to be younger members of old established families; New Elite=Notables found only in the Mutation après décès bearing surnames not previously well-known in the cities.

Source: Electoral lists of 1847-48 and Mutation après décès, 1852-69, for Reims and St. Etienne; Departmental Archives of the Marne and the Loire, series 4M and series Q, non côté.

TABLE 6: THE CHANGING COMPOSITION OF THE WEALTHIER NOTABLES UNDER THE SECOND EMPIRE ACCORDING TO OCCUPATIONAL CATEGORIES (PERCENTAGES)

REIMS	1	2	3	4	5	6	7	8	9	10	11	12	13	14	15	16	17	18	19	20	21
Old elite	0	3	0	1	63	3	0	10	4	4	12	38	7	18						47	91 cases 192
Notable names	0	3	0	2	49	2	0	10	6	7	21	36	6	7						24	66 cases 277
New names	8	3	0	8	49	8	0	5	3	5	11	23	16	10						13	38 cases 296

ST. ETIENNE	1	2	3	4	5	6	7	8	9	10	11	12	13	14	15	16	17	18	19	20	21
Old elite	0	2	0	0	51	4	0	4	5	4	30				34	7	0	2	5	51	55 cases 109
Notable names	0	0	2	0	43	2	0	6	6	2	39				35	0	2	2	4	28	64 cases 231
New names	6	0	3	0	28	3	0	6	9	13	32				19	0	0	0	9	13	32 cases 241

KEY: 1=Unknown; 2=Agriculture; 3=Mining; 4=Building; 5=All Manufacturing; 6=Banking; 7=Transportation; 8=Dealing; 9=Public Servants; 10=Liberal Professions; 11=Landlords; Manufacturing at Reims (A breakdown of column 5): 12=Woolens Manufacturing; 13=Wine Manufacturing; 14=Other Manufacturing; Manufacturing at St. Etienne: 15=Ribbon Manufacturing; 16=Small Metallurgy (quincaillerie); 17=Arms Manufacturing; 18=Iron and Steel Manufacturing; 19=Other Manufacturing; For both cities: 20=The proportion of the richer notables in each category (old elite, etc.); expressed as a percentage of all the notables in each category in both the 1847-48 electoral lists and in the Mutation après décès; Old Elite=Notables listed in both the 1847-48 electoral lists and in the Mutation après décès; Notable Names=Notables listed only in the Mutation après décès, but with prominent local family names, and assumed to be younger members of established families; New Elite=Notables not previously well-known in the cities.

Source: Electoral lists of 1847-48 and Mutation après décès, 1852-69, for Reims and St. Etienne; Departmental Archives of the Marne and the Loire, series 4M, and series Q, non côté.

TABLE 7: INVESTMENTS BY THE NOTABLES IN LOCAL BUSINESS ACCORDING TO OCCUPATIONAL CATEGORIES UNDER THE SECOND EMPIRE

REIMS	1	2	3	4	5	6	7	8	9	10	11	12	13	14	15	16	17	18	19	20	21
1852–1860																					
Old elite	0	0	0	4	48	0	0	17	9	0	22	31	4	13						30	23 cases 76
Notable names	14	0	0	0	43	0	0	10	5	9	19	38	0	5						18	21 cases 118
New names	13	13	0	0	24	13	0	0	0	13	24	24	0	0						7	8 cases 113
1861–1869																					
Old elite	3	0	0	0	51	3	3	13	7	10	10	38	3	10						25	20 cases 79
Notable names	0	0	0	3	48	8	0	15	5	13	8	38	5	5						25	40 cases 159
New elite	3	0	0	8	45	5	0	5	8	8	18	38	0	7						17	38 cases 220

ST. ETIENNE	1	2	3	4	5	6	7	8	9	10	11	12	13	14	15	16	17	18	19	20	21
1852–1860																					
Old elite	29	0	0	0	42	0	0	0	0	0	29				42	0	0	0	0	14	7 cases 50
Notable names	0	0	0	0	60	0	0	10	0	0	30				30	10	0	0	20	9	10 cases 112
New elite	0	0	14	0	28	0	0	0	0	14	44				14	0	0	0	14	6	7 cases 117
1861–1869																					
Old elite	0	0	0	0	55	9	0	0	0	18	18				37	9	0	0	9	29	11 cases 38
Notable names	10	0	0	0	80	0	0	0	0	0	10				30	30	0	0	20	8	10 cases 119
New elite	0	0	6	0	34	0	0	11	11	21	17				6	0	11	11	6	12	18 cases 153

KEY: 1=Unknown; 2=Agriculture; 3=Mining; 4=Building; 5=All Manufacturing; 6=Banking; 7=Transportation; 8=Dealing; 9=Public Servants; 10=Liberal Professions; 11=Landlords; Manufacturing at Reims (A breakdown of column 5): 12=Woolens Manufacturing; 13=Wine Manufacturing; 14=Other Manufacturing; Manufacturing at St. Etienne: 15=Small Metallurgy; 16=Ribbon Manufacturing; 17=Other Manufacturing (quincaillerie); 17=Arms Manufacturing; 18=Iron and steel manufacturing; 19=Other Manufacturing; 20=Percentage of investors within each category of the elite; 21=Total number of notables within each category of the elite (old elite, etc.)

Source: Electoral lists of 1847-48 and Mutation après décès, 1852-69, for Reims and St. Etienne; Departmental Archives of the Marne and the Loire, series 4M, and series Q, non côté.

TABLE 8: INVESTMENTS BY THE NOTABLES AT REIMS IN LOCAL BUSINESS UNDER THE SECOND EMPIRE ACCORDING TO OCCUPATIONAL CATEGORIES (PERCENTAGES)

FRANCS	1	2	3	4	5	6	7	8	9	10	11	12	13	14	15	cases
50,000–200,000	6	0	0	3	48	6	0	9	8	0	20	34	3	11	5	35 cases
20,000–49,999	0	4	0	0	66	4	0	4	9	9	4	53	9	4	3	3 cases
10,000–19,999	13	4	0	8	33	0	4	0	4	17	17	29	0	4	23	3 cases
5,000–9,999	0	0	0	4	50	0	0	8	4	17	17	46	4	0	3	24 cases
2,000–4,999	0	0	0	0	44	9	0	14	9	0	24	39	0	5	3	24 cases
1,000–1,999	0	0	0	6	38	6	0	25	9	19	6	19	0	19	21	21 cases
1–999	0	0	0	0	41	6	0	29	6	6	12	29	0	12	2	16 cases
0	6	5	1	3	37	4	2	18	5	4	15	15	3	19	29	79 cases
TOTAL	5	4	1	3	39	4	2	16	6	5	15	20	3	16		605 cases
																765 cases

KEY. 1=Unknown; 2=Agriculture; 3=Mining; 4=Building; 5=All Manufacturing; 6=Banking; 7=Transportation; 8=Dealing; 9=Public Servants; 10=Liberal Professions; 11=Landlords; A breakdown of manufacturing in column 5: 12=Woolens Manufacturing; 13=Wine Manufacturing; 14=Other Manufacturing; 15=Percentage of notables within each investing category.

Source: Mutation après décès, 1852–1869, for Reims and St. Etienne; Departmental Archives of the Marne and the Loire, series Q, non côté.

TABLE 9: INVESTMENTS BY THE NOTABLES AT ST. ETIENNE IN LOCAL BUSINESS UNDER THE SECOND EMPIRE ACCORDING TO OCCUPATIONAL CATEGORIES (PERCENTAGES)

REIMS

FRANCS	1	2	3	4	5	6	7	8	9	10	11	12	13	14	15	16	17	
50,000-200,000	6	0	6	0	50	6	0	0	0	13	19	<u>44</u>	6	0	0	0	3	16 cases
20,000-49,999	10	0	0	0	50	0	0	0	0	0	40	<u>30</u>	0	0	0	20	2	10 cases
10,000-19,999	0	0	0	0	47	0	0	13	7	20	13	<u>26</u>	7	0	7	7	3	15 cases
5,000-9,999	0	0	0	0	43	0	0	14	0	14	29	0	0	0	0	43	1	7 cases
2,000-4,999	0	0	14	0	28	0	0	0	0	14	44	0	0	0	0	28	1	7 cases
1,000-1,999	100	0	0	0	0	0	0	0	0	0	0	0	0	0	0	0	2	1 case
1-999	0	0	0	0	43	0	0	0	14	14	29	15	0	14	14	0	1	7 cases
0	2	1	2	1	37	2	1	13	5	2	34	20	3	3	2	9	89	522 cases
TOTAL	4	1	2	1	37	2	1	11	5	4	32	20	3	3	2	9		585 cases

KEY: 1=Unknown; 2=Agriculture; 3=Mining; 4=Building; 5=All Manufacturing; 6=Banking; 7=Transportation; 8=Dealing; 9=Public Servants; 10=Liberal Professions; 11=Landlords: A breakdown of manufacturing in column 5: 12=Ribbon Manufacturing; 13=Small Metallurgy (quincaillerie); 14=Arms Manufacturing; 15=Iron and Steel Manufacturing; 16=Other Manufacturing; 17=Percentage of notables within each investing category.

Source: Mutation après décès, 1852-69, for Reims and St. Etienne; Departmental Archives of the Loire, series Q, non côté.

TABLE 10: INVESTMENTS BY THE NOTABLES AT REIMS UNDER THE SECOND EMPIRE ACCORDING TO OCCUPATIONAL CATEGORIES (PERCENTAGES)

	1	2	3	4	5	6	7	8	9	10	11	12	13	14	15	16
Personal loans																
1852–1860	7	3	0	4	35	3	3	15	5	4	21	17	2	16	79 / 243	307 cases
1861–1869	3	5	1	3	38	5	2	17	7	6	13	20	3	15	86 / 393	458 cases
Local business																
1852–1860	8	2	0	2	42	2	0	11	6	6	21	32	2	8	17 / 52	307 cases
1861–1869	1	1	0	4	48	6	1	11	6	10	12	40	4	4	25 / 108	458 cases
French business																
1852–1860	0	0	0	0	23	6	0	12	12	12	35	23	0	0	5 / 17	307 cases
1861–1869	2	5	0	1	37	9	1	14	8	9	14	27	4	6	22 / 99	458 cases
Railroads																
1852–1860	3	0	0	3	44	0	0	14	3	8	25	36	3	5	12 / 36	307 cases
1861–1869	3	3	0	2	30	10	10	8	10	12	12	18	4	8	28 / 128	458 cases
Bonds																
1852–1860	3	5	0	2	36	3	2	11	4	6	28	19	0	17	21 / 64	307 cases
1861–1869	6	5	1	1	34	6	3	12	9	10	13	19	6	9	23 / 107	458 cases

KEY: 1=Unknown; 2=Agriculture; 3=Mining; 4=Building; 5=All Manufacturing; 6=Banking; 7=Transportation; 8=Dealing; 9=Public Servants; 10=Liberal Professions, 11=Landlords; A breakdown of column 5: 12=Woolens Manufacturing; 13=Wine Manufacturing; 14=Other Manufacturing; 15=Percentage of all notables investing in each category (local business, etc.); 16=The total number of notables in 1852-60 or 1861-69; Personal Loans=Loans either to individuals or families; there is no indication whether these are private loans, or outstanding business credits at time of death; Local business=Investments in local industry, almost invariably in Reims' mechanized woolens mills; French Business=Investments in French businesses outside the immediate area of Reims; Railroads=Investments in either French or foreign railroad companies; Bonds=Investments in either French or foreign government bonds.

Source: _Mutation après décès_, 1852-1869, for Reims; Departmental Archives of the Marne, Series Q, non côté.

TABLE 11: INVESTMENTS BY THE NOTABLES AT ST. ETIENNE UNDER THE SECOND EMPIRE
ACCORDING TO OCCUPATIONAL CATEGORIES (PERCENTAGES)

	1	2	3	4	5	6	7	8	9	10	11	12	13	14	15	16	17	18
Personal loans																		
1852–1860	5	2	3	0	40	1	2	13	3	2	29	20	2	2	2	14	45 / 123 cases	275 cases
1861–1869	1	1	1	1	35	4	1	15	6	6	29	19	1	3	2	10	75 / 232 cases	310 cases
Local business																		
1852–1860	9	0	4	0	46	0	0	4	0	4	33	29	4	0	0	13	9 / 24 cases	275 cases
1861–1869	3	0	3	0	44	3	0	5	5	18	19	20	3	3	5	13	13 / 39 cases	310 cases
French business																		
1852–1860	19	0	0	0	36	9	0	0	0	0	36	27	0	0	0	9	4 / 11 cases	275 cases
1861–1869	4	0	8	0	29	4	0	4	13	17	21	29	0	0	0	0	8 / 24 cases	310 cases
Railroads																		
1852–1860	9	0	0	0	46	9	0	0	0	9	27	37	9	0	0	0	4 / 11 cases	275 cases
1861–1869	4	0	4	0	26	0	4	10	13	13	26	22	0	4	0	0	7 / 23 cases	310 cases
Bonds																		
1852–1860	8	0	0	0	29	8	0	0	0	0	55	15	0	0	0	14	5 / 13 cases	275 cases
1860–1869	6	0	3	0	30	12	3	3	9	3	31	10	0	10	0	10	10 / 32 cases	310 cases

KEY: 1=Unknown; 2=Agriculture; 3=Mining; 4=Building; 5=All Manufacturing; 6=Banking; 7=Transportation; 8=Dealing; 9=Public Servants; 10=Liberal Professions; 11=Landlords; A breakdown of column 5: 12=Ribbon Manufacturing; 13=Small Metallurgy (quincaillerie); 14=Arms Manufacturing; 15=Iron and Steel Manufacturing; 16=Other Manufacturing; 17=Percentage of all notables investing in each category (local business etc.); 18=The total number of notables in 1852-60 and 1861-69; Personal loans=Loans either to individuals or families; there is no indication whether these are private loans, or outstanding business credits at time of death; Local business=Investments in local industry, almost invariably in heavy industry around St. Etienne; French Business=Investments in French businesses outside of the immediate area of St. Etienne; Railroads=Investments in either French or foreign railroad companies; Bonds=Investments in either French or foreign government bonds.
Source: Mutation après décès, 1852-1869, for St. Etienne, Departmental Archives of the Loire, series Q, non côte.

TABLE 12: THE SIZE OF INVESTMENTS BY THE NOTABLES UNDER THE SECOND EMPIRE (PERCENTAGES)

REIMS	1	2	3	4	5	6	7	8
Personal loans	17	16	17	10	8	4	11	17
Local business	5	3	3	3	3	2	2	79
French business	1	2	3	2	3	1	3	85
Railroads	4	5	3	3	2	2	2	79
Bonds	2	3	4	3	4	2	4	78

ST. ETIENNE	1	2	3	4	5	6	7	8
Personal loans	8	15	12	7	8	3	8	39
Local business	3	2	3	1	1	1	1	88
French business	1	1	1	1	1	1	1	93
Railroads	1	1	1	1	1	1	1	93
Bonds	1	1	1	1	2	1	1	92

KEY: 1=Fr 50,000 to 200,000; 2=Fr 20,000 to 49,999; 3=Fr 10,000 to 19,999; 4=Fr 5,000 to 9,999;
5=Fr 2,000 to 4,999; 6=Fr 1,000 to 1,999; 7=Fr 1 to 999; 8=Fr 0; Personal Loans=Loans listed in the
Mutation après décès made either to individuals or families; there is no indication whether these are
private loans, or outstanding business credits at time of death; Local business=Investments in local
industry, almost invariably either in Reims' mechanized woolens mills, or in heavy industry around
St. Etienne; French Business=Investments in French businesses outside of the immediate area of Reims or
St. Etienne; Railroads=Investments in either French or foreign railroad companies; Bonds=Investments
in either French or foreign government bonds.

Source: Mutation après décès, 1852-1869, for Reims and St. Etienne; Departmental Archives of the Marne and
the Loire, series Q, non côté.

TABLE 13: THE FORTUNES OF THE NOTABLES UNDER THE SECOND EMPIRE (PERCENTAGES)

REIMS

FRANCS	1	2	3	4	5	6	7	8	9	10	11	12	13	14	20	21	cases
500,000–2,000,000	3	0	0	0	70	3	0	6	12	3	3	49	12	9	4	4	33
200,000–499,999	1	3	0	1	57	5	0	9	4	5	15	39	9	9	11	6	81
100,000–199,999	2	5	0	4	46	3	2	13	2	6	17	26	3	17	16	9	125
50,000–99,999	7	4	1	4	34	4	2	18	7	4	15	17	1	16	27	16	209
20,000–49,999	7	5	1	3	33	4	2	20	6	5	14	14	2	17	42	24	317

ST. ETIENNE

FRANCS	1	2	3	4	5	6	7	8	9	10	11	15	16	17	18	19	20	21	cases
500,000–2,000,000	0	0	0	0	50	5	0	0	5	0	40	45	5	0	0	0	3	1	18
200,000–499,999	0	0	0	0	50	2	0	2	5	2	39	34	2	2	5	7	7	3	42
100,000–199,999	3	1	2	0	39	2	0	6	7	6	34	28	2	0	3	6	16	7	95
50,000–99,999	5	1	2	2	30	4	1	15	4	1	35	13	2	3	2	10	23	10	132
20,000–49,999	5	2	2	1	36	2	2	13	4	4	29	17	4	4	1	10	51	22	298

KEY: 1=Unknown; 2=Agriculture; 3=Mining; 4=Building; 5=All Manufacturing; 6=Banking; 7=Transportation; 8=Dealing; 9=Public Servants; 10=Liberal Professions; 11=Landlords; Manufacturing at Reims (A detail of column 5): 12=Woolens Manufacturers; 13=Wine Manufacturing; 14=Other Manufacturing; Manufacturing at St. Etienne: 15=Ribbons Manufacturing; 16=Small Metallurgy (quincaillerie); 17=Arms Manufacturing; 18=Iron and Steel Manufacturing; 19=Other Manufacturing; 20=The percentage of the notables in each category (Fr 20,000 to 49,999, etc.) within each city; 21=The combined percentage of the notables in both cities.

Source: Mutation après décès, 1852–1869, for Reims and St. Etienne; Departmental Archives of the Marne and the Loire, series Q, non coté.

TABLE 14: THE PROPORTION OF INDIGENCE WITHIN EACH OCCUPATIONAL CATEGORY OF THE WORKING CLASS UNDER THE SECOND EMPIRE (PERCENTAGES)

REIMS	1	2	3	4	5	6	7	8	9	10	11	12	13	14	15	16	17
INDIGENT WORKERS	83	52	72	74	57	77	63	46	65	39	18	68					67
(CASES)	178	44	13	34	243	219	5	37	34	48	6	183					813 cases
ALL WORKERS	214	85	18	46	426	285	8	80	52	124	33	269					1214 cases

ST. ETIENNE	1	2	3	4	5	6	7	8	9	10	11	12	13	14	15	16	17
INDIGENT WORKERS	98	60	89	91	81	89	89	61	92		77		75	92	83		84
(CASES)	371	77	187	59	749	248	42	73	184		233		131	142	244		1978 cases
ALL WORKERS	379	129	212	65	925	279	47	119	200		302		175	154	294		2355 cases

KEY: 1=Unknown; 2=Agriculture; 3=Mining; 4=Building; 5=All Manufacturing; 6=Day Laborers (journaliers); 7=Transportation; 8=Dealing (shop clerks, peddlers, etc); 9=Public Servants (soldiers, policemen, etc.); Occupations at Reims: 10=Woolens workers; 11=Wine workers; 12=Workers employed in all other kinds of manufacturing; Manufacturing at St. Etienne: 13=Ribbon workers (passementiers and veloutiers); 14=Arms making; 15=Metal workers (both quincailleurs and workers in the iron and steel industry); 16=Workers employed in all other kinds of manufacturing; For both cities: 17=Total; All Workers=Indicated as the number of cases.

Source: Enregistrement des Successions et Absences, 1852, 1862 and 1869, for Reims and St. Etienne; Departmental Archives of the Marne and the Loire, series Q, non côté.

TABLE 15: THE WEALTH OF THE SMALLER BOURGEOISIE AND WORKERS AT REIMS UNDER THE SECOND EMPIRE (PERCENTAGES)

	1	2	3	4	5	6	7	8	9	10	11	12	13	14	15
PETTY BOURG.	2	10	1	1	17	4	0	13	2	15	35	5	2	10	229 cases
Fr 2,000–4,999	2	20	0	0	48	8	0	19	3			5	8	35	8 — 90 cases
1,000–1,999	11	11	0	1	44	17	1	14	1			20	10	14	6 — 72 cases
500–999	8	11	0	0	42	21	0	9	9			17	2	23	4 — 53 cases
1–499	12	4	3	6	45	19	1	6	4			25	4	16	16 — 197 cases
INDIGENT	22	5	2	4	30	27	1	5	4			6	1	23	66 — 804 cases
ALL WORKERS	17	7	2	4	35	24	1	6	4			10	3	22	1216 cases

KEY: 1=Unknown; 2=Agriculture; 3=Mining; 4=Building; 5=All Manufacturing; 6=Day Laborers (journaliers); 7=Transportation; 8=Dealing (Small shopkeepers, shop clerks and peddlers); 9=Public Servants (soldiers, policemen, etc.); 10=Liberal Professions; 11=Landlords; 12=Woolens workers; 13=Wine workers; 14=All other workers employed in manufacturing; 15=The total number of workers within each category of wealth; Petty Bourg.=The smaller bourgeoisie, consisting of all persons with fortunes between Fr 5,000 and 19,999. Indigent=Indigent workers;

Source: Enregistrement des Successions et Absences, 1852, 1862 and 1869, for Reims; Departmental Archives of the Marne, series Q, non côté.

TABLE 16: THE WEALTH OF THE SMALLER BOURGEOISIE AND WORKERS AT ST. ETIENNE UNDER THE SECOND EMPIRE (PERCENTAGES)

FRANCS	1	2	3	4	5	6	7	8	9	10	11	12	13	14	15	16
PETTY BOURG.	4	6	1	1	22	1	1	8	1	12	43	11	5	3	3	317 cases
2,000–4,999	4	15	6	3	32	8	0	17	4		15	7	5	16	4	14 cases
1,000–1,999	3	20	6	7	26	7	0	8	3		23	8	4	11	3	69 cases
500–999	4	11	7	0	33	11	0	17	6		14	16	1	13	3	56 cases
1–499	8	11	5	0	37	8	2	9	4		22	15	3	13	6	150 cases
INDIGENT	19	4	9	3	26	12	2	4	9		12	6	7	13	84	1993 cases
ALL WORKERS	16	5	9	3	21	12	2	5	9		13	7	7	7		2363 cases

KEY: 1=Unknown; 2=Agriculture; 3=Mining; 4=Building; 5=All Manufacturing; 6=Day Laborers (journaliers); 7=Transportation; 8=Dealing (small shopkeepers, shop clerks and peddlers); 9=Public Servants (soldiers, policemen, etc); 10=Liberal Professions; 11=Landlords; 12=Ribbon Workers (passementiers and veloutiers); 13=Arms Making; 14=Metal Workers (both quincailleurs and workers in the iron and steel industry); 15=Workers employed in all other kinds of manufacturing; 16=The percentage of the workers in each category of wealth; Petty Bourg.=The smaller bourgeoisie, consisting of all persons with fortunes between Fr 5,000 and 19,999.

Source: Enregistrement des Succession et Absences, 1852, 1862 and 1869, for St. Etienne; Departmental Archives of the Loire, series Q, non côté.

Notes

Introduction

1. Theodore Zeldin, *The Political System of Napoleon III* (New York, 1958).
2. Adeline Daumard, *Les fortunes françaises au XIXième siècle: Enquête sur la répartition et la composition des capitaux privés à Paris, Lyon, Lille, Bordeaux et Toulouse d'après l'enregistrement des droits de succession* (Paris, 1973).

Chapter 1

1. Roger Price, *The Economic Modernization of France, 1730-1880* (New York, 1975).
2. Charles Tilly, "How Protest Modernized in France, 1845-1855," in William Aydelotte, ed., *Dimensions of Quantitative Research in History* (Reading, Mass., 1971), p. 226.
3. Eric J. Hobsbawm, *The Age of Capital, 1848-1875* (New York, 1975).
4. Karl Marx, *The Communist Manifesto* (New York, 1947), p. 10.
5. Roger Price, *The French Second Republic: A Social History* (Ithaca, 1972), pp. 234-36.
6. For a detailed description of Reims, see Georges Boussinesq and Gustave Laurent, *Histoire de Reims depuis ses origines jusqu'à nos jours* (Reims, 1933).
7. Ribbon manufacturing in the Forez dated from the sixteenth century, but it was only during the last years of the *ancien régime* that it became centered around St. Etienne, St. Chamond, and Montbrison. Following a prolonged and severe depression under the empire, the industry revived under the Restoration and the July Monarchy, stimulated by the introduction of new articles such as velours, and especially by the introduction of new technology. By 1840 the industry employed more than 30,000 workers (12,500 men, 18,000 women, and 2,000 children) and was on the eve of the most prosperous period of its history. See Yves Lequin, *Les ouvriers de la région lyonnaise, 1848-1914*, 2 vols. (Lyons, 1977), 1:31-32.

8. Armand Audiganne, *Les populations ouvrières et les industries de la France*, 2 vols. (Paris, 1860), 2:80.

9. Flora Tristan, *Le tour de France: Journal inédit, 1843-1844* (Paris, 1845). Other observers such as Bonnefous were struck by the black clouds, caused by the burning of large amounts of coal, which perpetually hung over St. Etienne. See Bonnefous, *Histoire de St. Etienne* (St. Etienne, n.d.), pp. 424-25.

10. Claude Fohlen, *L'industrie textile au temps du Second Empire* (Paris, 1956), p. 330.

11. The reduction of tax requirements for voting after 1830 from Fr 300 to Fr 200 and of age requirements from thirty to twenty-five years had expanded the electorate from 90,000 to 170,000 voters.

12. The electoral laws of the July Monarchy also enfranchised members of the Institute de France and retired army officers (the so-called *demi-censeurs*) who paid only Fr 100 in direct taxes. For a detailed treatment of the changing laws governing the suffrage between 1814 and 1870, see Félix Ponteil, *Les institutions de la France de 1814 à 1870* (Paris, 1966).

13. Adeline Daumard, *La bourgeoisie parisienne de 1815 à 1848* (Paris, 1963); and André-Jean Tudesq, *Les grands notables en France, 1840-1849* (Paris, 1964). The *grands notables* were the small group of voters who paid at least Fr 1,000 in direct taxes.

14. Sherman Kent, *Electoral Procedure under Louis Philippe* (New Haven, 1937), p. 30.

15. The tables are located in the appendix.

16. Both the *personelle et mobilière*, which was levied in an attempt to tax large incomes by taxing the external attributes of wealth, and the *portes et fenêtres* have been disregarded in this study, as they are not representative of important differences between various occupational groups within the elite.

17. It remains uncertain to what extent these *propriétaires* were in fact landowners. As Theodore Zeldin remarks, *"propriétaire"* is the closest approximation in French to the English honorific appellation of "gentleman" and may have been used as loosely to define people who no longer directly participated in trade. See Zeldin, *The Political System of Napoleon III* (New York, 1958), p. 58.

18. David Landes, "French Entrepreneurship and Industrial Growth in the Nineteenth Century," *Journal of Economic History* 9 (May 1949): 45-61; also see George V. Taylor, "Noncapitalist Wealth and the French Revolution," *American Historical Review* 72 (1967): 469-96. Taylor's study of "proprietary" capitalism, the investment in land, urban property, and offices in order to "live nobly" on an income unconnected with trade, is as relevant to nineteenth-century bourgeois life as it is to that of the *ancien régime*. By the nineteenth century, however, the atavistic purchase of land, which Taylor believes reflected the "profoundly rural" values of most Frenchmen, had begun to show important regional variations, as the comparison between Reims and St. Etienne demonstrates.

19. Boussinesq and Laurent, *Histoire de Reims*, pp. 520-21.

20. Pierre Delautel, *Notice sur l'histoire de la laine et de l'industrie textile* (Paris, 1907), p. 15.

21. Evelyne Taquet, "L'industrie textile à Reims," *La Champagne économique*, no. 5 (May 1970), p. 198.

22. Departmental Archives of the Marne, 169M7, Expositions of 1839 and 1844.

23. Delautel, *Notice sur l'histoire de la laine*, p. 15.

24. These firms included Lachapelle-Levarlet, founded by the wealthiest of the prerevolutionary woolens manufacturers, Baron Ponsardin; Bertherand-Sutaine, a wealthy Legitimist whose *filature* was the largest within the walls of Reims; and the *filature* of Henriot frères, soeur et Cie, which had previously pioneered in the development of the artisanal weaving of merinos and flannels. See Departmental Archives of the Marne, 169M7, Expositions of 1839 and 1844.

25. *Statistique de la France*, 1835-73, 1st ser., vol. 13.

26. Fohlen, *L'industrie textile*, p. 336; and Delautel, *Notice sur l'histoire de la laine*, pp. 15-16.

27. "Jean-Baptiste David," in Lucien Thiollière, *Notices industrielles: La Chambre de Commerce, bustes et portraits* (St. Etienne, 1894).

28. J. A. de la Tour-Varen, *Note statistique industrielle sur la ville de St. Etienne* (St. Etienne, 1851), pp. 60-61.

29. "Jean-Baptiste David," in Thiollière, *Notices industrielles*. For a discussion of the successive technological improvements of the ribbon looms, see Arthur L. Dunham, *The Industrial Revolution in France, 1815-1848* (New York, 1955), pp. 311-13.

30. C. P. Testenoire-Lafayette, *Histoire de St. Etienne* (St. Etienne, n.d.), p. 118.

31. "Denis Epitalon" and "Jean-Baptiste David," in *Foreziens dignes de mémoire* (St. Etienne, 1889).

32. Louis J. Gras, *Histoire de l'armurerie stéphanoise* (St. Etienne, 1905), pp. 115-22.

33. Testenoire-Lafayette, *Histoire de St. Etienne*, pp. 118-19.

34. Louis J. Gras, *Essai sur l'histoire de la quincaillerie et petite métallurgie* (St. Etienne, 1904), p. 77.

35. Price, *French Second Republic*, pp. 32, 69.

36. For a discussion of the place of the *conseils généraux* in the political reforms of the empire, see Ponteil, *Institutions de la France*, pp. 374-78.

37. André-Jean Tudesq, *Les conseillers généraux en France au temps de Guizot, 1840-1848* (Paris, 1967), p. 273.

38. Bernard Le Clerc and Vincent Wright, *Les préfets du Second Empire* (Paris, 1973), p. 141.

39. Ibid., p. 153.

40. The imperial government's hesitation in appointing the unpopular Edouard Werlé mayor of Reims in 1852 and its unwillingness to support him

in the legislative elections of 1852 and 1857 demonstrates the care that even the dictatorship took in appeasing local bourgeois opinion. Werlé's career will be discussed in detail in the following chapters.

41. Louis J. Gras, *Histoire économique de la métallurgie de la Loire* (St. Etienne, 1908), pp. 32-33.

42. W. F. Jackson, *James Jackson et ses fils* (St. Etienne, 1893), pp. 21-26.

43. Dunham, *Industrial Revolution in France*, p. 134.

44. Jackson, *James Jackson*, pp. 36-37.

45. Gras, *Histoire économique de la métallurgie*, pp. 43-44.

46. Dunham, *Industrial Revolution in France*, p. 141.

47. In 1835 the Terrenoire company operated two smelting furnaces, fourteen puddling furnaces, and a large piston hammer and produced ten thousand tons of iron and steel; by 1838 it employed sixty workers and had acquired a smelting furnace and engine factory at Vienne, four smelting furnaces and a cannonball factory at La Voulte, and coke ovens at Rive-de-Gier. See Gras, *Histoire économique de la métallurgie*, p. 45.

48. Jackson, *James Jackson*, p. 74.

49. Traditionally inexpensive coal had even played a special role in St. Etienne's Mardi Gras celebrations, when in a rare display of prodigality masses of coal were piled in the streets and allowed to burn through the night. Despite the suffocating smoke, workers danced in the streets, the light provided by the coal reminding Bonnefous, who witnessed the scene in 1851, of a scene from the Inferno. See Louis J. Gras, *Histoire économique générale des mines de la Loire*, 2 vols. (St. Etienne, 1922), 1:403-4.

50. Pierre Guillaume, "Les débuts de la grande industrie houillière dans la Loire: Les mines de Roche-la-Molière et de Firminy sous la Restauration," *Cahiers d'histoire* 4 (1959): 125.

51. Pierre Guillaume, *La compagnie des mines de la Loire, 1846-1854* (Paris, 1966), pp. 18-19.

52. Dunham, *Industrial Revolution in France*, p. 105.

53. Guillaume, *La compagnie des mines de la Loire*, p. 135.

54. Ibid., pp. 69, 79, 167-68, 171.

55. Ibid., pp. 102, 160, 181.

56. The miners (of whom there were 4,632 in the St. Etienne basin in 1848) were convinced, as were many members of the local elite, that the Compagnie générale was attempting to reduce wages in order to offset the enormous cost of its purchase of many mines at inflated prices. Tensions were further exacerbated by the company's disregard of the limits of the twelve-hour day, as well as by the brutal discipline to which the miners were subjected by company engineers and supervisors. The 1846 strike at St. Etienne had begun when a divisional engineer told the miners that they were lazy and incompetent and would soon be obliged to survive on a diet of bread, water, and potatoes like miners in other basins. See Petrus Faure, *Histoire du mouvement ouvrier dans le département de la Loire* (St. Etienne, 1955), pp. 124-25; and Guillaume, *La compagnie des mines de la Loire*, p. 164.

57. As early as 1840 the striking miners had received the almost unanimous sympathy of the local population, which blamed the strike on wage reductions imposed by the large coal companies. See Guillaume, *La compagnie des mines de la Loire*, p. 189.

58. *Le Mémorial de la Loire*, April 5, 1846.

59. Guillaume, *La compagnie des mines de la Loire*, p. 187.

60. Archives Nationales, BB18 1440 (1881), *Procureur général* to the garde des sceaux, April 2, 1846.

61. Louis Chevalier, "Les fondements économiques et sociaux de l'histoire politique de la région parisienne, 1848-1870" (Ph.D. dissertation, Sorbonne, 1950), p. 715.

62. Boussinesq and Laurent, *Histoire de Reims*, p. 500.

63. Léon Faucher, the opposition deputy elected in 1846, had been born in Limoges in 1803. Although from a very poor family, he had eventually become a journalist and occasional contributor to the *Revue des deux mondes*, in which he championed prison reforms as well as free trade. In 1847 he was a leader of Reims's banquet campaign but refused to participate in the planned meeting in Paris. After February 1848 he opposed the establishment of the national workshops, the government guarantee of full employment, and any limitation of working hours. Faucher's conservatism recommended him to Louis-Napoleon Bonaparte, and he was appointed minister of public works in December 1848; he later became minister of the interior. He was obliged to resign in May 1849 after blatantly using the prefects and police to ensure a conservative victory in the legislative elections. Faucher was, however, still able to participate in government policy making. He was a member of the commission that drafted the law of May 31, 1850, establishing residency requirements for voting, which disenfranchised many urban workers. He became a minister in the government again in April 1851 but resigned in October in protest over the repeal of the 1850 electoral law. Following the establishment of the Second Empire, he played a role in the creation of the Crédit mobilier and died in Marseilles in 1854.

64. The Legitimist party, led by *grands notables* such as Bertherand-Sutaine, as well as other wealthy families such as the Goulets, Rogelets, and Brimonts, opposed the Orleanist elite on religious as well as political grounds. The party owed its popular following to the philanthropies of its leading members. It had supported the conservative candidate Chaix d'Este-Ange in the legislative election of 1844 but later became disillusioned with him. By 1846 its leaders created a new alliance with the liberal opposition, which they attempted to preserve until 1848. See Georges Boussinesq, *Reims à la fin de la Monarchie de Juillet et pendant la période révolutionnaire de 1848* (Reims, 1923), pp. 13-16.

65. Boussinesq and Laurent, *Histoire de Reims*, p. 514.

66. Archives Nationales, Fic III 3 Marne, Prefect to the minister of the interior, August 16, 1846.

67. Boussinesq and Laurent, *Histoire de Reims*, p. 538.

68. Untitled electoral pamphlet for the legislative election of 1849, CR II 408 MM 3ième liasse, Municipal Library of Reims.

69. Departmental Archives of the Marne, 30M15, Reports of the *police politique*, February 19, 1847.

70. Boussinesq and Laurent, *Histoire de Reims*, pp. 544-45.

Chapter 2

1. Marx's works on French political developments between 1848 and 1850, which first appeared in the *Neue Rheinische Zeitung*, have been collected in Karl Marx, *Class Struggles in France, 1848-1850* (New York, 1964).

2. Karl Marx, *The Eighteenth Brumaire of Louis Bonaparte* (New York, 1963), pp. 22-23.

3. Roger Price, *The French Second Republic: A Social History* (Ithaca, 1972); Maurice Agulhon, *La république au village* (Paris, 1970); John Merriman, *The Agony of the Republic* (New Haven, 1978); and Ted Margadant, *French Peasants in Revolt: The Insurrection of 1851* (Princeton, 1979).

4. Price, *French Second Republic*, p. 123.

5. Jean Lhomme, *Economie et histoire* (Paris, 1967), p. 70; also see Charles Tilly, "The Changing Place of Collective Violence," in Peter Stearns and Daniel Walkowitz, eds., *Workers in the Industrial Revolution* (New Brunswick, 1974), p. 130.

6. For examples of modern studies of provincial political life under the Second Republic, see William H. Sewell, Jr., *Work and Revolution in France* (Cambridge, Mass., 1980); Margadant, *French Peasants in Revolt*; Leo Loubère, "The Emergence of the Extreme Left in Lower Languedoc, 1848-1851: Social and Economic Factors in Politics," *American Historical Review* 73 (1968): 1019-51; Georges Dupeux, *Aspects de l'histoire sociale et politique du Loir-et-Cher, 1848-1914* (Paris, 1962); C. Marcilhacy, "Les caractères de la crise sociale et politique de 1846 à 1852 dans le département du Loiret," *Revue d'histoire moderne et contemporaine* 6 (1959): 5-59; and Philippe Vigier, *La Seconde République dans la région alpine*, 2 vols. (Paris, 1953).

7. Price, *French Second Republic*, p. 189.

8. Ibid., p. 133.

9. Tilly, "Changing Place of Collective Violence," pp. 130-31.

10. Georges Boussinesq, *Reims à la fin de la Monarchie de Juillet et pendant la période révolutionnaire de 1848* (Reims, 1923), p. 52.

11. Georges Clause, "L'industrie lainière rémoise à l'époque napoléonienne," *Revue d'histoire moderne et contemporaine* 17 (July-September 1970): 93; and Georges Boussinesq and Gustave Laurent, *Histoire de Reims depuis les origines jusqu'à nos jours* (Reims, 1933), p. 642.

12. Louis Villermé, *Tableau de l'état physique et moral des ouvriers* (Paris, 1840), pp. 235-38.

13. Boussinesq and Laurent, *Histoire de Reims*, pp. 642-48. Wages paid in 1847 to male wool combers had fallen from Fr 1.75 to Fr 1.50, and to women from Fr 1.20 to Fr 1; the wages of weavers of fine woolens goods fell from Fr 1.25 to Fr 1 and from Fr 1.75 to Fr 1.60 for weavers of *nouveautés*. See Departmental Archives of the Marne, 134M1, Cost of Living.

14. Boussinesq and Laurent, *Histoire de Reims*, p. 568.

15. Radical revolutionary demands seem to have been widely publicized among artisans from the earliest days of the revolution. These included the incorporation of all men aged twenty-one and over in the National Guard, control of bread prices, the elimination of *livrets* and the tax (*octroi*) on foodstuffs, and the reduction of rents. See Armand Audiganne, *Les populations ouvrières et les industries de la France*, 2 vols. (Paris, 1860), 2:133.

16. Leo A. Loubère, "The Intellectual Origins of French Jacobin Socialism," *International Review of Social History* 4 (1959): 422, cited in Robert J. Bezucha, *The Lyon Uprising of 1834: Social and Political Conflict in the Early July Monarchy* (Cambridge, Mass., 1974), p. 117, and Price, *French Second Republic*, p. 72. For a more detailed discussion of the connection between the corporate tradition of artisan workers and the development of political organizations during the period of the Second Republic, see William Sewell, "Social Change and the Rise of Working Class Politics in Nineteenth Century Marseilles," *Past and Present*, no. 65 (November 1974), pp. 75-109, and "The Working Class of Marseilles under the Second Republic: Social Structure and Political Behavior," in Stearns and Walkowitz, eds., *Workers in the Industrial Revolution*, pp. 75-116.

17. Boussinesq and Laurent, *Histoire de Reims*, p. 649.

18. *Le Républicain*, March 10, 13, 21, April 7, 1848.

19. Boussinesq, *Reims à la fin de la Monarchie de Juillet*, p. 34.

20. Ponce Nollet, *Organisation industrielle: la place de Reims* (1845), pamphlet in the Municipal Library of Reims.

21. Boussinesq, *Reims à la fin de la Monarchie de Juillet*, pp. 96-97. In April both the sub-prefect and the municipal government requested the billeting of cavalry at Reims to maintain order. See Departmental Archives of the Marne, 194M4, Strikes, 1834-79, sub-prefect to the citizen commissar, April 11, 1848.

22. *Le Courrier de la Champagne*, March 13, 1848.

23. Boussinesq and Laurent, *Histoire de Reims*, pp. 582-83.

24. *Le Républicain*, March 21, April 14, 1848.

25. Price, *French Second Republic*, p. 129.

26. Boussinesq, *Reims à la fin de la Monarchie de Juillet*, p. 117; and *Le Républicain*, April 18, 1848.

27. Boussinesq and Laurent, *Histoire de Reims*, p. 607.

28. For a more detailed discussion of the consequences of the change from the *scrutin d'arrondissement* to the *scrutin de liste*, see André-Jean Tudesq, *Les grands notables en France, 1840-1849* (Paris, 1964), pp. 1228-30.

29. Louis Chevalier believes David, the government commissioner at Reims, approved of these measures; see "Les fondements économiques et

sociaux de l'histoire politique de la région parisienne, 1848-1870" (Ph.D. dissertation, Sorbonne, 1950), p. 267.

30. Boussinesq, *Reims à la fin de la Monarchie de Juillet*, pp. 121-22.

31. *L'Indicateur de la Champagne*, July 20, 1848.

32. *L'Industriel de la Champagne*, July 29, 1848.

33. Boussinesq and Laurent, *Histoire de Reims*, p. 626.

34. Price, *French Second Republic*, pp. 140, 190-91.

35. Departmental Archives of the Marne, 12M236, Municipal Council Reports, 1848-70, Report of August 2, 1848.

36. This is Price's assessment of the country's political mood during the presidential elections; see *French Second Republic*, p. 214.

37. Price believes this latter attitude was especially widespread among the workers in larger cities, such as Paris and Lyons; see ibid., p. 215.

38. Both Royet and Robichon were ribbon manufacturers; Paliard was an arms *fabricant*. See Stanislas Bossakiewicz, *Histoire générale de St. Etienne* (St. Etienne, 1905), p. 245.

39. Bezucha, *Lyon Uprising of 1834*, p. 88.

40. Bossakiewicz, *Histoire générale de St. Etienne*, pp. 246-47.

41. *L'Avenir républicain*, May 10, 1848.

42. *Société populaire: Liste des candidats à la représentation nationale*, electoral pamphlet, Municipal Library of St. Etienne.

43. Pierre Guillaume, "La situation économique et sociale du département de la Loire d'après l'enquête sur le travail agricole et industriel du 25 mai 1848," *Actes du 86ième congrès national des sociétés savants: section d'histoire moderne et contemporaine* (1961), pp. 22, 29.

44. Petrus Faure, *Histoire du mouvement ouvrier dans le département de la Loire* (St. Etienne, 1955), pp. 120-23.

45. Archives Nationales, BB18 1390 (1590), St. Etienne: Organization of *maîtres et ouvriers passementiers*, 1841-42, minister of the interior to the garde des sceaux, March 5, 1841. The Investigative Commission of 1848 found that a married master weaver (*chef d'atelier*) with two looms could hope to earn Fr 1,296 a year, which after expenses yielded a profit of Fr 886, a sum clearly insufficient to support a family of four. Other workers earned even less; *devideuses* earned 60 to 90 centimes for a sixteen hour day, ordinary ribbon workers 50 to 80 centimes, and the highest paid *ourdisseuses* Fr 1.40; others earned only 70 centimes a day. See Faure, *Histoire du mouvement ouvrier*, p. 113; and Departmental Archives of the Loire, 84M7, Medical Commission Attached to the Industrial and Agricultural Inquiry for the Two Cantons of St. Etienne.

46. Archives Nationales, BB 18 (1590), St. Etienne: Organization of *maîtres et ouvriers passementiers*, 1841-42; minister of the interior to the garde des sceaux, June 4, 25, 1841; *procureur général* to the garde des sceaux, January 11, 1842.

47. Guillaume, "Situation du département de la Loire," pp. 31-33. The masters also demanded payment in money rather than chits, which were

frequently discounted by the merchants. These demands were met after 1848 by the government of the Second Republic, which also stipulated that prompt payment be made to workers by the merchants' agents (*commissionnaires*) or other intermediaries upon receipt of finished work. See Departmental Archives of the Loire, 84M7, Industrial Work, Correspondence, 1825-50, minister of agriculture and commerce to the prefect, July 15, 1850.

48. Robert Bezucha believes that a similar union was possible at Lyons because the journeymen, who had the most serious grievances, were a floating population, constantly leaving and entering the trade and thus unable to formulate demands that might have threatened the masters; see *Lyon Uprising of 1834*, pp. 45-46.

49. *Le Mercure seguisien*, April 16, 1848.

50. Bossakiewicz, *Histoire générale de St. Etienne*, p. 248.

51. *Le Mercure seguisien*, April 14, 1848.

52. Untitled pamphlets on the legislative election of 1849, Municipal Library of St. Etienne; also see *L'Avenir républicain*, March 30, 1848.

53. Bossakiewicz, *Histoire générale de St. Etienne*, pp. 439-40.

54. *La Sentinelle populaire*, August 9, 1848.

55. Departmental Archives of the Loire, 2M1, Presidential Election of 1848.

56. Boussinesq and Laurent, *Histoire de Reims*, p. 629.

57. This activity included a petition presented by workers to the minister of the interior in April 1849 requesting the creation of a commission of employers, foremen, and artisans to set a uniform scale of wages for woolens workers that would be enforced in the countryside as well as in the city. See Archives Nationales, F12 2370-74, Subsistence.

58. Boussinesq and Laurent, *Histoire de Reims*, p. 636.

59. Ibid., p. 638.

60. Ibid.

61. *L'Association rémoise*, June 2, 1850.

62. Departmental Archives of the Marne, 7M28, Legislative Election of 1849. Louis Chevalier believes the liberals received most of their support from small and middle bourgeois groups in the towns who were still anxious to preserve the republic and the constitution. See Chevalier, "Les fondements économiques et sociaux," p. 435.

63. Price, *French Second Republic*, pp. 231, 236-39.

64. Boussinesq and Laurent, *Histoire de Reims*, pp. 644-45, 648, 650. Eugène Courmeaux was a champagne salesman for J. H. Mumm in Asia Minor and the Crimea before his return to France. Dérodé, who later re-entered political life, ran unsuccessfully in the legislative election of 1857 and died in 1864. See ibid., p. 738.

65. *L'Association rémoise*, June 2, 1850.

66. The electoral law of May 31, 1850, required that all voters be residents of one place for three years, attested to by a tax receipt or an employer's affidavit; this policy primarily affected industrial workers, who were at once both the most migratory and radical element in the population.

67. Boussinesq and Laurent, *Histoire de Reims*, pp. 661-62.

68. Departmental Archives of the Marne, 194M9, Strikes, 1834-79.

69. Price, *French Second Republic*, p. 133.

70. Boussinesq and Laurent, *Histoire de Reims*, pp. 667-71.

71. This is the opinion of Chevalier, "Les fondements économiques et sociaux," p. 622.

72. Theodore Zeldin, *The Political System of Napoleon III* (New York, 1958), p. 11.

73. Georges Lallement, *Edouard Werlé, négociant en vins de Champagne, maire de la ville de Reims, député au Corps législatif (1801-1884)*, pamphlet of the Société des amis de vieux Reims.

74. *La Concorde*, December 9, 1852; Price, *French Second Republic*, p. 275.

75. Departmental Archives of the Marne, 12M236, Municipal Council Reports, 1848-70, Report of August 28, 1852.

76. Departmental Archives of the Marne, 7M31, Legislative Election of 1852. The Corps législatif, which under the Second Empire replaced the National Assembly, had only 260 members and was required to meet for only three months a year to approve the budget and legislation presented by the government. It could not introduce legislation, and its debates were published only in brief official summaries that prevented any criticism of the regime from becoming known. The powers of this body began to approximate those of a true parliament only in the last years of the empire.

77. Archives Nationales, BB30 383, Reports of the *procureur général* to the minister of justice, October 15, December 20, 1852.

78. M. E. Brossard, *Les élections et les répresentants du département de la Loire aux assemblés législatifs, 1789-1889* (St. Etienne, 1889), p. 62.

79. Departmental Archives of the Loire, 3M7, Legislative Election of 1849.

80. Archives Nationales, BB30 379, Reports of the *procureur général* to the minister of justice, June 7, 1850.

81. Price, *French Second Republic*, pp. 232-33.

82. Archives Nationales, BB30 379, Reports of the *procureur général* to the minister of justice, June 7, 1850.

83. Archives Nationales, Fic III, 4, Loire (270), July 16, 1850.

84. Bossakiewicz, *Histoire générale de St. Etienne*, p. 255.

85. *L'Avenir républicain*, October 1, 26, 1850.

86. Archives Nationales, BB30 379, Reports of the *procureur général* to the minister of justice, February 3, April 23, May 20, 1851.

87. Departmental Archives of the Loire, 2M2, Plebiscite of 1851.

88. *L'Industrie* (the former *L'Avenir républicain*), March 3, 1852.

89. Departmental Archives of the Loire, 10M39, Political Events, February to June 1852, Reports of February 15-25, 1852.

90. Balay was one of the very few local notables to invest heavily in the Compagnie générale des mines de la Loire. See Archives Nationales, BB30 379, Reports of the *procureur général* to the minister of justice, March 8, 1852.

91. Martin had previously defeated General de Grammont, the commanding officer of the local military government, in the legislative by-election of 1850. See Departmental Archives of the Loire, 10M39, Political Events, February to June 1852, Report of April 24, 1852.

92. *L'Industrie*, September 3, 1852.

93. Departmental Archives of the Loire, 6M15, Municipal Council Elections, 1837-55, Election of 1852.

94. Archives Nationales, BB30 379, Reports of the *procureur général* to the minister of justice, December 11, 1852.

Chapter 3

1. Fernand Braudel and Ernest Labrousse, *Histoire économique et sociale de la France*, 7 vols. (Paris, 1976), 3: 484.

2. Georges Boussinesq and Gustave Laurent, *Histoire de Reims depuis les origines jusqu'à nos jours* (Reims, 1933), p. 720.

3. Claude Fohlen, *L'industrie textile au temps du Second Empire* (Paris, 1956), p. 344.

4. Georges Le Guesnier, *Reims et le pays rémois en 1872* (Reims, 1873), p. 83. Holden also operated factories at St. Denis and at Croix near Roubaix; in 1867 the payroll of these three plants was in excess of Fr 350,000F. See Louis Reybaud, *La laine: Nouvelle série des études sur le régime des manufactures* (Paris, 1867), p. 142.

5. Recent studies of social structure based on the use of the *Mutation après décès* and the *Tables des successions et absences* include Adeline Daumard, *La bourgeoisie parisienne de 1815 à 1848* (Paris, 1963), and *Les fortunes françaises au XIXième siècle: Enquête sur la répartition et la composition des capitaux privés à Paris, Lyon, Lille, Bordeaux, et Toulouse d'après l'enregistrement des droits de succession* (Paris, 1973); M. C. Aboucaya, *Les structures sociales et économiques de l'agglomeration lyonnaise à la veille de la révolution de 1848* (Lyons, 1963); Félix Codaccioni, "Lille: Etude sociale, 1850-1914" (Ph.D. dissertation, University of Lille, 1971); Jesus Ibarrola, *Structure sociale et fortune mobilière et immobilière à Grenoble en 1847* (Grenoble, 1965); and Pierre Léon, *Geographie de la fortune et structures sociales à Lyon au XIXième siècle, 1815-1914* (Lyons, 1974).

6. For a more detailed discussion of community property, see Daumard, *Les fortunes françaises*, pp. 80-85.

7. It is also difficult to assess the wealth of members of the bourgeoisie who owned little property but received high salaries not indicated in the *Mutation*. As Adeline Daumard points out, however, a bourgeoisie without patrimony, though not unknown (especially among state officials), represented a negligible portion of the provincial bourgeoisie in this period (*Les fortunes françaises*, pp. 100, 589).

8. Roger Price also blames low profit margins in the woolens industry for limited investment in machinery before the 1860s (*The Economic Modernization of France, 1730-1880* [New York, 1975], p. 105).

9. Fohlen, *L'industrie textile*, p. 96.

10. Theodore Zeldin, *France, 1848-1945: Love, Ambition and Politics* (Oxford, 1973), p. 68.

11. Fohlen, *L'industrie textile*, pp. 124-25; also see pp. 176-77.

12. Departmental Archives of the Marne, 186M7, Industrial Statistics, 1850-60, sub-prefect to the prefect, October 8, 1856.

13. Boussinesq and Laurent, *Histoire de Reims*, p. 720.

14. Departmental Archives of the Marne, 186M8, Industrial Statistics, Industrial Census of 1860.

15. Fohlen, *L'industrie textile*, pp. 124-25.

16. Henri See, *La vie économique de la France sous la Monarchie de Juillet* (Paris, 1927), p. 62.

17. See Tihomir J. Markovich, "Le revenu industriel et artisanal sous la Monarchie de Juillet et le Second Empire," *Economies et sociétés* 8 (April 1967): 91-93.

18. Price, *Economic Modernization of France*, pp. 164-65.

19. César Poulain, *L'agriculture et les traités de commerce* (Paris, 1879), Tables synoptiques de l'industrie lainière, 1789-1879. The growth of the French woolens industry was reflected in the consumption of raw wool, which rose from 90,000 tons in 1850 to 160,000 tons in 1870. See Price, *Economic Modernization of France*, p. 106.

20. Fohlen, *L'industrie textile*, pp. 335-36.

21. Ibid., pp. 18, 128, 336.

22. Boussinesq and Laurent, *Histoire de Reims*, p. 720.

23. Departmental Archives of the Marne, 172M3, Chamber of Commerce, 1859-1911, Report of the Chamber of Commerce to the prefect, July 26, 1858. The woolens boom, which encouraged mechanization, also helped prolong the life of artisan industry. The breakdown of occupations within the industry published by Louis Reybaud in 1867 shows thirty-eight thousand workers still employed on hand looms both in the city and its immediate suburbs, as compared with only nine hundred workers serving thirteen hundred mechanized looms. The survey also reveals one thousand workers engaged in wool combing and seventy-four hundred in wool spinning. See Reybaud, *La laine*, p. 334.

24. Departmental Archives of the Marne, 194M9, Strikes, 1834-79, mayor to the prefect, March 1, 1850.

25. Fohlen, *L'industrie textile*, pp. 335-36.

26. Price, *Economic Modernization of France*, p. 152.

27. *Le comptoir d'escompte Chapuis et Cie, 1854-1924* (Reims, 1925), p. 49, Municipal Library of Reims.

28. Departmental Archives of the Marne, Q non côté, *Mutation après décès*, Reims.

29. Departmental Archives of the Marne, 186M7, Industrial Statistics, 1850-60, sub-prefect to the prefect, May 9, 1860.

30. The law of May 23, 1863, allowed the creation of joint stock companies without government authorization if capitalization did not exceed Fr 20 million. This restriction was abandoned in 1867. As a result, the 110 share companies (with a capitalized value of Fr 11 billion) traded on the Paris Bourse in 1851 increased by 1869 to 307 companies capitalized at Fr 31 billion. The *société en commandite*, which made a distinction between those responsible for the administration of a company and a sleeping partner enjoying limited liability, had already begun to facilitate economic expansion in the 1850s. See Price, *Economic Modernization of France*, p. 147.

31. Julien Turgan, *Les grandes usines: Etudes industrielles en France et à l'étranger*, 18 vols. (Paris, 1871), 8: 121-22.

32. Fohlen, *L'industrie textile*, pp. 335-36.

33. Adeline Daumard has found similar developments in manufacturing centers such as Lyons and Lille, where the growth of industrial fortunes under the Second Empire was also accompanied by a marked increase of investment in joint stock companies (*Les fortunes françaises*, pp. 145, 164-65).

34. In 1848 only 5 percent of bourgeois wealth was invested in share companies, as compared with 58 percent in land and houses, but by 1900 the proportion of wealth in real estate had fallen to 45 percent and investments in shares had risen to 31 percent. See Zeldin, *France*, pp. 59-60.

35. Departmental Archives of the Marne, 186M7, Industrial Statistics, 1850-60, sub-prefect to the prefect, September 1, 1865.

36. Le Guesnier, *Reims et le pays rémois*, p. 1.

37. Departmental Archives of the Marne, 186M7, Industrial Statistics, 1866-68, Report of the sub-prefect, May 30, 1868.

38. Arthur L. Dunham, *The Anglo-French Treaty of Commerce of 1860 and the Progress of the Industrial Revolution in France* (Ann Arbor, 1930), p. 235.

39. Departmental Archives of the Marne, 186M7, Industrial Statistics, 1850-60, sub-prefect to the prefect, June 19, 1860.

40. Departmental Archives of the Marne, 172M3, Chamber of Commerce, 1859-1911, Report of the Chamber of Commerce to the prefect, August 6, 1860.

41. Maurice Hollande, *La Chambre de Commerce de Reims, 1801-1951* (Reims, 1951), pp. 72-76; and Departmental Archives of the Marne, 169M10, International Exposition of 1867, sub-prefect to the prefect, November 21, 1866.

42. Departmental Archives of the Marne, 186M7, Industrial Statistics, 1869-74, Chamber of Commerce to the sub-prefect, December 20, 1869; and 172M12, Chamber of Commerce of Reims, Elections, 1819-72.

43. Departmental Archives of the Marne, 87M61, Société industrielle, undated report; mayor to the sub-prefect, July 12, 1861; prefect to the minister of the interior, April 11, 1861; and mayor to the sub-prefect, September 11, 1866.

44. Ibid., prefect to the minister of the interior, April 11, 1861; mayor to the sub-prefect, September 11, 1866.

Chapter 4

1. Lucien Thiollière, "Rubannerie," *Association française pour l'avancement des sciences*, 26th sess., 2 (August 1897): pp. 83-84, 88-89.

2. *Statistique de la France*, 1835-73, 1st ser., vol. 13.

3. Departmental Archives of the Loire, Industrial Inquiry of 1848, Arrondissement of St. Etienne, Canton of St. Etienne.

4. By 1856 St. Etienne had fifteen thousand looms; the value of ribbon sales rose from Fr 45 million (Lequin claims 37) to 97 million. See Thiollière, "Rubannerie," p. 70; and Yves Lequin, *Les ouvriers de la région lyonnaise, 1848-1914*, 2 vols. (Lyons, 1977), 1: 70.

5. Departmental Archives of the Marne, 186M8, Statistique industrielle, Industrial Census of 1860.

6. The seriousness of this problem was reflected in the decline of the city's population, which fell from more than one hundred thousand people (after the annexation of its suburban communes in 1855) to ninety-two thousand in 1861. See Louis J. Gras, *Histoire du commerce local* (St. Etienne, 1910), pp. 614-20.

7. Thiollière, "Rubannerie," p. 69.

8. Several of the most important ribbon manufacturers made some efforts to modernize production in the face of foreign competition; factories were built by Vignat at Bourg-Argental, by Colcombet at La Seauve, and by Balay at Sainte-Foy (in the department of the Rhône). The hostility of St. Etienne's artisans to factory work prevented similar experiments in the city. See Louis J. Gras, *Histoire de la rubannerie et des industries de la soie à St. Etienne et dans la région stéphanoise* (St. Etienne, 1906), p. 623.

9. Archives Nationales, BB30 379, Reports of the *procureur général* to the minister of justice, January 4, 1859.

10. In 1862 a local commentator complained of the fickleness of fashion, which had abandoned ribbons in favor of lace, and lamented the insecure base upon which the prosperity of the entire *fabrique* was built. See Gras, *Histoire de la rubannerie*, pp. 622-23.

11. Archives Nationales, BB30 379, Reports of the *procureur général* to the minister of justice, Report of April 2, 1863.

12. Arthur L. Dunham, *The Anglo-French Treaty of Commerce of 1860 and the Progress of the Industrial Revolution in France* (Ann Arbor, 1930), pp. 154-55.

13. Louis J. Gras, *Histoire de la Chambre de Commerce de St. Etienne, 1833-1898* (St. Etienne, 1898), p. 176.

14. Gras, *Histoire de la rubannerie*, pp. 610-16; also see Archives Nationales, BB30 379, Reports of the *procureur général* to the minister of justice, July

9, 1870. By 1867 the number of ribbon manufacturing houses had fallen back to 250, and the number of active looms had fallen to 8,000 (ibid., p. 618).

15. Thiollière, "Rubannerie," p. 79.

16. Louis J. Gras, *Histoire de l'armurerie stéphanoise* (St. Etienne, 1905), pp. 238-42.

17. The growth of the arms industry was chiefly responsible for the increase of the city's population from 92,000 in 1861 to 110,000 in 1872. See ibid., p. 241.

18. Frank E. Manuel, "The Luddite Movement in France," *Journal of Modern History* 10 (1938): 181-83; and Gras, *Histoire de la rubannerie*, p. 210. Artisans had protested against the introduction of machinery in the arms industry in 1790 and again in 1831, when a riot left dozens wounded. See Petrus Faure, *Histoire du mouvement ouvrier dans le département de la Loire* (St. Etienne, 1955), pp. 109-10.

19. The wider distribution of orders was also a result of Escoffier's inefficiency. See Gras, *Histoire de l'armurerie stéphanoise*, pp. 243-44.

20. Société industrielle et agricole de St. Etienne, *Rapport de la commission chargé de réchercher les causes de la décadence de la quincaillerie à St. Etienne, et les moyens de la régénérer*, 1852, Municipal Library of St. Etienne.

21. Artisan *quincailleurs* lived in the worst housing in the city and subsisted on a diet of potatoes and thin soup. A fourteen-hour work day combined with malnutrition made them particularly susceptible to tuberculosis. See Departmental Archives of the Loire, 84M7, Medical Commission Attached to the Industrial and Agricultural Inquiry for the Two Cantons of St. Etienne.

22. Société industrielle, *Rapport de la commission*.

23. Though some new methods, including the use of steam-powered air pumps, were introduced into coal mining under the Second Empire, the industry remained unaffected by major technological changes and continued to depend heavily upon manual labor. See Fernand Braudel and Ernest Labrousse, *Histoire économique et sociale de la France*, 7 vols. (Paris, 1976), 2: 489.

24. Jean Vial, *L'industrialisation de la sidérurgie française, 1814- 1864* (Paris, 1967), pp. 112, 169-70, 232-33.

25. Ibid., pp. 169-70.

26. Chambre de Commerce de St. Etienne, *Rapport des délibérations relatifs à l'adjonction des mines de la Grand' Combe (Gard) à la Compagnie des mines de la Loire*, October 20, 1852, Municipal Library of St. Etienne.

27. The Compagnie générale des mines de la Loire was replaced by four independent companies: the Société anonyme des houillères de St. Etienne, the Société anonyme des houillères de Montrambert et de la Berardière, the Société anonyme des mines de la Loire, and the Société anonyme des houillères de Rive-de-Gier. In 1854 the four companies accounted for 55 percent of all production in the region; in 1869 they and two others accounted for 75 percent of all production. See Lequin, *Les ouvriers de la région lyonnaise*, 1: 53; and Louis J. Gras, *Histoire économique générale des mines de la Loire*, 2 vols. (St. Etienne, 1922), 2: 729-31.

28. Pierre Guillaume, *La compagnie des mines de la Loire, 1846-1854* (Paris, 1966), p. 223; and Guillaume, "La mine de houille dans la Loire sous le Second Empire," (Master's thesis, 1956), pp. 60-61. Other ties between the coal and steel industries were created by Charles Jackson's seat on the board of the Rive-de-Gier coal company. Other members of the local elite on coal boards included Antoine Neyrand (also in the Rive-de-Gier company), Ernest Neyron on the board of the St. Etienne company, and Francisque Balay on the Montrambert board. See Gras, *Histoire économique générale des mines*, 1: 460.

29. For a recent discussion of the importance of the "steel revolution" in the development of French industry under the Second Empire, see Braudel and Labrousse, *Histoire économique et sociale de la France*, 3: 487-89, also pp. 113, 129.

30. Steelworkers were also among the first to be subjected to modern factory discipline. According to the rules of the Terrenoire company in the 1820s, a ten-minute lateness was punished with the loss of a half day's pay and more than ten minutes with the loss of a full day's pay; a full day's absence cost two days' wages. Insubordination and drunkenness were also punished by fines. See Louis J. Gras, *Histoire économique de la métallurgie de la Loire* (St. Etienne, 1908), p. 46.

31. Guy Thuillier, *Georges Dufaud et les débuts de grande capitalisme dans la métallurgie en Nivernais au XIXième siècle* (Paris, 1959), p. 41.

32. Claude Fohlen, "Bourgeoisie française: Liberté économique et intervention de l'état," *Revue économique* 7 (May 1956): 416.

33. W. F. Jackson, *James Jackson et ses fils* (St. Etienne, 1893), pp. 150-51.

34. Thuillier, *Georges Dufaud*, pp. 40-41.

35. Jackson, *James Jackson*, pp. 94-96.

36. Ibid., pp. 96-101.

37. Ibid., pp. 103-05.

38. Gras, *Histoire économique de la métallurgie*, pp. 130-32.

39. Archives Nationales, BB30 379, Reports of the *procureur général* to the minister of justice, July 10, 1859.

40. Georges Duchêne, *L'économie politique de l'Empire* (Paris, 1870), pp. 69-70.

41. Gras, *Histoire économique de la métallurgie*, p. 217. "Having raised itself to the level of a public institution," one commentator wrote, "the company remained unaffected by the crisis created by free trade" (Jacques Valserres, *Les industries de la Loire* [St. Etienne, 1862]).

42. Julien Turgan, *Les grandes usines: Etudes industrielles en France et à l'étranger*, 18 vols. (Paris, 1865), 4: 207.

43. Gras, *Histoire économique de la métallurgie*, p. 251. Le Creusot also grew rapidly in this period, expanding its operations to include the building of locomotives as well as ships at its naval yard at Chalons-sur-Saone. See Braudel and Labrousse, *Histoire économique et sociale de la France*, 3: 516.

44. Departmental Archives of the Loire, 80M5, Letters of Jullien, the director of Terrenoire, to the prefect, August 21, December 4, 1872. By 1869

Terrenoire had six Bessemer and four Martin furnaces, as well as 114 puddling furnaces, all fed by the company's smelting furnaces in the Ardèche. See Lequin, *Les ouvriers de la région lyonnaise*, 1: 54; and Gras, *Histoire économique de la métallurgie*, p. 218.

45. Gras, *Histoire économique de la métallurgie*, pp. 224-27. Before the Revolution of 1848, the Holtzer company had produced only seven hundred tons of cast iron and puddled steel per year. But in 1852 it introduced the Wolf and Langwiller puddling process, making it one of the first French companies to produce puddled steel in large quantities. It began the manufacture of bells and other cast pieces in 1857 and by 1860 employed more than five hundred workers on a payroll of Fr 452,000. See ibid., pp. 224-25, 269.

46. Ibid., pp. 223-24. The company, originally a *société en commandite*, had been founded by François-Félix Verdié, the brother of Xavier Verdié, the director of the foundries at Lorette. It was later transformed into a joint stock company in 1867. Verdié had been born in the Ariège and began life as a draftsman. He worked at Assailly in 1831 and founded a small steel factory at Lyons in 1838. Ruined by the events of 1848, he later founded the Firminy company to exploit a process he had invented for strengthening iron machine parts by surfacing them with steel. The introduction of mixed iron and steel pieces resulted in a considerable savings for steel users and was highly praised at the Industrial Exposition of 1855. Verdié remained an innovator in the industry, helping in the 1860s to perfect the electric Siemens-Martin furnaces. See ibid., pp. 223, 267-68.

47. Darmancier, "Material de guerre," *Association française pour l'avancement des sciences*, 26th sess., 2 (August 1897): 214-16.

48. Gras, *Histoire économique de la métallurgie*, p. 177. The government had provided a fifty-year state guarantee for the P-L-M bond issue of 1860, while also guaranteeing government support for the amortization of new and existing lines; this represented a total commitment of more than Fr 1.125 billion. See Albert Meinadier, *La Compagnie des chemins de fer de Paris à Lyon et à la Méditerranée* (Paris, 1908), p. 109.

49. L. Babu, "La métallurgie dans la Loire," *Association française pour l'avancement des sciences*, 26th sess., 2 (August 1897): 153-57; and Braudel and Labrousse, *Histoire économique et sociale de la France*, 3: 567.

50. Guillaume, "La mine de houille dans la Loire," pp. 93-94; also see Gras, *Histoire économique de la métallurgie*, pp. 180-81; and *Lettre du duc de Persigny à son excellence M. le Marquis de Talhouet*, 1870, Municipal Library of St. Etienne.

51. For a discussion of this development, see Braudel and Labrousse, *Histoire économique et sociale de la France*, 2: 145-47.

52. David Landes, "French Entrepreneurship and Industrial Growth in the Nineteenth Century," *Journal of Economic History* 9 (May 1949): 51.

53. Unlike investors at Reims, the elite of St. Etienne invested in only a few major railroad companies, notably those of the Nord, Est, and Paris à Lyon et à la Méditerranée.

54. The Société de Commentry-Fourchamboult et Decazeville, for example, never distributed a dividend of more than Fr 60 between 1854 and 1914, though its average earning per share exceeded Fr 200. Similarly, though the average earnings of the Société des forges de St. Etienne was over Fr 300 a share between 1869 and 1914, it never paid a dividend above Fr 90. See Roger Price, *The Economic Modernization of France, 1730-1880* (New York, 1975), p. 74.

55. The size of capital investments in metallurgy in the 1850s can be appreciated by comparing the Fr 49 million invested in steelmaking and the Fr 1 million in armsmaking. See Gras, *Histoire économique de la métallurgie*, p. 238.

56. Jean Bouvier, *Naissance d'une banque: Le Crédit lyonnais* (Paris, 1968), pp. 147-48.

57. Quoted in Theodore Zeldin, *France, 1848-1945: Love, Ambition and Politics* (Oxford, 1973), pp. 81-82.

58. Jacques Lafitte, Louis-Philippe's banker, was a pioneer in the development of modern French banking, and attempted to mobilize national capital resources to finance promising new industries. Lafitte's ideas received full development only after 1852 under the direction of two former St. Simonians, Emile and Isaac Pereire, who helped found the Crédit mobilier. See ibid., p. 82.

59. The willingness of national banks to lend to industry began to decline by the late 1860s because of growing uncertainty about international conditions; the investment portfolio of the Crédit lyonnais, for example, declined between 1866 and 1869 from Fr 6.5 to 2.3 million. But it was only after the crash of 1882 that the bank began to invest solely in safer utility and government bond issues. See Price, *Economic Modernization of France*, p. 156.

60. Ibid., p. 155.

61. Bertrand Gille, *La sidérurgie française au XIXième siècle* (Paris, 1968), pp. 147-48.

62. In the 1860s, 86 percent of the notables at Reims made these loans, which were often under Fr 100. Seventy-five percent of the elite at St. Etienne made similar loans in the same period, which are labeled personal loans in Tables 10-11.

63. Gras, *Histoire de la Chambre de Commerce*, pp. 19-22.

64. Gras, *Histoire économique de la métallurgie*, pp. 70-71.

65. Gras, *Histoire de la Chambre de Commerce*, pp. 22, 461-72.

Chapter 5

1. Georges Boussinesq and Gustave Laurent, *Histoire de Reims depuis les origines jusqu'à nos jours* (Reims, 1933), pp. 694-95.

2. Departmental Archives of the Marne, 190M7, Length of the Working Day, 1848-1913, Chamber of Commerce to the minister of the interior,

January 8, 1853; and 189M2, *Livrets*, Conseil des prudhommes to the sub-prefect, September 25, 1854; also see Archives Nationales, BB30 282, Reports of the *procureur général* to the minister of justice, 1850-59, Report of July 25, 1859.

3. Boussinesq and Laurent, *Histoire de Reims*, pp. 696-97.

4. Several of the sentences were subsequently increased by the Ministry of Justice. See Archives Nationales, BB30 383, Reports of the *procureur général* to the minister of justice, 1850-59, Report of February 21, 1855.

5. Boussinesq and Laurent, *Histoire de Reims*, pp. 693-94.

6. Departmental Archives of the Marne, 172M3, Recommendations of the Chamber of Commerce, 1859-1911, Chamber of Commerce to the prefect, August 2, 1859; and 195M1, Unemployment, 1848-1912, sub-prefect to the prefect, January 23, 1862.

7. Archives Nationales, BB30 383, Reports of the *procureur général* to the minister of justice, 1850-59, Report of August 20, 1858.

8. Departmental Archives of the Marne, 30M24, Report of the *police politique*, June 14, 1863.

9. Georges Le Guesnier, *Reims et le pays rémois en 1872* (Reims, 1873), pp. 70-71. A mutual aid society was established in conjunction with the retirement home. Workers could deposit one sou daily from the time they were twenty until the age of sixty into the fund, thus assuring themselves a pension of Fr 365 a year. With a small additional savings a worker could afford the annual fee of Fr 400 charged by the home; many of the city's employers made up this difference out of their own pockets. In 1867, however, Louis Reybaud found only 494 subscribers to the society out of a total working population of more than 60,000, an indication of the low level of wages that prevented this reform from benefiting many workers (*La laine: Nouvelle série des études sur la régime des manufactures* [Paris, 1867], pp. 147-50).

10. Evelyne Taquet, "L'industrie textile à Reims," *La Champagne économique* 5 (May 1970): 208.

11. Ibid., pp. 208-09; and Departmental Archives of the Marne, 194M9, Strikes, 1834-79, police commissioner to the sub-prefect, August 3, 1864. Pierre Pierrard has found the same lack of paternalism at Lille under the Second Empire. As the old Lille *patron*, whose style of life was similar to that of his workers, began to disappear, even employers who offered their workers an annual banquet became rare. Thomas R. Christofferson found a similar decline of paternalism at Marseilles under the Second Republic. See Pierrard, *La vie ouvrière à Lille sous le Second Empire* (Lille, 1965), p. 185; and Christofferson, "Urbanization and Political Change: The Political Transformation of Marseilles under the Second Republic," *Historian* 36, no. 2 (February 1974): 192-93.

12. Le Guesnier, *Reims et le pays rémois*, p. 77.

13. Since it was impossible for an unaided wool comber to process one kilogram per day, actual daily wages were approximately Fr 1.10. Subtracting the occupational costs of heating the combs and cleaning the wool, which amounted to at least 20 centimes, the average wool comber's wages were

hardly more than 90 centimes a day. Armand Audiganne estimated that yearly wages were approximately Fr 225, which after allowing for rent (Fr 75) left Fr 150, or 42 centimes per day, for other expenses, including food and clothing. Audiganne found one wool-combing family composed of a father, mother, and eight children. Two children were domestic servants living outside the household; the eldest remaining son worked in a weaving mill for Fr 16 a month; a ten-year-old daughter was an apprentice *couturière*, and earned 40 centimes daily. Two other children helped their mother in the auxiliary combing operations. The wages for the entire group, not counting time lost by unemployment and small expenses, amounted to Fr 680, or less than 24 centimes per person per day. This family and others were dependent on local charities, which distributed bread monthly (six kilos in the winter and three in the summer). Audiganne also found some families so poor they could not afford rent and were obliged to live like nomads (*Les populations ouvrières et les industries de la France* [Paris, 1860], pp. 118-24).

14. Reybaud, *La laine*, p. 138. César Poulain claims that wages for some groups of woolens workers reached Fr 5 by 1868. These must certainly have been paid to power-loom weavers, whose wages were at least one-third higher than those of artisan weavers. Male operators faced other dangers, however, because they could easily be replaced by women at great savings to their employers. See César Poulain, *L'agriculture et les traités de commerce* (Paris, 1879), Tableau synoptique de l'industrie lainière, 1789-1879; and Reybaud, *La laine*, pp. 144-52.

15. In the mid-1860s bread cost 30 to 35 centimes per kilogram, meat Fr 1.20 to 1.60, butter Fr 2.40, and potatoes Fr 2.30 the hectoliter. See Reybaud, *La laine*, p. 153.

16. Departmental Archives of the Marne, 189M8, Industrial and Agricultural Inquiry of 1848; and Le Guesnier, *Reims et le pays rémois*, pp. 70-73.

17. Archives Nationales, BB30 379, Reports of the *procureur général* to the minister of justice, September 9, 1852, June 4, 1853.

18. Ibid., Report of July 17, 1856.

19. Archives Nationales, BB18 1624 (4224), St. Etienne: Illicit Workers' Organizations, 1861.

20. *Le Courrier de St. Etienne*, May 23, 25, 31, November 26, 1863, June 15, 1864. Robin, the editor of *Le Courrier*, had attempted to vote at the Hotel-de-Ville without a voting card and was abused by the police. See ibid., June 26, 1864.

21. Archives Nationales, BB30 379, Reports of the *procureur général* to the minister of justice, Report of November 8, 1857, July 6, 1861.

22. In place of the meager benefits offered by other companies (the Compagnie des mines de Chazotte, for example, had established a *caisse* in 1845 funded by workers' contributions which paid an indemnity of only 50 centimes to severely injured workers), the Compagnie générale paid Fr 1 per day to disabled workers and 50 centimes to widows; families also received 25 centimes per day for each dependent child under twelve. By 1852 the

company claimed to have spent Fr 70,000 for medical services and pensions and to have invested another Fr 298,000 in infirmaries and schools. Additional company benefits included an extra half-day's pay on the feast of St. Barbara, the miners' patron saint. See Louis J. Gras, *Histoire économique générale des mines de la Loire*, 2 vols. (St. Etienne, 1922), 1: 400, 515-24.

23. Pierre Guillaume, "La mine de houille dans la Loire sous le Second Empire" (Master's thesis, 1956), p. 162.

24. Archives Nationales, BB30 379, Reports of the *procureur général* to the minister of justice, July 6, 1861.

25. Quoted in Charles Robert, *La suppression des grèves par l'association aux bénéfices* (Paris, 1870), p. 10. The brutal treatment of the miners by mine supervisors almost resulted in strikes at Roche-le-Molière in 1864 and 1867.

26. Guillaume, "La mine de houille dans la Loire," p. 161.

27. Archives Nationales, BB30 379, Reports of the *procureur général* to the minister of justice, January 8, 1866; and Departmental Archives of the Loire, 92M11, Strikes, 1860-68, prefect to a senator, January 11, 1866.

28. The custom of allowing the partition of small estates immediately before death, though more common in the countryside than in the city, could also have contributed to an inflated number of indigent workers in the *Successions et absences*. See Adeline Daumard, *Les fortunes françaises au XIXième siècle: Enquête sur la répartition et la composition des capitaux privés à Paris, Lyon, Lille, Bordeaux, et Toulouse d'après l'enregistrement des droits de succession* (Paris, 1973), p. 82.

29. William Sewell, "Social Change and the Rise of Working Class Politics in Nineteenth Century Marseilles," *Past and Present* 65 (November 1974): 82.

30. The category of "metalworkers" combines both steelworkers and *quincailleurs* because the two are indistinguishable in the occupational listing in the *Successions et absences*. The high level of indigence among metalworkers (87.5 percent) reflects the greater proportion of *quincailleurs* in the town.

31. This group is defined as all individuals listed in the *Successions et absences* with fortunes of between Fr 5,000 and 19,999.

32. *Statistique de la France*, 1st ser., 1835-73, vol. 21.

33. Departmental Archives of the Marne, 172M3, Recommendations of the Chamber of Commerce, 1859-1911, untitled brochure, January 1859.

34. Boussinesq and Laurent, *Histoire de Reims*, p. 731.

35. Departmental Archives of the Marne, 194M9, Strikes, 1834-79, police commissioner to the sub-prefect, January 26, 1861, August 3, 1864.

36. Departmental Archives of the Marne, 30M19, Reports of the *police politique*, 1856-67, sub-prefect to the prefect, "Rapport sur l'état générale de l'opinion et de la situation électorale dans l'arrondissement de Reims," February 26, 1864.

37. Departmental Archives of the Marne, 30M26, Reports of the *police politique*, 1863-64, April 29, 1864.

38. The price of many necessities also began to rise in the same period; the price of bread rose 25 percent between 1867 and 1871 over the previous five years, while in the same period the price of potatoes rose 28 percent, beef

19 percent, and pork 26 percent. See Departmental Archives of the Marne, 128M11-13, *Mercuriales*, Arrondissement of Reims, Principal market: Reims.

39. Departmental Archives of the Marne, 186M9, Industrial Statistics, 1861-65, July 4, 1865.

40. Departmental Archives of the Marne, 186M10, Industrial Statistics, 1866-68, Report of May 30, 1868; and 186M12, Industrial Statistics, 1869-74, Report of 1869.

41. Joan Scott found a similar response among artisan glass workers of Carmaux, who also became more radical when their skills were made obsolete by technological changes (*The Glassworkers of Carmaux* [Cambridge, Mass., 1974], chapters entitled "Mechanization" and "Socialism").

42. Taquet, "L'industrie textile à Reims," p. 210.

43. Claude Fohlen, *L'industrie textile au temps du Second Empire* (Paris, 1956), p. 392; and Departmental Archives of the Marne, 30M29, Reports of the *police politique*, 1868, Report of March 30, 1868.

44. Departmental Archives of the Marne, 186M12, Industrial Statistics, 1867-74, Report of November 30, 1869. Inspired by the English Combinations Act of 1825 and the writings of John Stuart Mill, the law also guaranteed "freedom of work" by preventing harassment of nonstriking workers. The law was denounced by republican deputies in 1864 for preventing the creation of permanent trade unions. In 1869, the decision to enforce the "right to work" provisions during the coal strike in the Loire was to have grave consequences for the imperial government. See Theodore Zeldin, *Emile Ollivier and the Liberal Empire of Napoleon III* (Oxford, 1963), p. 79.

45. Departmental Archives of the Marne, 186M10, Industrial Statistics, 1867, Report of October 1867; also see 30M29, Reports of the *police politique*, Report of August 28, 1867; and 194M9, Strikes, 1834-79, Report of the sub-prefect to the prefect, March 30, 1868. In 1867 a group of weavers had petitioned the prefect to allow the creation of a Société de prévoyance et de solidarité des ouvriers tisseurs de tous genres to maintain wages; the group hoped to create a permanent fund to pay any worker Fr 2.50 per day for refusing to work for employers paying less than the minimum wage established by the society. After some consideration, the government decided to prevent the establishment of the society. See Archives Nationales, F12 2370-74, Subsistence.

46. Departmental Archives of the Marne, 30M30, Reports of the *police politique*, 1868, Report of the prefect to the minister of the interior, July 1868; and 30M31, Reports of the *police politique*, 1869-70, Report of February 27, 1869. The stipulation in the law of public assembly of June 1869 that a police officer be present at all meetings might have contributed to the spirit of moderation in which they were held; within months, however, discussions about economic problems had given way to political attacks on the regime all over France.

47. Departmental Archives of the Marne, 186M12, Industrial Statistics, 1869-74, Report of June 29, 1870; and 87M61, La Société de résistance, 1870, Report of April 4, 1870.

48. Departmental Archives of the Marne, 30M31, Reports of the *police politique*, 1869-70, Reports of June 29, December 29, 1869; and Departmental Archives of the Marne, 87M61, La Société de résistance, 1870, prefect of the Ardennes to prefect of the Marne, November 24, 1869. By April 1870 the Société de résistance had gained members throughout the departments of the Marne and Ardennes. See ibid., Report of the minister of the interior to the prefect, April 6, 1870.

49. Departmental Archives of the Marne, 30M31, Reports of the *police politique*, 1869-70, Reports of January 27, February 26, 1870.

50. Departmental Archives of the Marne, 87M61, La Société de résistance, 1870, Reports of the commissioner of police at Pontfaverger and of the justice of the peace at Bourgogne, to the sub-prefect, both dated December 2, 1869.

51. Zeldin, *Emile Ollivier*, p. 134.

52. Departmental Archives of the Marne, 87M61, La Société de résistance, sub-prefect to the prefect, February 7, 1870; and pamphlet dated March 30, 1870. The Association internationale des travailleurs was also weakened immediately before the plebiscite in May 1870 by Ollivier's order to arrest all members of the organization. See Zeldin, *Emile Ollivier*, p. 159.

53. Departmental Archives of the Marne, 30M31, Reports of the *police politique*, Report of May 30, 1870.

54. Departmental Archives of the Marne, 30M64, Political Associations, Secret Societies, Free Masons, etc., 1814-92, Reports of May 16, 29, 31, 1871.

55. Only Toulouse, Mulhouse, and Roubaix grew as rapidly. See Jacques Schnitzler, "St. Etienne et ses problèmes urbains," *La vie urbaine dans le département de la Loire et ses abords* (St. Etienne, 1969), p. 197.

56. Although Yves Lequin estimates that more than half of the workers in St. Etienne in the early 1850s were born outside of the city, the great majority of ribbon weavers came from the Forez; many came from immediately outside of St. Etienne. Most were also from families already engaged in the ribbon trade, and most married within the industry's artisanal community. Corporate traditions were equally strong among artisan armsmakers, over 70 percent of whom followed the occupations of their fathers. Only miners came from rural, peasant backgrounds, fitting easily into an industry that occasionally required only physical strength. See Yves Lequin, *Les ouvriers de la région lyonnaise, 1848-1914*, 2 vols. (Lyons, 1977), 1: 208-38.

57. Charles Tilly, "How Protest Modernized in France, 1845-1855," in William Aydelotte, ed., *Dimensions of Quantitative Research in History* (Reading, Mass., 1971), p. 203.

58. Under the Second Republic most migrants came from within a forty-kilometer radius of the city. See D. Tenand, "Les origines de la classe ouvrière stéphanoise" (Master's thesis, University of Lyons II, 1972), pp. 84, 151.

59. Audiganne, *Les populations ouvrières et les industries de la France*, pp. 103-05.

60. Louis Reybaud, *Etude sur le régime des manufactures: Condition des ouvriers en soie* (Paris, 1859), p. 222.

61. Departmental Archives of the Loire, 84M7, Medical Commission Attached to the Industrial and Agricultural Inquiry in the Two Cantons of St. Etienne, 1848.

62. Louis J. Gras, *Histoire du commerce local* (St. Etienne, 1910), p. 370.

63. A three-year apprenticeship was free but obliged the apprentice to help the master for very low wages; a one-year term cost Fr 100. See Lequin, *Les ouvriers de la région lyonnaise*, 2: 5.

64. More than eighteen hundred houses were built by master weavers in the 1850s. Audiganne found the masters to be the most literate section of the working class because they were obliged to read their contracts with merchants. The literacy level for the whole of the ribbon-weaving population was lower. The Investigatory Commission of 1848 found only one-third of all ribbon workers able to read and write and another third able only to read; only 10 percent of women in the trade were literate. See Audiganne, *Les populations ouvrières*, pp. 101-03 and 110; and Petrus Faure, *Histoire du mouvement ouvrier dans le département de la Loire* (St. Etienne, 1955), p. 113.

65. In the hard times that began at the end of the 1850s weavers were obliged to sell their looms, which had cost Fr 1,500 or more, for as little as Fr 300 or 400. See Audiganne, *Les populations ouvrières*, pp. 220-21, 229.

66. Archives Nationales, BB30 379, Reports of the *procureur général* to the minister of justice, April 7, July 10, 1859.

67. The Chamber of Commerce tried to change these conditions in 1869 when it proposed to distribute monetary prizes and medals inscribed "Honneur au travail" to outstanding ribbon workers. Stating that it had already raised Fr 1,400 for similar prizes for artisan armsmakers, the chamber told the prefect that it hoped in this way to improve relations between employers and workers. See Archives Nationales, F12, 2370-74, Chamber of Commerce to the prefect, June 30, 1869, and report of April 7, 1859.

68. *Notes sur le projet de démembrement du département de la Loire* (1852), pp. 20-21, Municipal Library of St. Etienne.

69. Jacky Meaudre, "Les débuts de l'amanagement urbain de Saint Etienne (1815-1872)," *Etudes foreziennes*, 1971, pp. 85-90; and J. Meaudre, "La pousse urbaine à Saint Etienne" (Master's thesis, University of Lyons, 1966), p. 189.

70. Meaudre, "La pousse urbaine," p. 191. By 1853 the population was growing so rapidly that houses were rented before they were built; rents rose 30 percent between 1853 and 1856. See Lequin, *Les ouvriers de la région lyonnaise*, 2: 17.

71. Louis J. Gras, *Histoire de la rubannerie et les industries de la soie à St. Etienne et dans la région stéphanoise* (St. Etienne, 1906), p. 622. A similar cooperative, the Société commerciale et industrielle des veloutiers réunis, was founded in the same period but was dissolved in 1867 before it began production. See ibid., p. 622.

72. The strike was particularly well organized. Workers divided themselves into groups of fifteen to nineteen men, thus obviating the government's ruling against large coalitions; these groups were coordinated by a central committee of six members. See Faure, *Histoire du mouvement ouvrier*, pp. 162-63.

73. Tensions were further exacerbated by the fall of artisan wages in the decade after 1856-57. By 1867 the minimal wage paid to ribbon weavers had fallen from Fr 1.50 (in 1857) to Fr 1; the late 1860s also saw an increase in the price of necessities, which further depressed real wages. See Departmental Archives of the Loire, 85M2, Industrial Salaries for 1857 and 1867; and 90M1, Industrial Inquiry of 1872, St. Etienne.

74. Faure, *Histoire du mouvement ouvrier*, pp. 162-63; and Archives Nationales, BB30 379, Reports of the *procureur général* to the minister of justice, Reports of October 7, 1865, March 27, 1866.

75. Lucien Thiollière, "Rubannerie," *Association française pour l'avancement des sciences*, 26th sess., 2 (August 1897): 85.

76. The number of miners increased at the following rates: 1851-55, 21.92 percent; 1856-60, 21.41; 1861-65, 31.81; 1866-70, 16.92. Despite this rate of growth the mining companies continued to complain of a shortage of workers, which they claimed was the only obstacle to greater production. See Lequin, *Les ouvriers de la région lyonnaise*, 1: 125-26.

77. Ibid., 2: 201; 1: 536. The companies did not object to worker participation in the management of individual company funds as long as members of the Caisse fraternelle were not involved. Following the example of the accident fund of the Unieux et Fraisses mines (owned by Petin and Gaudet), the Loire mining company's fund included workers in its management. Its council was composed of seven engineers and other company employees and an equal number of miners elected by their fellow workers. See ibid., pp. 534, 541.

78. Archives Nationales, BB30 379, Reports of the *procureur général* to the minister of justice, Report of March 27, 1866. Between 1865 and 1866 a number of companies, including the mines operated by Petin and Gaudet and the Loire mining company, had established pensions of 50 centimes and Fr 1 respectively for workers over the age of sixty who had been employed by the company for twenty-five years. See Gras, *Histoire économique générale des mines*, 1: 533-35; also see H. Baret, *Histoire local du travail* (St. Etienne, 1932), p. 124; Bernard Delabre, "La grève de 1869 dans le bassin minier stéphanois," *Etudes foreziennes*, 1971, p. 109; and Departmental Archives of the Loire, 92M11, Strikes, 1860-68, Reports of January 5, 11, 1866.

79. V. Brechignac, *Les caisses de secours des ouvriers mineurs dans le bassin de la Loire* (St. Etienne, 1869), pp. viii-ix.

80. Guillaume, "La mine de houille dans la Loire," p. 217.

81. Departmental Archives of the Loire, 10M61, Political Reports of 1868, police commissioner of the first arrondissement to the prefect.

82. Delabre, "La grève de 1869," pp. 110-13; and Guillaume, "La mine de houille dans la Loire," p. 213.

83. The miners demanded a 50 centime increase, which would have brought the wages of pick men to Fr 5.50, of timber men to Fr 5, of wagon men to Fr 4, and of workers outside the pits to Fr 3. See Faure, *Histoire du mouvement ouvrier*, p. 166; and Gras, *Histoire économique générale des mines*, 2: 753.

84. Fernand L'Huillier, *La lutte ouvrière à la fin du Second Empire* (Paris, 1957).

85. Delabre, "La grève de 1869," pp. 127-28.

86. Victor Jannesson, *Monographie et histoire de la ville de St. Etienne depuis ses origines jusqu'à nos jours* (St. Etienne, 1892), p. 130.

87. Delabre, "La grève de 1869," p. 134.

88. Guillaume, "La mine de houille dans la Loire," p. 217; and Departmental Archives of the Loire, 10M61, Political reports of 1868, Report of the police commissioner to the prefect, May 24, 1868.

89. After the strike two other mining companies, Beaubrun and Villeboeuf, joined the Loire, Montrambert, St. Etienne, and La Peronnière companies in creating a central accident fund for miners; it provided a pension of Fr 300 for miners aged fifty-five or older who had worked for the companies for thirty years (with a Fr 25 supplement for each additional year worked). The Montrambert company also raised its widows' pension from 50 to 60 centimes a day and began paying miners daily sick leave of Fr 1. See Gras, *Histoire économique générale des mines*, 1: 536-37.

90. Delabre, "La grève de 1869," pp. 134-35; and Gras, *Histoire économique générale des mines*, 1: 532.

91. Guillaume, "La mine de houille dans la Loire," pp. 217-18.

92. Departmental Archives of the Loire, 92M12, Strikes, 1869-70, minister of the interior to the prefect, October 29, 1869, and report of November 8, 1869.

93. Louis J. Gras, *Histoire économique de la métallurgie de la Loire* (St. Etienne, 1908), pp. 143, 146. Even in the 1840s metalworkers had been among the healthiest in the department, despite the heavy physical labor they performed and the enormous amounts of wine they consumed (forge men at Terrenoire, exposed to the heat of the furnaces, supposedly drank eight liters of wine daily). See Departmental Archives of the Loire, 84M7, Medical Commission Attached to the Industrial and Agricultural Inquiry for the Two Cantons of St. Etienne.

94. The families of some steelworkers at St. Chamond enjoyed combined incomes of more than Fr 3,000 and lived in "proper bourgeois households." See Gras, *Histoire économique de la métallurgie*, p. 152.

95. Eric J. Hobsbawm, "The Labor Aristocracy in Nineteenth Century Britain," in Peter Stearns and Daniel Walkowitz, eds., *Workers in the Industrial Revolution* (New Brunswick, 1975), p. 139. Steelworkers' jobs were also usually secure, a tradition dating from the earliest days of the industry, when employers were anxious to create a permanent work force to protect manufacturing secrets. In the 1830s the Jackson company had made four- to twelve-year contracts with individual workers that imposed penalties of Fr

1,000 to 5,000 for the party who broke them. See W. L. Jackson, *James Jackson et ses fils* (St. Etienne, 1893), pp. 64-65 and 87-88.

96. Gras, *Histoire économique de la métallurgie*, p. 97; and Departmental Archives of the Loire, 94M3, Mutual Aid Societies, 1852-69, sub-prefect to the prefect, January 26, 1852. Paternalistic programs were common in the steel industry, especially among older firms such as de Wendel and Schneider. See Jean Vial, *L'industrialisation de la sidérurgie française, 1814-1864* (Paris, 1967), p. 427; Louis J. Gras, *Histoire de la Chambre de Commerce de St. Etienne, 1833-1898* (St. Etienne, 1898), p. 316; and Gras, *Histoire économique de la métallurgie*, p. 93.

97. Georges Duveau, *La vie ouvrière sous le Second Empire* (Paris, 1946), pp. 362, 440.

98. Robert, *La suppression des grèves*, p. 54.

99. Michael Hanagan, *The Logic of Solidarity: Artisans and Industrial Workers in Three French Towns, 1871-1914* (Urbana, 1980); and Vial, *L'industrialisation de la sidérurgie française*, p. 350.

100. *La Loire*, May 18, 1869; also see Robert, *La suppression des grèves*, p. 54; and untitled electoral pamphlet for Rochetaillée, Legitimist, for the 1867 Conseil général election, C37 (43), Municipal Library of St. Etienne.

101. Archives Nationales, BB30 379, Reports of the *procureur général* to the minister of justice, Report of October 22, 1866.

102. *L'Eclaireur*, May 9, 1870.

103. Ibid., August 10, 1870.

104. *La Sentinelle populaire*, May 8, 1869.

105. Departmental Archives of the Loire, 6M3, Municipal Council of St. Etienne, 1870-71, Report of November 8, 1870.

106. *La Commune*, February 6, 22, 24, 1871.

107. Yves Lequin believes that different groups of workers provided some mutual assistance in the strikes of 1869-70. This phenomenon, however, remained unimportant during the last years of the Second Empire. See Lequin, *Les ouvriers de la région lyonnaise*, 2: 206.

108. More than 37 percent of the members of the secret society Pères de familles were ribbon weavers (77 percent of the total membership was working class), but this group comprised only a little over 17 percent of the membership of the Alliance républicaine in 1871; the total working-class membership was over 66 percent. It is possible that by 1871 a portion of the ribbon workers had forsaken the moderate republicans for more radical groups such as the Société civil de prévoyance des passementiers, which had joined the Association internationale des travailleurs in 1870. See ibid., 2: 175, 210.

109. Different groups of workers remained divided even during their leisure hours. Miners, for example, belonged to gymnastic clubs, while armsmakers joined rifle clubs; workers also tended to congregate in separate cafes according to occupation. The largest single group of workers continued to be employed in ribbon weaving. In 1872 the city's ribbon-manufacturing population was estimated at 45,000 persons (27,000 women, 16,000 men, and

2,000 children), the arms-manufacturing population at about 10,000 (9,900 men and 100 women), and the metalworkers and miners respectively at 12,000 and 16,036 men. See Theodore Zeldin, *France, 1848-1945: Love, Ambition and Politics* (Oxford, 1973), 270; and Departmental Archives of the Loire, 90M1, Industrial Inquiry of 1872, St. Etienne.

110. *Le Mémorial de la Loire*, February 8, 1871; also see *La Commune*, February 22, 1871, and *La Loire en 1870-71*, a reprinted series of documents in the Municipal Library of St. Etienne.

111. *La Commune*, February 26, 1871.

112. Gras, *Histoire du commerce local*, pp. 606-09. By the late 1860s bread prices had risen 26 percent and potato prices 16 percent. Throughout the period of the empire wages nationally had consistently lagged behind profits. It has been estimated that between 1850 and 1870 wages rose 45 percent and real wages 28 percent, while profits increased by 286 percent. See Archives Nationales, BB30 390, Reports of the *procureur général* to the minister of justice, July 9, 1870; and Zeldin, *Emile Ollivier*, p. 135.

113. *La Commune*, March 12, 1871.

114. Communes were also established in late March at Marseilles, Toulouse, Narbonne, Brest, Limoges, and Le Creusot. See Louis M. Greenberg, *Sisters of Liberty: Marseilles, Lyon, Paris and the Reaction to a Centralized State, 1868-1871* (Cambridge, Mass., 1971), pp. 140-42.

115. *L'Eclaireur*, March 25, 1871; and Stanislas Bossakiewicz, *Histoire général de Saint Etienne* (St. Etienne, 1905), pp. 266-70.

116. *La Loire en 1870-71*, p. 62.

117. Bossakiewicz, *Histoire général de Saint Etienne*, pp. 272-73.

118. Ibid., p. 274; and *L'Eclaireur*, March 26, 27, 29, 1871.

119. *L'Eclaireur*, April 7, 28, May 1, June 4, 1871.

Chapter 6

1. For a recent discussion of the division between the conservative politics of the champagne industry and the more liberal politics of elements within the woolens industry, see Maurice Crubellier and Charles Juillard, *Histoire de la Champagne* (Reims, 1969), pp. 100-02.

2. *Annuaire de la Marne*, 1852.

3. Archives Nationales, BB30 383, Reports of the *procureur général* to the minister of justice, Reports of October 15, November 13, and December 20, 1852.

4. Archives Nationales, BB18 1523 (3676), *La Concorde*, Report of the *procureur général* to the minister of justice, October 28, 1853.

5. Departmental Archives of the Marne, 30M64, Political Associations: Secret Societies, Free Masonry, etc., 1814-92, Report of the commissioner of police, August 25, 1852.

6. Archives Nationales, BB30 383, Reports of the *procureur général* to the minister of justice, Reports of October 15, November 13, 1852.

7. *Le Courrier de la Champagne*, May 30, 1855.

8. Georges Boussinesq and Gustave Laurent, *Histoire de Reims depuis les origines jusqu'à nos jours* (Reims, 1933), p. 733.

9. Elizabeth Picard, "Un notaire rémois de la première moitié du XIX-ième siècle: Nicolas-Henri Carteret, 1807-1862" (Master's thesis, University of Reims, 1974).

10. Boussinesq and Laurent, *Histoire de Reims*, p. 733.

11. Theodore Zeldin, *The Political System of Napoleon III* (New York, 1958), p. 14. Carteret was soon dropped by the government because of his independence in the Corps législatif.

12. Georges Lallement, *Edouard Werlé, négociant en vins de Champagne, maire de la ville de Reims, député au Corps législatif, 1801-1884*, pamphlet of the Société des amis de vieux Reims.

13. Boussinesq and Laurent, *Histoire de Reims*, pp. 722-24.

14. Archives Nationales, BB30 384, Reports of the *procureur général* to the minister of justice, 1860-67, Report of February 13, 1860.

15. Departmental Archives of the Marne, 30M23, Reports of the *police politique*, Report of the sub-prefect to the prefect, January 30, 1860.

16. Simon Dauphinot, *Discours pronouncées aux funerailles des victimes de l'accident du 23 juillet à Reims*, 1868, Municipal Library of Reims.

17. Departmental Archives of the Marne, 30M23, Reports of the *police politique*, Report of the sub-prefect to the prefect, August 28, 1860.

18. Departmental Archives of the Marne, 30M22, Reports of the *police politique*, Report of the prefect to the minister of the interior, November 30, 1859.

19. Workers continued to regard most of the bourgeoisie with hostility. They feared the middle-class clubs in which they believed manufacturers met to conspire against labor and frequently denounced middle-class "circles" to the police for harboring political aims. "It is the same refrain heard since 1848," wrote the commissioner of police, "that of the war of the rich against the poor." The ability of the middle-class opposition in the 1860s at least partially to overcome this attitude was a considerable achievement. See Departmental Archives of the Marne, 30M64, Political Associations: Secret Societies, Free Masonry, etc., 1814-92, Report of the commissioner of police to the sub-prefect, April 14, 1858.

20. Carteret had died in 1862. See Departmental Archives of the Marne, 7M39, Legislative Election of 1862, Report of the prefect to the minister of the interior, February 21, 1862.

21. Archives Nationales, BB30 383, Reports of the *procureur général* to the minister of justice, Report of June 16, 1862.

22. Departmental Archives of the Marne, 30M25, Reports of the *police politique*, 1862, Reports of January 14, February 15, 1862.

23. Louis Chevalier also notes a certain rebelliousness (*tempérément frondeur*) which colored the politics of Reims's Orleanist elite ("Les fondements

économiques et sociaux de l'histoire politique de la région parisienne" [Ph.D. dissertation, Sorbonne, 1950], p. 410).

24. Antoine Barthelemy Villeminot-Huard, one of the most important manufacturers in the city, had begun work as a mechanic at the age of eleven. He subsequently founded a workshop for the manufacture of machinery for the woolens industry and eventually built one of the largest spinning mills in the city. See *Almanach Matot-Braine*, 1878.

25. Departmental Archives of the Marne, 8M12, The Conseil général, 1861-63, Reports of the sub-prefect to the prefect, March 29, April 17, May 3, 1862.

26. Departmental Archives of the Marne, 7M40, Legislative Election of 1863, Reports of the prefect to the sub-prefect and minister of the interior to the prefect, May 11, 1863.

27. Departmental Archives of the Marne, 30M26, Reports of the *police politique*, Report of June 14, 1863.

28. Both Zeldin and Chevalier have suggested that bourgeois politics between 1815 and 1870 can be explained in generational terms. According to Chevalier, the oldest manufacturing houses founded at Reims before the Revolution produced the leaders of the Legitimist party, whereas newer manufacturers, liberals under the Restoration, became Orleanists after 1830. Hostile to the Revolution of 1848, they were opposed by a younger group who either supported the republic or later rallied to the empire. A subsequent generation, rivals of the Bonapartist elite in the 1860s, eventually joined the republican opposition. See Zeldin, *Political System of Napoleon III*, p. 7; and Chevalier, "Les fondements économiques et sociaux," pp. 716-18.

29. Archives Nationales, BB30 384, Reports of the *procureur général* to the minister of justice, Report of January 1866.

30. Eugène Maumené, Victor Rogelet and Jules Warnier, members of the administrative council of the Société industrielle, *Lettre à M. le président de la Société industrielle de Reims sur l'adoption de l'absolu comme base unique de condition-nement*, 1858, Municipal Library of Reims.

31. Jules Warnier, who was to remain the leader of the republican party after 1870, was born in 1826 in a poor peasant family. His widowed mother moved to Reims, where he began working for Adolphe David. Warnier subsequently acquired a municipal scholarship and eventually married Elisa David, the daughter of his patron. He was co-founder of the firm of Warnier-Francard, which in the last years of the Second Empire merged with David's company to form the firm of Warnier-David. First elected secretary of the Société industrielle (founded in 1833 by Adolphe David and Croutelle-Neveu), he became its president in 1860 and served until 1866. See Marie-Claude Genet, "Un républicain liberal, Jules Warnier, vu à travers sa corre-spondence avec Jules Simon, 1874-1896," *Etudes champenoises*, no. 2 (1976), pp. 67-69.

32. Departmental Archives of the Marne, 30M19, Reports of the *police politique*, 1856-57, Report of the sub-prefect to the prefect, October 8, 1865;

and Archives Nationales, BB30 384, Reports of the *procureur général* to the minister of justice, Report of August 4, 1864.

33. Departmental Archives of the Marne, 30M27, Reports of the *police politique*, Report of April 2, 1865.

34. The government remained neutral in the 1864 Conseil général elections despite Werlé's request for official support. See Departmental Archives of the Marne, 30M26, Reports of the *police politique*, Report of May 14, 1864; and Archives Nationales, BB30 384, Reports of the *procureur général* to the minister of justice, 1860-67, Report of February 15, 1864.

35. *Le Courrier de la Champagne*, July 19, 1865. The list drawn up by the Legitimist electoral committee, headed by Henri Goulet, ignored most of the government's candidates. It did include liberals such as Lelegard and Houzeau, as well as important Legitimists Paris and Maille. See Departmental Archives of the Marne, 8M13, Conseil général, 1864, Reports of the sub-prefect to the prefect, February 20, 29, 1864; and *Le Courrier de la Champagne*, July 21, 1865.

36. Departmental Archives of the Marne, 30M27, Reports of the *police politique*, 1865, Report of April 28, 1865; and *Le Courrier de la Champagne*, July 20, 1865.

37. Departmental Archives of the Marne, 30M27, Reports of the *police politique*, Report of August 1865; and 12M236, Election of the Municipal Council, 1865.

38. Gilles Derrole, "L'anticléricalisme à Reims de 1870 à 1906" (Master's thesis), pp. 10-11, Municipal Library of Reims; and *Obseques de M. Victor Diancourt*, undated pamphlet, ibid. The Ligue d'enseignement had been founded nationally the previous year by Jean Macé as an offshoot of Masonry dedicated to the development of lay education in France. See Adrien Dansette, *The Religious History of Modern France* (New York, 1961), p. 315.

39. Departmental Archives of the Marne, 30M19, Reports of the *police politique*, 1856-67, Report of the sub-prefect to the prefect, October 8, 1865.

40. Archives Nationales, BB30 394, Reports of the *procureur général* to the minister of justice, Report of February 14, 1867.

41. Departmental Archives of the Marne, 30M26, Reports of the *police politique*, Report of December 16, 1864.

42. Derrole, "L'anticléricalisme à Reims," pp. 10-11.

43. Archives Nationales, BB30 394, Reports of the *procureur général* to the minister of justice, Report of May 20, 1867; and Departmental Archives of the Marne, 30M19, Reports of the *police politique*, 1856-67, Report of the commissioner of police to the prefect, March 22, 1867.

44. Archives Nationales, BB30 394, Reports of the *procureur général* to the minister of justice, Report of May 20, 1867.

45. *Le Courrier de la Champagne*, August 13, 1867.

46. Archives Nationales, BB30 384, Reports of the *procureur général* to the minister of justice, Report of February 15, 1868.

47. Departmental Archives of the Marne, 30M30, Reports of the *police politique*, 1868, Report of March 2, 1868.

48. *Le Courrier de la Champagne*, December 19, 1868; and Archives Nationales, BB30 384, Reports of the *procureur général* to the minister of justice, 1860-67, Report of October 1869.

49. Departmental Archives of the Marne, 30M31, Reports of the *police politique*, 1869-70, Report of February 27, 1869.

50. *L'Indépendent rémois*, June 19, 1868.

51. Ibid., October 10, April 9, 1869.

52. Departmental Archives of the Marne, 7M40, Legislative Election of 1863, Report of the sub-prefect to the prefect, May 30, 1863; for a more general discussion of the role of the smaller bourgeoisie in the radical movement, see Jean Bouvier, "Aux origines de la Troisième République: Les réflexes sociaux des milieux d'affaires," *Revue historique* 210 (October-December 1953): 299-300.

53. *L'Indépendent rémois*, September 13, 1869. Though the paper questioned the method of electing the Chamber of Commerce for its own political ends, this issue had first been raised by *Le Courrier de la Champagne*, January 20, 1869.

54. Departmental Archives of the Marne, 7M44, Legislative Election of 1869, Report of the sub-prefect to the prefect, May 7, 1869.

55. The constitution was ambiguous about parliamentary responsibility. Ministers were declared responsible to the Chamber of Deputies, yet also "depended on the Emperor alone." See Theodore Zeldin, *Emile Ollivier and the Liberal Empire of Napoleon III* (Oxford, 1963), p. 126; and Zeldin, *Political System of Napoleon III*, p. 142.

56. Departmental Archives of the Marne, 7M44, Legislative Election of 1869, Report of the sub-prefect to the prefect, May 20, 1869; and *Le Courrier de la Champagne*, May 22, 1869.

57. *L'Indépendent rémois*, May 25, 1869.

58. *Le Courrier* repeatedly warned its readers against the revolutionary program which Jules Simon, as a Socialist and anarchist, represented. See *Le Courrier de la Champagne*, April 6-May 4, 1869.

59. Departmental Archives of the Marne, 8M14, Conseil général, 1815-67, Report of February 2, 1867.

60. *L'Indépendent rémois*, May 25, 26, 1869.

61. Departmental Archives of the Marne, 8M13, Conseil général, Report of the sub-prefect to the prefect, June 1869.

62. Departmental Archives of the Marne, 2M25, Plebiscite of 1870, Police reports to the prefect, Reports of May 3, 6, 1870.

63. *L'Indépendent rémois*, May 5, 1870.

64. Departmental Archives of the Marne, 2M25, Plebiscite of 1870, Report of April 9, 1870.

65. At Reims, 6,848 affirmative and 4,650 negative votes were cast out of a total registered population of 16,462. Nationally, the new constitution was approved by 7,358,786 votes to 1,571,939. See ibid., Report of the results of the plebiscite.

66. *L'Indépendent rémois*, May 20, 1870.

67. Boussinesq and Laurent, *Histoire de Reims*, pp. 742-43.

68. Ibid., p. 746; and Arthur Barbat de Bignicourt, *Les hommes politique de la Marne* (Reims, 1872).

69. Following the election, Dauphinot attempted to resign as mayor. He suggested creating a committee of five municipal councillors, including Houzeau and Paris, to run the local administration; the Germans, however, refused to accept this plan, and Dauphinot continued to serve. See Boussinesq and Laurent, *Histoire de Reims*, p. 759.

70. Ibid., p. 761.

71. Ibid., pp. 759, 763-64.

72. *Le Courrier de la Champagne*, May 6, 1871.

73. This was the course adopted by financiers such as Casimir-Perier and Henri Germain, as well as industrialists Magnin and Feray. The economist Léon Say also declared himself "a son of the Revolution" and opposed the restoration of the monarchy. Even as cautious a figure as Alfred Deseilligny, director of Le Creusot, wrote in 1867 that he believed it possible to "moralize" the workers and "to substitute free and honest discussions of wage questions for useless and ruinous strikes." For a detailed discussion of the confidence with which many industrialists approached the question of regime in the early 1870s, see Bouvier, "Aux origines de la Troisième République," pp. 276-77.

74. Jean Bouvier, "Les banquiers devant l'actualité politique en 1870-1871," *Revue d'histoire moderne et contemporaine* 5 (April-June 1958): 138; and Claude Fohlen, "Bourgeoisie française: Liberté économique et intervention de l'état," *Revue économique*, no. 7 (May 1956), pp. 424-25.

75. Departmental Archives of the Marne, 12M237, Municipal Council, 1870-80, Results of the Municipal Elections of 1871.

76. Following the municipal election of 1871, Diancourt had been offered the post of mayor but declined it; Warnier, who received the second largest number of votes, was already a deputy and so could not serve. Poulain therefore was chosen. See Boussinesq and Laurent, *Histoire de Reims*, pp. 767-68.

77. Departmental Archives of the Marne, 30M64, Political Associations: Secret Societies, Free Masonry, etc., 1814-92, Reports of May 16, 29, 31, 1871. The three defeated candidates were Dauphinot, Paris, and Rome, a former deputy mayor under Werlé's administration. See *Le Courrier de la Champagne*, October 6, 1871.

78. Eugène Courmeaux, "République ou royauté," letter to the editor of *La Champagne*, Municipal Library of Reims. In January 1871 thirty conservatives, including Henri Paris, petitioned the government to allow them to establish a Catholic society for workers as an alternative to more radical organizations. Alfred Werlé, the son of the former mayor, was proposed as president of this organization. See Departmental Archives of the Marne, 87M52, Political and Confessional Associations, Report of the secretary general to the minister of the interior, January 15, 1871.

79. *Le Courrier de la Champagne*, October 13, 1871.

Chapter 7

1. Balay was typical of the deputies elected to the Corps législatif in 1852. As Zeldin points out, Napoleon's parliament contained almost as many politically new men as that of 1848, though many more were successful businessmen. See Theodore Zeldin, *The Political System of Napoleon III* (New York, 1958), p. 63.

2. Archives Nationales, BB30 379, Reports of the *procureur général* to the minister of justice, Report of March 8, 1852.

3. The opposition won again in the Conseil général elections in August. St. Etienne elected the republican leaders Sain and Favre despite government attempts to coerce voters into supporting the official candidates. See Archives Nationales, BB30 379, Reports of the *procureur général* to the minister of justice, Reports of August 12, December 11, 1852.

4. Departmental Archives of the Loire, 6M2, Municipal Council, 1852-69, Report of the sub-prefect to the prefect, June 10, 1853.

5. Departmental Archives of the Loire, 6M15, Municipal Council Elections of 1853, *procès-verbaux* of the second *tour de scrutin*. Having succeeded in destroying the local opposition, the prefect filled departmental as well as municipal offices with men from the conservative party. In April he supported Antoine Neyron for the Conseil général seat for Montbrison. One of St. Etienne's seats was offered to Quantin. The sub-prefect reported that although there was still organized opposition to government candidates at St. Etienne, he planned to find measures to eliminate all opponents of the regime. See Archives Nationales, Fic III 4 Loire, Report of the prefect to the minister of police, April 19, 1853.

6. Voting was very light in 1855; Paliard, an arms manufacturer who received the most votes, got only 2,272 out of a registered population of 15,708; the thirty-sixth councillor elected received 195 votes. The ribbon industry was represented by Claudius Vignat, Passerat, Merllié, and Girinon. See Departmental Archives of the Loire, 5M67, Municipal Council Election of 1855, *procès-verbaux* of the second *tour de scrutin*.

7. Departmental Archives of the Loire, 4M11, Conseil général, Elections of 1855.

8. Departmental Archives of the Loire, 10M53, Political Events of 1856-57, Report of August 11, 1856.

9. *Le Mémorial de la Loire*, June 15-16, 18, 21, 1857.

10. The victory of the opposition over one of the city's most important merchant manufacturers was accomplished without any press support. The *procureur général* thought this demonstrated once again the government's inability to win the support of working-class voters, who he said remained "obsessed with ideas of economic equality." See Archives Nationales, BB30 379, Reports of the *procureur général* to the minister of justice, Report of July 1857.

11. Sain received 4,011 votes and Charpin 4,261. The government had divided St. Etienne into two electoral districts to split the city's republican majority. The city's two western cantons were combined with St. Héand, Rive-de-Gier, Pelussin, and St. Chamond; its two eastern ones were linked with Bourg-Argenteuil, Le Chambon, and St. Genest Malifaux. Balay received 13,224 votes in the whole of the electoral district; Pelletan got 7,218. See Departmental Archives of the Loire, 3M10, Legislative Election of 1857, *procès-verbaux*.

12. This policy was in keeping with the government's decision to increase political controls nationally. Although the Orsini assassination attempt in 1858 gave the government a pretext for the creation of the Loi de Sûreté générale, which permitted the arbitrary arrest of political dissidents, the decision to increase police powers had been taken in 1857 after the reemergence of the republican opposition. See Zeldin, *Political System of Napoleon III*, pp. 76-77.

13. Archives Nationales, BB30 379, Reports of the *procureur général* to the minister of justice, Report of October 22, 1866; and Antonin Portallier, *Le Chambre de Commerce de St. Etienne* (St. Etienne, 1909), pp. 204, 233.

14. Departmental Archives of the Loire, 5M70, Municipal Council Elections of 1860.

15. This local experiment with a freer press was part of a national attempt to introduce liberal reforms into the imperial system. In 1860 the government allowed the Corps législatif for the first time to reply to the address from the throne and permitted the publication of legislative debates. Until the final liberalization of the press laws in 1868, however, a newspaper continued to need government permission to write about political questions.

16. Robin was a former Parisian journalist and republican. By 1861 he had become a supporter of a free press loyal to what he hoped would be an increasingly liberal empire. In *Le Courrier*'s first issue he wrote that he did not intend to allow "those men who are notorious for their antiliberal ideas to be presented to the suffrage as government candidates. . . . We recall the words of M. de Persigny in our program, 'Abuses in government and society should always be brought to light. The acts of the administration should always be examined, and conflicting ideas and opinions be debated in political as well as in commercial life.' " See Charles Robin, *Les confessions d'un journaliste* (Paris, 1862), pp. 23-24, 159-60; and *Le Courrier de St. Etienne*, May 30, 1861.

17. Archives Nationales, BB18 1643, *Le Courrier de St. Etienne*, Report of the *procureur général* to the minister of justice, December 19, 1861. Robin was originally supposed to have been defended by Jules Favre, the republican leader. See ibid., Reports of February 16, 25, 1862.

18. *Le Courrier de St. Etienne*, February 3, 1862.

19. Jules Balay died in November 1862 and left his entire fortune to his daughter. She married her cousin Francisque Balay. See *Le Mémorial de la Loire*, May 24-25, 1863.

20. Denis Descreux, "Notes biographiques stéphanois," Municipal Library of St. Etienne, pp. 155-56.

21. See *Le Courrier de St. Etienne*, May 16, 1863.

22. For a more general discussion of the politically destabilizing effects of rapid industrial growth and the particular application of this problem to nineteenth-century France, see Marcus Olsen, "Rapid Growth as a Destabilizing Force," *Journal of Economic History* 23 (December 1963): 529-52; and Zeldin, *Political System of Napoleon III*, pp. 65, 164-65.

23. *Annuaires de la Loire*, 1857-61.

24. Gaudet and de Bouchaud, a director of Terrenoire, were among the other representatives of heavy industry on the Conseil général in 1863. Older bourgeois interests were represented by David, Faure-Belon, and Philip-Thiollière. See Departmental Archives of the Loire, 4M12, Conseil général elections.

25. Zeldin, *Political System of Napoleon III*, p. 97.

26. *Le Courrier de St. Etienne*, May 16, 25, 27, 31, 1863. Dorian also exercised considerable control over the lives of his workers. During the fiercely contested legislative election in 1869, the radical press accused him of having offered the prefect of the Haute Loire a banquet at the expense of the workers at his Pont Solomon factory. Foremen there had distributed fishing rods to workers as they went home with instructions to return with enough trout for the banquet, an interesting comment on the demands that even liberal manufacturers could make on their workers. See *La Sentinelle populaire*, May 22, 1869.

27. Balay received 10,218 votes in the entire electoral district, while Fourneyron received 8,951 votes. Dorian beat Charpin by 7,932 votes to 7,254. See Departmental Archives of the Loire, 3M11, Legislative Election of 1863, *procès-verbaux*.

28. Archives Nationales, BB18 1643, *Le Courrier de St. Etienne*, Report of November 26, 1863.

29. *Le Courrier de St. Etienne*, June 2, 1863.

30. Archives Nationales, BB30 379, Reports of the *procureur général* to the minister of justice, Report of June 27, 1863. The government again campaigned vigorously against Dorian in the Conseil général elections in 1864 and convinced some major industrialists to support its candidates. Verdié, the director of the steel works at Firminy, wrote an open letter supporting the candidacy of Charpin, Dorian's opponent. (Verdié was an important collaborator of Talabot, who with the help of the imperial government had organized a vast system of interlocking railroad and industrial interests.) Ultimately both Fourneyron and Dorian were defeated, victims, *Le Courrier* claimed, of the influential men controlled by the government. Dorian, the paper said, had been defeated by Verdié's letter, while Fourneyron was defeated by de Bouchaud, who owed his success to his control of the Terrenoire company workers. Following the election, St. Etienne's four representatives on the Conseil général were de Bouchaud, Philip-Thiollière, and two ribbon manufacturers, André Chateauneuf and Victor Colcombet. See *Le Mémorial de la Loire*, June 18, 1864; *Le Courrier de St. Etienne*, June 27, 1864; Theodore Zeldin, *Emile Ollivier and the Liberal Empire of Napoleon III*

(Oxford, 1963), p. 80; and Departmental Archives of the Loire, 4M14, Conseil général elections, 1862-64.

31. *Le Courrier de St. Etienne*, August 31, 1864. Once Robin decided voluntarily to cease publication, Persigny arranged to have all charges against him dropped. The minister continued, however, to believe in the importance of the press in shaping public opinion in large urban centers. In 1865 he wrote to the emperor that "I concluded, and I still do, that it is the press which made and will make the elections in Paris, and that it is therefore necessary to capture the press at all costs." See Archives Nationales, BB18 1643, *Le Courrier de St. Etienne*, November 24, 1864; and Zeldin, *Political System of Napoleon III*, p. 112.

32. *Le Courrier de St. Etienne*, August 31, 1864.

33. Robin claimed that "if the candidates of the opposition win, the empire is lost. But one must act now, for in six years the Prince Imperial will have reached his majority, and the empire will have been firmly established." See Archives Nationales, BB18 1643, *Le Courrier de St. Etienne*, Report of June 15, 1863.

34. *Le Courrier de St. Etienne*, June 28, 1864.

35. Hutter, whose family was of German origin, had studied law in Paris before becoming a notary at Rive-de-Gier, where his father and several brothers had founded the Compagnie générale des verreries de la Loire et du Rhône. Jacques Claudinon, another republican industrialist, was a local metalworker who in 1852 had founded a small factory at Chambon; it subsequently prospered through the manufacture of anvils and other forged pieces. All members of the liberal committee benefited from the unpopularity of the ribbon manufacturers, for whom, the prefect wrote, the workers reserved their greatest hostility. See Louis J. Gras, *Histoire économique générale des mines de la Loire* (St. Etienne, 1922), 1: 462-63; Departmental Archives of the Loire, 4M15, Conseil général elections, 1865-67, Minister of the interior to the prefect, June 6, 1867; and Archives Nationales, BB30 379, Reports of the *procureur général* to the minister of justice, Reports of January 8, October 22, 1866.

36. Some of the new councillors had only modest incomes, but others were quite wealthy. A report on the taxes paid by municipal councillors in 1872 shows that Chillet paid a total tax of Fr 722, higher than that of Faure-Belon, one of the wealthiest ribbon manufacturers. See Departmental Archives of the Loire, 6M16, Municipal Council Elections, 1865-78.

37. Buisson, a cabaret keeper, had been appointed mayor in August 1865 but was soon obliged to resign because of incompetence. See Stanislas Bossakiewicz, *Histoire générale de St. Etienne* (St. Etienne, 1905), p. 48; and Archives Nationales, BB30 379, Reports of the *procureur général* to the minister of justice, Report of October 6, 1866.

38. Archives Nationales, BB30 379, Reports of the *procureur général* to the minister of justice, Report of December 22, 1866.

39. Departmental Archives of the Loire, 4M15, Conseil général Elections, 1865-67, Report of the prefect to the minister of the interior, July 31, 1867.

40. *Le Mémorial de la Loire*, August 3, 1867.

41. Departmental Archives of the Loire, 4M16, Conseil général, Elections of 1867.

42. Departmental Archives of the Loire, 10M61, Political Events of 1868, Reports of the police to the prefect, July 24, 1868.

43. Many workers who could not afford to buy newspapers depended for their news on *Le Progrès de Lyon*, which was always available in the city's working-class shops and cabarets. See Departmental Archives of the Loire, 10M60, Political Events of 1867, Reports of the prefect to the minister of the interior, September 16, November 23, 1867.

44. Archives Nationales, BB18 1775, *L'Eclaireur*, 1868-71, Report of August 11, 1868.

45. Departmental Archives of the Loire, 10M63, *L'Eclaireur*, undated report.

46. Sanford Elwitt has suggested that smaller industrialists, fearful of the growth of large businesses supported by the government, became republicans, while larger manufacturers remained Bonapartists. Large manufacturers such as Dorian and Jullien, however, worked to destroy the empire in order to increase their own political influence. Elwitt, *The Making of the Third Republic: Class and Politics in France, 1868-1884* (Baton Rouge, 1975), pp. 81-85.

47. Terrenoire supported the Legitimist cause because of Jullien's family. His wife was a granddaughter of de Pommerd, a royalist deputy under the Restoration. Charles de Wendel, who had also married into the Legitimist nobility (a Commingues-Guitant), similarly wavered in his loyalty to the empire. He finally resigned from the Corps législatif in 1867. See Guy Palmade, *French Capitalism in the Nineteenth Century* (New York, 1972), p. 156.

48. Archives Nationales, BB18 1776, *La Loire*, Report of August 24, 1868.

49. Ibid.; and Archives Nationales, BB30 379, Reports of the *procureur général* to the minister of justice, Report of October 12, 1868.

50. Archives Nationales, BB18 1776, *La Loire*, Report of November 17, 1868.

51. *La Loire*, January 15, 20, 1869. *L'Eclaireur* also continued its attacks on the government, and compared the approaching legislative elections in 1869 with the opening of the Estates General in 1789. See Archives Nationales, BB18 1775, *L'Eclaireur*, Report of February 21, 1869.

52. Archives Nationales, BB18 1775, *L'Eclaireur*, Reports of February 13, 22, 1869. Le Nordez was again tried in May 1869, when he was fined Fr 1,200 and given a month in prison for attacks on the government.

53. For a full discussion of the complex industrial and social background of the 1869 elections in the Loire, see Jean Merley, "Les élections de 1869 dans le département de la Loire," *Cahiers d'histoire* 6, no. 1 (1961): 59-93.

54. An abortive challenge to the claims of the liberal Union démocratique to speak for the workers had come from Renault, the leader of the miners' Caisse fraternelle, when he had run for the Conseil général in 1867. Renault, however, had received only 185 votes as compared with 1,065 for Dorian.

55. *L'Eclaireur*, February 21, 1869.

56. Antide Martin, *Elections générales de 1869: Devoirs des citoyens électeurs* (1868), Municipal Library of St. Etienne.

57. The paper also accused Dorian of adding his salary as deputy to his already large income rather than using it to buy books for the *bibliothèques populaires*. See *La Sentinelle populaire*, May 8, 22, 1869.

58. Boudarel, Clapeyron, and Tiblier-Verne were among the leaders of the Comité de la démocratie radicale, the official name of the Union démocratique, who supported Bernard. See Merley, "Les élections de 1869," p. 75; and *L'Eclaireur*, May 21, 1869.

59. Martin was blamed for the destruction of the convents in 1848. See *L'Eclaireur*, May 9, 1869.

60. Departmental Archives of the Loire, 10M62, Political Events of 1869, Report of April 1869.

61. *L'Eclaireur* singled out Euverte, a director of Terrenoire, whose political support it claimed guaranteed the votes of several hundred industrial workers. See *La Sentinelle populaire*, May 22, 1869; and *L'Eclaireur*, May 21, 1869.

62. Departmental Archives of the Loire, 10M62, Political Events of 1869-70, Report of January 24, 1869.

63. Departmental Archives of the Loire, 10M60, Political Events of 1867, Police report to the prefect; and Merley, "Les élections de 1869," p. 75.

64. The government had by 1869 given up any hope of reducing St. Etienne's republican majority. It therefore redrew the department's electoral districts, reuniting the city, and placed the smaller industrial centers around St. Etienne in another district. Charpin defeated César Bertholon in this latter district, which included Chambon, Rive-de-Gier, St. Chamond, Argenteuil, and Pelussin.

65. Merley, "Les élections de 1869," p. 87. Nationally, thirty republican deputies were elected to the Corps législatif.

66. *Le Mémorial de la Loire*, May 25, 1869.

67. The threat of popular violence increased steadily in France during the last months of 1869. The Parisian *Le Père Duchesne* wrote in December after the police seized one of its issues that "they have broken our pens. When the revolution comes, we shall break their heads." See Zeldin, *Emile Ollivier*, p. 132.

68. *La Loire*, September 5, 1869; and Bernard Delabre, "La grève de 1869 dans le bassin minier stéphanois," *Etudes foreziennes*, 1971, p. 123. *La Loire* complained that tensions between capital and labor were the fundamental cause of the strike and claimed that the miners were being manipulated for the benefit of the liberal opposition. See *La Loire*, September 5, 1869.

69. Departmental Archives of the Loire, 92M12, Strikes, 1869-70, Minister of the interior to the prefect, October 29, 1869, and report of the prefect to the minister of the interior, November 8, 1869.

70. A decline in the number of subscribers had also made the paper more costly to operate. See Archives Nationales, BB18 1776, *La Loire*, Report of

February 8, 1870; and BB30 390, Reports of the *procureur général* to the minister of justice, Report of April 10, 1870.

71. The most important reform from the Legitimist point of view was the government's plan for placing local government in the hands of the departmental Conseils généraux, which the royalists believed they could control. See Zeldin, *Emile Ollivier*, p. 125.

72. *Le Mémorial de la Loire*, April 30, 1870.

73. Archives Nationales, BB30 390, Reports of the *procureur général* to the minister of justice, Report of January 21, 1870.

74. These promises do seem to have helped incubate the strike and thus contributed to the shooting at La Ricamerie. See *L'Indépendent rémois*, July 25, 1869.

75. Delabre, "La grève de 1869," p. 126.

76. The commission included Duplay-Balay, the president of the Chamber of Commerce, Faure, the president of the Conseil des prudhommes, Nicolas Guitton, Denis Epitalon, Giron aîné, and Peyret-Gerin. See Departmental Archives of the Loire, 6M3, Municipal Council, 1870-71, Report of the prefect to the minister of the interior, June 21, 1869.

77. *L'Eclaireur*, May 4, 1870.

78. There were 19,957 votes cast during the plebiscite out of a registered population of more than 26,000; 5,293 votes supported the liberal empire, and 14,000 opposed it.

79. *L'Eclaireur*, May 9, 1870.

80. Among the other councillors elected were Dorian, Crozet, Boudarel, Clapeyron, and Tiblier-Verne. See Departmental Archives of the Loire, 5M79, Municipal Council Elections of 1870.

81. Departmental Archives of the Loire, 6M13, Municipal Commissions: Acts of the prefect of the Loire, Act of September 26, 1870; and *L'Eclaireur*, September 6, 1870.

82. *L'Eclaireur*, September 5, 1870. Tiblier-Verne died in December 1870 and was replaced by Boudarel.

83. Departmental Archives of the Loire, 6M3, Municipal Council, Minister of the interior to the prefect, November 8, 1870.

84. Bossakiewicz, *Histoire générale de St. Etienne*, pp. 264-65. The liberal administration was also faced with a resurgent conservative movement supported by the town's mercantile interests and the industrialists who had previously supported *La Loire*. A new conservative newspaper, *Le Défenseur*, was founded in October. The editor, Pierre-Auguste Callet, was a convert to Catholicism and to the Legitimist cause. He had welcomed the fall of the empire in 1870 and by 1871 had become an important figure on the Right. Called Veuillot's monkey by *L'Eclaireur*, he referred to the republicans as "the sons of Robespierre, the monkeys of Marat, and agitators who, like Fouquier-Tinville, are always ready to become public accusers." Callet worked hard to promote a union of the Right against those whom he styled "the new tyrants of the Left" and printed gory accounts of the massacres of 1793 as examples

of what France could expect under a new republic. See *L'Eclaireur*, February 4, 8, 1871; and *Le Défenseur*, February 8, 1871.

85. *L'Eclaireur*, February 5, 1871. The republican leadership had also been forced to take harsh measures against conservatives and Legitimists such as closing religious schools in November and replacing them with nineteen lay schools. At the same time *L'Eclaireur* encouraged the elite to contribute to the emergency fund established in September for the defense of the city, warning that if contributions were not made voluntarily, the administration would impose assessments. See Marcel Sapey, "La commune de St. Etienne," *Europe* 70 (October 1951): 88; Bossakiewicz, *Histoire générale de St. Etienne*, p. 264; and *Le Défenseur*, October 6, 7, 11, 1870.

86. Albert de Lalarge, *Plus de révolutions: Appel à la bourgeoisie* (1871), Municipal Library of St. Etienne.

87. The Alliance républicaine was founded by Bertholon during the Franco-Prussian War to organize support for the republic; it was dissolved in 1872 by the government, which feared the growing influence of radical elements within the organization. See: *Le Mémorial de St. Etienne*, February 3, 1871; and Elwitt, *Making of the Third Republic*, pp. 104-7.

88. The list included Duchamps, Durbize, and Durand, the latter two former editors of *L'Eclaireur* who had been fired by the paper's more moderate directors. See *Le Mémorial de la Loire*, February 3, 1871.

89. The government party had called itself "Liberal-Conservative" during the 1869 legislative elections. After 1870 a coalition of monarchists and former Bonapartists created a new conservative group to defend bourgeois interests from the supposed threat of radical revolution.

90. Lucien Arbel, originally from the Jura, had begun work as a draftsman in a Paris firm. He subsequently worked for the railroads and later became a mining engineer at Rive-de-Gier. He founded the Forges Arbel, Deflassieux, and Pcillon, which manufactured wagon wheels for the railroads and employed 150 workers in 1861. See Louis J. Gras, *Histoire économique de la métallurgie de la Loire* (St. Etienne, 1908), p. 221.

91. Adolphe Robert et al., *Dictionnaire des parlémentaires français*, 5 vols. (Paris, 1891).

92. Arbel was not a true conservative; following his election he voted with the Republican Left. See Jacques Gouault, *Comment la France est devenue républicaine, 1870-1875* (Paris, 1954), p. 214.

93. *Le Mémorial de la Loire*, February 8, 1871.

94. *Annuaire de la Loire*, 1871. The others were Cunit and three landowners, Bouillier, de Sugny, and de Meaux; the latter was a Legitimist with a national political reputation. Several major industrial manufacturers also remained the mayors of their localities. Jullien was mayor at Pelussin, Euverte at Terrenoire, and Verdié at Firminy. But Petin was replaced by the republican Richarme at Rive-de-Gier, and the radical leader Duchamps was appointed mayor at St. Chamond.

95. Departmental Archives of the Loire, 10M69, Political Events of 1871, Report of the prefect to the minister of the interior, April 25, 1871; and *L'Eclaireur*, April 28, 1871.

96. Dorian, who as minister of works in the government of National Defense was in charge of arms production, remained popular during the period of the Commune among workers both in Paris and St. Etienne. His name headed all the electoral lists during the first abortive Paris Commune proclaimed in October of 1870, when it was proposed that the city continue to fight alone against the German invaders. See Stewart Edwards, *The Paris Commune of 1871* (London, 1971), pp. 78 and 88.

97. *L'Eclaireur*, June 23, 1871.

98. *Le Défenseur*, April 28, 1871; and *Le Mémorial de la Loire*, April 29, 1871.

99. The new councillors included Crozet, Boudarel, Chillet, Duchamps, and Bertholon.

100. Departmental Archives of the Loire, 5M82, Municipal Council Elections of 1871; and *Le Mémorial de la Loire*, May 2, 1871.

101. The council claimed that the creation of the Commune had been justified by fears of the monarchist majority in the National Assembly. See *La Loire en 1870-71*, a collection of printed documents in the Municipal Library of St. Etienne, pp. 79-80.

102. The members of the commission included Faure, Duplay-Balay, Escoffier, Fraisse-Brossard, Tézénas, and Thiollière. See Departmental Archives of the Loire, 6M13, Municipal commissions; and Bossakiewicz, *Histoire générale de St. Etienne*, p. 277.

103. *L'Eclaireur*, June 21, 1871.

104. Departmental Archives of the Loire, 10M70, Trial of the Members of the Alliance républicaine, 1871-72; and Sapey, "La commune de St. Etienne," p. 94.

105. Departmental Archives of the Loire, 6M3, Municipal Council, Report of the prefect to the minister of the interior, May 28, 1872. Dorian had been a major backer of *Le Républicain de la Loire*, a departmental newspaper dedicated to the support of a bourgeois republic. See Elwitt, *Making of the Third Republic*, p. 101.

106. Laurent Boyer, "Le département de la Loire entre la République et la Monarchie après la chute du Second Empire," *Etudes foreziennes*, Melanges I, 1968, p. 140.

107. Bossakiewicz, *Histoire générale de St. Etienne*, p. 49.

Conclusion

1. Theodore Zeldin, *The Political System of Napoleon III* (New York, 1958).

2. Eric J. Hobsbawm, *The Age of Capital, 1848-1875* (New York, 1975), p. 248.

Bibliography

Archival Sources

Archives Nationales

Fic III 3 Marne and Fic IV Loire
F12 Subsistence
BB18 Political Reports
BB30 Reports of the *Procureurs généraux* to the Minister of Justice

Bibliothèque Nationale

Statistique de la France, 1st ser., 1835-73

Departmental Archives of the Marne and the Loire

Series M: National, departmental, and municipal elections; plebiscites; reports of the *police politique* and the *police de la presse*; elections and recommendations of the Conseils généraux, Conseils d'arrondissement, Conseils municipaux, and Chamber of Commerce; industrial statistics; reports on industrial expositions and strikes; *mercuriales* and reports on charitable and social organizations.

Series Q: The *Mutation après décès* and the *Successions et absences*

Newspapers in the Municipal Library of Reims

L'Association rémoise
La Concorde

Le Courrier de la Champagne
L'Indépendent rémois
L'Indicateur de la Champagne
L'Industriel de la Champagne
Le Républicain

Newspapers in the Municipal Library of St. Etienne

L'Avenir républicain; later *L'Industrie*
La Commune
Le Courrier de St. Etienne
Le Défenseur
L'Eclaireur
La Loire
Le Mémorial de la Loire
Le Mercure seguisien
La Sentinelle populaire

Pamphlets, Almanacs, and Other Material in the Municipal Library of Reims

Almanachs Matot-Braine
A Messieurs les électeurs du conseil municipal de la ville de Reims. 1865.
Annuaires de la Marne, 1840-71
Association vinicole de la Champagne.
Le comptoir d'escompte Chapuis et Cie, 1854-1924. Reims, 1925.
Courmeaux, Eugène. "République ou royauté," Letter to the editor of *La Champagne.*
Dauphinot, Simon. *Discours pronouncées aux funerailles des victimes de l'accident de 23 juillet à Reims.* 1866.
Derrole, Gilles. "L'anticléricalisme à Reims de 1870 à 1906." Master's thesis.
Lallement, Georges. *Edouard Werlé, négociant en vins de Champagne, maire de la ville de Reims, député au Corps législatif, 1801-1884.* Société des amis de vieux Reims, Reims.
Maumené, E., Rogelet, V., and Warnier, J. *Lettre à M. le président de la Société industrielle de Reims sur l'adoption de l'absolu comme base unique de conditionnement.* 1858.
Medoc, L. J. *Rapport à M. Simon Diancourt, Maire de Reims, sur la situation morale et materielle des salles d'aisle et des écoles primaires de Reims.* 1869.
Nollet, Ponce. *Organisation industrielle: La place de Reims.* 1845.
Notice sur la Maison Vve Pommery fils et Cie.
Obseques de M. Victor Daincourt.
Paris, Henri. *Lettres à MM. les conseillers municipaux de la ville de Reims.* 1865.

———. *A Messieurs les électeurs du conseil municipal de la ville de Reims.* 1865.
Paris, Louis. *Questionnaire: Appel aux honnêtes gens de tous les partis.* 1846.

Pamphlets and Almanacs in the Municipal Library of St. Etienne

Annuaires de la Loire, 1840-71.
Aux électeurs de canton sud-est: Deuxième tour de scrutin.
Chambre de Commerce de St. Etienne. *Rapport des déliberations relatifs à l'adjonction des mines de la Grand' Combe (Gard) à la Compagnie des mines de la Loire.* 1852.
Chapelles, F. *L'insalubrité stéphanois: Infection de la ville.* 1868.
Encoure des électiouns. In the St. Etienne dialect.
Jacollist, M. *Reponse aux attaques contre les bibliothèques populaires à St. Etienne.* 1867.
de Lalarge, Albert. *Plus de révolutions: Appel à la bourgeoisie.* 1871.
La Loire en 1870-1871. A collection of documents.
Martin, Antide. *Elections générales de 1869: Devoirs des citoyens électeurs.* 1868.
Note sur le projet de démembrement du département de la Loire. 1852.
Persigny, duc de. *Lettre du duc de Persigny à son excellence M. le Marquis de Talhouet.* 1870.
Peyret-Lallier. *Dépenses municipales.* 1851.
Revenues municipales: Hotel de Prefecture. 1851.
Société industrielle et agricole de St. Etienne. *Rapport de la commission chargé de réchercher les causes de la décadence de la quincaillerie à St. Etienne, et les moyens de la régénérer.* April 14, 1852.
Société populaire: Liste des candidats à la réprésentation nationale.
Terme, C. *Les élections municipales à St. Etienne en 1865.* 1865.

Books

Aboucaya, M. C. *Les structures sociales et économiques de l'agglomeration lyonnaise à la veille de la révolution de 1848.* Lyons, 1963.
Agulhon, Maurice. *La république au village.* Paris, 1970.
Audiganne, Armand. *Les populations ouvrières et les industries de la France.* 2 vols. Paris, 1860.
Balzac, Honoré de. *The Deputy of Arcis.* Boston, 1896.
Barbat de Bignicourt, Arthur. *Les hommes politiques de la Marne.* Reims, 1872.
Baret, H. *Histoire locale du travail.* St. Etienne, 1932.
Bezucha, Robert J. *The Lyon Uprising of 1834: Social and Political Conflict in the Early July Monarchy.* Cambridge, Mass., 1974.
Bonnefous. *Histoire de St. Etienne.* St. Etienne, n.d.
Bossakiewicz, Stanislas. *Histoire générale de St. Etienne.* St. Etienne, 1905.

Boussinesq, Georges. *Reims à la fin de la Monarchie de Juillet et pendant la période révolutionnaire de 1848*. Reims, 1923.

Boussinesq, Georges, and Laurent, Gustave. *Histoire de Reims depuis les origines jusqu'à nos jours*. Reims, 1933.

Bouvier, Jean. *Naissance d'une banque: Le Crédit lyonnais*. Paris, 1968.

Braudel, Fernand, and Labrousse, Ernest. *Histoire économique et sociale de la France*. 7 vols. Paris, 1976.

Brechignac, V. *Les caisses de secours des ouvriers mineurs dans le bassin de la Loire*. St. Etienne, 1869.

Brossard, M. E. *Les élections et les répresentants du département de la Loire aux assemblés législatifs, 1789-1889*. St. Etienne, 1889.

Les célébrités du vin de Champagne. Reims, 1880.

Codaccioni, Félix. "Lille: étude sociale, 1850-1914." Ph.D. dissertation, University of Lille, 1971.

Crubellier, Maurice, and Juillard, Charles. *Histoire de la Champagne*. Reims, 1969.

Dansette, Adrien. *The Religious History of Modern France*. New York, 1961.

Daumard, Adeline. *La bourgeoisie parisienne de 1815 à 1848*. Paris, 1963.

————. *Les fortunes françaises au XIXième siècle: Enquête sur la répartition et la composition des capitaux privés à Paris, Lyon, Lille, Bourdeaux, et Toulouse d'après l'enregistrement des droits de succession*. Paris, 1973.

Delaroa, Joseph. *Foreziens dignes de mémoire*. St. Etienne, 1889.

Delautel, Pierre. *Notice sur l'histoire de la laine et de l'industrie textile*. Paris, 1907.

Descreux, Denis. "Notes biographiques stéphanois." 1868. Manuscript notes in the Municipal Library of St. Etienne.

Duchêne, Georges. *L'économie politique de l'Empire*. Paris, 1870.

Dunham, Arthur L. *The Anglo-French Treaty of Commerce of 1860 and the Progress of the Industrial Revolution in France*. Ann Arbor, 1930.

————. *The Industrial Revolution in France, 1815-1848*. New York, 1955.

Dupeux, Georges. *Aspects de l'histoire sociale et politique du Loir-et-Cher, 1848-1914*. Paris, 1962.

Duveau, Georges. *La vie ouvrière sous le Second Empire*. Paris, 1946.

Edwards, Stewart. *The Paris Commune of 1871*. London, 1971.

Elwitt, Sanford. *The Making of the Third Republic: Class and Politics in France, 1868-1884*. Baton Rouge, 1975.

Farat, Honoré. *Persigny: Un ministre de Napoleon III, 1808-1871*. Paris, 1957.

Faure, Petrus. *Histoire du mouvement ouvrier dans le département de la Loire*. St. Etienne, 1955.

Festy, Octave. *Le mouvement ouvrier au début de la Monarchie de Juillet*. Paris, 1908.

Fohlen, Claude. *L'industrie textile au temps du Second Empire*. Paris, 1956.

Gille, Bertrand. *La sidérurgie française au XIXième siècle*. Paris, 1968.

Girard, Louis. *Les élections de 1869*. Paris, 1960.

————. *La politique des travaux publiques du Second Empire*. Paris, 1951.

Gouault, Jacques. *Comment la France est devenue républicaine, 1870-1875*. Paris, 1954.

Gras, Louis J. *Essai sur l'histoire de la quincaillerie et petite métallurgie*. St. Etienne, 1904.

———. *Histoire de l'armurerie stéphanoise*. St. Etienne, 1905.

———. *Histoire de la Chambre de Commerce de St. Etienne, 1833-1898*. St. Etienne, 1898.

———. *Histoire de la rubannerie et les industries de la soie à St. Etienne et dans la région stéphanoise*. St. Etienne, 1906.

———. *Histoire du commerce local*. St. Etienne, 1910.

———. *Histoire économique de la métallurgie de la Loire*. St. Etienne, 1908.

———. *Histoire économique générale des mines de la Loire*. 2 vols. St. Etienne, 1922.

Greenberg, Louis M. *Sisters of Liberty: Marseilles, Lyon, Paris and Their Reaction to a Centralized State, 1868-1871*. Cambridge, Mass., 1971.

Guillaume, Pierre. *La compagnie des mines de la Loire, 1846-1854*. Paris, 1966.

Hanagan, Michael. *The Logic of Solidarity: Artisans and Industrial Workers in Three French Towns, 1871-1914*. Urbana, 1980.

Hobsbawm, Eric J. *The Age of Capital, 1848-1875*. New York, 1975.

Hollande, Maurice. *La Chambre de Commerce de Reims, 1801-1951*. Reims, 1951.

Ibarrola, Jesus. *Structure sociale et fortune mobilière et immobilière à Grenoble en 1847*. Grenoble, 1965.

Jackson, W. F. *James Jackson et ses fils*. St. Etienne, 1893.

Jannesson, Victor. *Monographie et histoire de la ville de St. Etienne depuis ses origines jusqu'à nos jours*. St. Etienne, 1892.

Kent, Sherman. *Electoral Procedure under Louis Philippe*. New Haven, 1937.

Le Clerc, Bernard, and Wright, Vincent. *Les préfets du Second Empire*. Paris, 1973.

Le Guesnier, Georges. *Reims et le pays rémois en 1872*. Reims, 1873.

Léon, Pierre. *Geographie de la fortune et structures sociales à Lyon au XIXième siècle, 1815-1914*. Lyons, 1976.

Lequin, Yves. *Les ouvriers de la région lyonnaise, 1848-1914*. 2 vols. Lyons, 1977.

Lhomme, Jean. *Economie et histoire*. Paris, 1967.

L'Huillier, Fernand. *La lutte ouvrière à la fin du Second Empire*. Paris, 1957.

Margadant, Ted. *French Peasants in Revolt: The Insurrection of 1851*. Princeton, 1979.

Marx, Karl. *Class Struggles in France, 1848-1850*. New York, 1964.

———. *The Communist Manifesto*. New York, 1947.

———. *The Eighteenth Brumaire of Louis Bonaparte*. New York, 1963.

Mazière, Adrien. *Origine et développement du commerce du vin de Champagne*. Reims, 1846.

Meinadier, Albert. *La Compagnie des chemins de fer de Paris à Lyon et à la Méditerranée*. Paris, 1908.

Merriman, John. *The Agony of the Republic*. New Haven, 1978.

Palmade, Guy. *French Capitalism in the Nineteenth Century*. New York, 1972.

Perrier, Maxime. *St. Etienne et sa région économique*. St. Etienne, 1937.

Pierrard, Pierre. *La vie ouvrière à Lille sous le Second Empire*. Lille, 1965.

Ponteil, Félix. *Les institutions de la France de 1814 à 1870*. Paris, 1966.

Portallier, Antonin. *Le Chambre de Commerce de St. Etienne.* St. Etienne, 1909.

Poulain, César. *L'agriculture et les traités de commerce.* Paris, 1879.

Price, Roger. *The Economic Modernization of France, 1730-1880.* New York, 1975.

———. *The French Second Republic: A Social History.* Ithaca, 1972.

Reybaud, Louis. *Etude sur le régime des manufactures: Condition des ouvriers en soie.* Paris, 1859.

———. *La laine: Nouvelle série des études sur le régime des manufactures.* Paris, 1867.

Robert, Adolphe, et al. *Dictionnaire des parlémentaires français.* 5 vols. Paris, 1891.

Robert, Charles. *La suppression des grèves par l'association aux bénéfices.* Paris, 1870.

Robin, Charles. *Les confessions d'un journaliste.* Paris, 1862.

Scott, Joan W. *The Glassworkers of Carmaux.* Cambridge, Mass., 1974.

See, Henri. *La vie économique de la France sous la Monarchie de Juillet.* Paris, 1927.

Sewell, William H., Jr. *Work and Revolution in France.* Cambridge, 1980.

Testenoire-Lafayette, C. P. *Histoire de St. Etienne.* St. Etienne, n. d.

Thiollière, Lucien. *Notices industrielles: La Chambre de Commerce; bustes et portraits.* St. Etienne, 1894.

Thuillier, Guy. *Georges Dufaud et les débuts du grande capitalisme dans la métallurgie en Nivernais au XIXième siècle.* Paris, 1959.

Tour-Varen, J. A. de la. *Note statistique industrielle sur la ville de St. Etienne.* St. Etienne, 1851.

Tristan, Flora. *Le tour de France: Journal inédit, 1843-1844.* Paris, 1845.

Tudesq, André-Jean. *Les conseillers généraux en France au temps de Guizot, 1840-1848.* Paris, 1967.

———. *Les grands notables en France, 1840-1849.* Paris, 1964.

Turgan, Julien. *Les grandes usines: Etudes industrielles en France et à l'étranger.* 18 vols. Paris, 1865-78.

Valserres, Jacques. *Les industries de la Loire.* St. Etienne, 1862.

Vial, Jean. *L'industrialisation de la sidérurgie française, 1814-1864.* Paris, 1967.

Vigier, Philippe. *La Seconde République dans la région alpine.* 2 vols. Paris, 1953.

Villermé, Louis. *Tableau de l'état physique et moral des ouvriers.* Paris, 1840.

Zeldin, Theodore. *Emile Ollivier and the Liberal Empire of Napoleon III.* Oxford, 1963.

———. *France, 1848-1945: Love, Ambition and Politics.* Oxford, 1973.

———. *The Political System of Napoleon III.* New York, 1958.

Articles and Theses

Babu, L. "La métallurgie dans la Loire." *Association française pour l'avancement des sciences.* 26th sess., 2 (August 1897): 128-85.

Bouvier, Jean. "Aux origines de la Troisième République: Les réflexes sociaux des milieux d'affaires." *Revue historique* 210 (October-December 1953): 271-301.

―――. "Les banquiers devant l'actualité politique en 1870-1871." *Revue d'histoire moderne et contemporaine* 5 (April-June 1958).

Boyer, Laurent. "Le département de la Loire entre la République et la Monarchie après la chute du Second Empire." *Etudes foreziennes*, Mélanges I, 1968.

Chevalier, Louis. "Les fondements économiques et sociaux de l'histoire politique de la région parisienne, 1848-1870." Ph.D. dissertation, Sorbonne, 1950.

Christofferson, Thomas R. "Urbanization and Political Change: The Political Transformation of Marseilles under the Second Republic." *Historian* 36 (February 1974): 189-206.

Clause, Georges. "L'industrie lainière rémoise à l'époque napoléonienne." *Revue d'histoire moderne et contemporaine* 17 (July-September 1970): 574-95.

Darmancier. "Material de guerre." *Association française pour l'avancement des sciences*. 26th sess., 2 (August 1897).

Daumard, Adeline. "L'évolution des structures sociales en France à l'époque de l'industrialisation, 1815-1914." *Revue historique* 502 (April-June 1972): 325-46.

Delabre, Bernard. "La grève de 1869 dans le bassin minier stéphanois." *Etudes foreziennes*, 1971.

Fohlen, Claude. "Bourgeoisie française: Liberté économique et intervention de l'état." *Revue économique* 7 (May 1956): 414-28.

―――. "La concentration dans l'industrie textile française au milieu du XIXième siècle." *Revue d'histoire moderne et contemporaine* 2 (January-March 1955): 46-58.

Genet, Marie-Claude. "Un républicain liberal, Jules Warnier, vu à travers sa correspondence avec Jules Simon, 1874-1896." *Etudes champenoises*, no. 1 (1976).

Guillaume, Pierre. "Les débuts de la grande industrie houllière dans la Loire: Les mines de Roche-le-Molière et de Firminy sous la Restauration." *Cahiers d'histoire* 4 (1959).

―――. "La mine de houille dans la Loire sous le Second Empire." Master's thesis, 1956.

―――. "La situation économique et sociale du département de la Loire d'après l'enquête sur le travail agricole et industriel du 15 mai 1848." *Actes du 86ième congrès national des sociétés savants: Section d'histoire moderne et contemporaine*, 1961.

Hobsbawm, Eric J. "The Labor Aristocracy in Nineteenth Century Britain." In Peter Stearns and Daniel Walkowitz, eds., *Workers in the Industrial Revolution*. New Brunswick, 1975.

Landes, David. "French Entrepreneurship and Industrial Growth in the Nineteenth Century." *Journal of Economic History* 9 (May 1949): 45-61.

Loubère, Leo. "The Emergence of the Extreme Left in Lower Langueduc, 1848-1851: Social and Economic Factors in Politics." *American Historical Review* 73 (1968): 1019-51.

Manuel, Frank E. "The Luddite Movement in France." *Journal of Modern History* 10 (1938): 180-211.

Marcilhacy, C. "Les caractères de la crise sociale et politique de 1846 à 1852 dans le département du Loiret." *Revue d'histoire moderne et contemporaine* 6 (1959): 5-59.

Markovitch, Timohir J. "Le revenu industriel et artisanal sous la Monarchie de Juillet et le Second Empire." *Economies et sociétés* 8 (April 1967): 3-138.

Meaudre, Jacky. "Les débuts de l'amanagement urbain de St. Etienne, 1815-1872." *Etudes foreziennes*, 1971.

————. "La pousse urbaine à St. Etienne," Master's thesis, University of Lyons, 1966.

Merley, Jean. "Les élections de 1869 dans le département de la Loire." *Cahiers d'histoire* 6, no. 1 (1961).

Merriman, John. "The Crown in Limoges in April of 1848." Paper presented at the American Historical Association meeting, December 1971.

Olsen, Marcus. "Rapid Growth as a Destabilizing Force." *Journal of Economic History* 2 (December 1963): 529-52.

Picard, Elizabeth. "Un notaire rémois de la première moitié du XIXième siècle: Nicolas-Henri Carteret, 1807-1862." Master's thesis, University of Reims, 1974.

Sapey, Marcel. "Le commune de St. Etienne." *Europe*, no. 70 (October 1951).

Schnitzler, Jacques. "St. Etienne et ses problèmes urbains." *La vie urbain dans le département de la Loire et ses abords*. St. Etienne, 1969.

Sewell, William. "Social Change and the Rise of Working Class Politics in Nineteenth Century Marseilles." *Past and Present* 65 (November 1974): 75-109.

————. "The Working Class of Marseilles under the Second Republic: Social Structure and Political Behavior." In Peter Stearns and Daniel Walkowitz, eds., *Workers in the Industrial Revolution*. New Brunswick, 1974.

Taquet, Evelyne. "L'industrie textile à Reims." *La Champagne économique*, no. 5 (May 1970).

Taylor, George V. "Noncapitalist Wealth and the French Revolution." *American Historical Review* 72 (1967): 469-76.

Tenand, D. "Les origines de la classe ouvrière stéphanoise." Ph.D. dissertation, University of Lyons II, 1971.

Thiollière, Lucien. "Rubannerie." *Association française pour l'avancement des sciences*, 26th sess., 1 (August 1897).

Tilly, Charles. "How Protest Modernized in France, 1845-1855." In William Aydelotte, ed., *Dimensions of Quantitative Research in History*. Reading, Mass., 1971.

————. "The Changing Place of Collective Violence." In Peter Stearns and Daniel Walkowitz, eds., *Workers in the Industrial Revolution*. New Brunswick, 1974.

Index

About the Author

David M. Gordon teaches history at the University of North Carolina at Charlotte. He received his bachelor of arts degree from Brooklyn College and his masters and doctorate from Brown University. This is his first book.